A Great Deal of Ruin

A Great Deal of Ruin provides an accessible introduction to the enduring problem of financial crises. Illustrated with historical analysis, case studies, and clear economic concepts, this book explains in three parts what financial crises are, how they are caused and what we can learn from them. It begins with a taxonomy of crises and a list of factors that increase the risk for countries experiencing a financial crisis. It then examines five of the most important crises in modern economic history, beginning with Great Depression and ending with the Subprime Crisis in the United States and its evolution into a debt crisis in the Eurozone. The book concludes with a set of lessons that can be learnt from the crises of the past. It will appeal to university students as well as general readers who are curious to learn more about the recent Subprime Crisis and other financial crises.

JAMES GERBER is a Professor of Economics, Emeritus at San Diego State University. He is the author of *International Economics* (2018), a best-selling textbook now in its 7th edition, and numerous works on US-Mexico economic relations, including *Fifty Years of Change on the US-Mexico Border: Growth, Development, and Quality of Life* (with Joan Anderson, 2008) which won the Association of Borderlands Studies Book Award.

A Great Deal of Ruin

Financial Crises since 1929

JAMES GERBER
San Diego State University

CAMBRIDGE
UNIVERSITY PRESS

University Printing House, Cambridge CB2 8BS, United Kingdom

One Liberty Plaza, 20th Floor, New York, NY 10006, USA

477 Williamstown Road, Port Melbourne, VIC 3207, Australia

314–321, 3rd Floor, Plot 3, Splendor Forum, Jasola District Centre, New Delhi – 110025, India

79 Anson Road, #06–04/06, Singapore 079906

Cambridge University Press is part of the University of Cambridge.

It furthers the University's mission by disseminating knowledge in the pursuit of education, learning, and research at the highest international levels of excellence.

www.cambridge.org
Information on this title: www.cambridge.org/9781108497343
DOI: 10.1017/9781108608589

First published 2019

Printed in the United Kingdom by TJ International Ltd. Padstow Cornwall

A catalog record for this publication is available from the British Library.

ISBN 978-1-108-49734-3 Hardback
ISBN 978-1-108-73990-0 Paperback

Contents

List of Tables — *page* x

Preface — xi

I. Introduction — 1

- I.1 More Frequent, More Expensive, Harder to Avoid — 1
- I.2 Economics, Finance, and History — 5
- I.3 Plan of the Book — 9

PART I: FINANCIAL CRISES — 15

1. Categories and Risk Factors — 17
   - 1.1 An Introduction to Financial Crises — 17
   - 1.2 Categories of Financial Crises — 20
   - 1.3 Seven Risk Factors — 22
     - 1.3.1 Asset Bubbles — 24
     - 1.3.2 Credit Booms — 28
     - 1.3.3 Weak Supervision and Regulation — 30
     - 1.3.4 Capital Market Liberalization — 31
     - 1.3.5 Overvalued Currencies — 33
     - 1.3.6 Large Trade Deficits — 35
     - 1.3.7 Excessive Debt Levels — 37
   - 1.4 What Do We Really Know? — 40

2. Growth, Globalization, and Financial Crises — 43
   - 2.1 Modern Economic Growth — 43
   - 2.2 Modern Globalization's First Wave: 1914–1950 — 46
     - 2.2.1 Open Capital Markets — 47
     - 2.2.2 The Gold Standard — 48
     - 2.2.3 Financial Crises — 49

2.3 Interwar Instability, 1914–1950 51
2.3.1 Deflation 52
2.3.2 Gold and the Great Depression 53
2.4 Bretton Woods and the Golden Age, 1950–1973 55
2.4.1 The Bretton Woods Exchange Rate System 57
2.4.2 The End of Bretton Woods 58
2.5 The Second Globalization Wave, 1973 to the Present 61
2.5.1 Factors Behind the Increase in Financial Crises 62
2.6 Conclusion 64

PART II: FIVE CASE STUDIES 67

3. The Great Depression, 1929–1939 69
3.1 Why Study the Great Depression? 69
3.2 Factors Leading Up to the Depression 72
3.3 What Caused the Great Depression? 76
3.4 The Keynesian Idea 79
3.5 The Monetarist Response 81
3.6 Two Complications to the Monetarist Story 83
3.7 Economic Recovery and Relapse 87
3.8 Conclusions 90

4. The Latin American Debt Crisis, 1982–1989 92
4.1 Conditions Leading Up to the Crisis 92
4.2 The IMF's First Global Crisis 94
4.3 The Credit Boom 97
4.4 Varieties of Crises 99
4.5 The Search for Solutions 103
4.6 The Return of Capital Flows 108
4.7 Lessons 109
4.8 From Latin America to East Asia 114

5. The Asian Crisis, 1997–1999 118
5.1 Stable Economies and Rapid Growth 118

5.2 Explanations for Rapid Growth 120
5.3 The Onset of the Crisis in Thailand 124
5.4 Contagion and Common Fundamentals 128
5.5 Crisis Resolution 132
5.6 The Fallout 135

6. The Subprime Crisis in the United States 143
6.1 Vulnerabilities 143
6.2 Chronology 152
6.2.1 Too Big to Fail 154
6.2.2 Maintaining Credit Availability 156
6.3 Financial Reforms 158
6.3.1 Crisis Prevention 159
6.3.2 Crisis Mitigation 161
6.3.3 Prognosis 163

7. The Financial Crisis in Europe 165
7.1 The Single Currency Project 165
7.2 An Uneven Crisis 169
7.3 Bank Debt Becomes National Debt 171
7.4 The Doom Loop 173
7.5 Emergency Actions 176
7.6 Recessions Prolonged 179

PART III: LESSONS 183

8. Markets Do Not Self-Regulate 185
8.1 Overconfidence in the Market 185
8.2 Market Reality 189
8.3 Empirically Speaking 193

9. Shadow Banks Are Banks 197
9.1 No Bailout? 197
9.2 Shadow Banks 199

9.3 Securitization 201
9.4 Regulators and Incentives 202
9.5 Shadow Bank Depositors 204
9.6 Bank Panics with Shadow Banks 206
9.7 The Rise of Finance 208

10. Banks Need More Capital, Less Debt 212
10.1 Other People's Money 212
10.2 Leverage 214
10.3 Limits to Risk Models 217
10.4 Resistance to Increasing Capital 219
10.5 Capital and Risk Reduction 221

11. Monetary Policy Does Not Always Work 224
11.1 Overconfidence 224
11.2 The Rise of Monetary Policy 225
11.3 New Classical Economics 228
11.4 The Great Moderation 230
11.5 Zero Lower Bound 232

12. Fiscal Multipliers Are Larger Than Expected 237
12.1 Acts of Nature 237
12.2 The Keynesian Consensus 239
12.3 The Multiplier 241
12.4 Expectations 243
12.5 Keynesians and Anti-Keynesians 245
12.6 Testing Ideas with a Crisis 248

13. Monetary Integration Requires Fiscal Integration 252
13.1 The Grand Experiment 252
13.2 The United States Is a Monetary and Fiscal Union 253
13.3 The Euro and Optimal Currency Areas 256
13.4 Promoting the Euro 257
13.5 Missing Institutions 261

14. Open Capital Markets Can Be Dangerous 266
- 14.1 Assume There Are Benefits 266
- 14.2 Capital Market Liberalization Defined 267
- 14.3 From Open Capital Markets to a Financial Crisis 270
- 14.4 Open Capital Markets and Economic Growth 274
- 14.5 Should Countries Close Their Capital Markets? 277

15. Not All Debt Is Created Equal 279
- 15.1 Fear of a US Debt Crisis 279
- 15.2 Households, Businesses, and Governments 282
- 15.3 Sovereign Debt Crises 284
- 15.4 A Second Look at the United States 288
- 15.5 Getting Out of Debt 292

Conclusion 296

Abbreviations and Acronyms 304
Bibliography 306
Index 327

Tables

1.1	Types of financial crises	*page* 21
1.2	Common risk factors associated with financial crises	24
2.1	Estimated average annual growth of real per capita income	45
5.1	Annual average rates of real GDP growth	120
5.2	Average annual current account balance, percent of GDP	140

Preface

In the 1970s, problems of economic instability and crisis began to be pushed into the background of the discipline of economics and replaced by a focus on economies in stable equilibria at full employment. This viewpoint has ample theoretical justification, but as an economist with a background in historical studies, I have a natural skepticism toward stories of long run equilibrium, or quick recoveries from a collapse of the macroeconomy. In the first years of my career, I was continually puzzled by the fact that twenty miles from where I worked was another world where the Mexican economy took nearly a decade to emerge from a crisis that cut wages in half and threw millions back into poverty. Plus, there was the problem of Japan in the 1990s. After several decades of spectacular growth on what appeared to be a stable trajectory that would soon surpass the United States in GDP, Japan fell into a lost decade of intractable economic problems. Solid institutions and competent macroeconomic management did not seem to be enough to avoid a prolonged crisis. While Japan was struggling to emerge from its problems, a group of institutionally strong, fast growing, stable models of economic development in East Asia experienced sudden and catastrophic breakdowns and then came the Subprime Crisis that many thought could never happen.

Watching the difficulties of regaining growth in Latin America, Europe and the United States, puzzling over the lost decade in Japan, and studying the collapse in East Asia, confirms my view that market economies have more than a little instability baked in, and that the natural tendency to return to full employment after a recession or a crisis could be obstructed by far more than simple human error or misguided government policies. If history teaches anything, it is that the world is a lot messier and more complex than the one described by economic theories emphasizing equilibrium and full employment.

Economic theory is a powerful tool for understanding the world but it requires institutional and historical context, as well as a sense of the limits to theoretical models, in order to avoid falling into scholasticism. I am fortunate that both my undergraduate and graduate programs were in universities where economic history was valued and taught beyond the bare minimum. And, in the university where I teach, I had the luck to become the "accidental director" of the Latin American Studies program. That good fortune gave me the opportunity to travel in Latin America, especially Mexico, to talk with scholars and friends abroad, and to think about the problems of economic instability from outside the lens of the US economy.

In 2009, colleagues in La Paz, Mexico, invited me to give a paper on the Subprime Crisis as part of a conference on that topic. I want to thank Antonina Ivanova, Alba Eritrea Gamez, and Manuel Ángeles for the opportunity to begin developing some of the ideas in this book. Shortly thereafter, I created a course on the subject of financial crises which enabled me to develop a set of topics for teaching about the Subprime Crisis and other historical episodes. I thank my colleagues for the space to develop this course. I benefited greatly from the several semesters of students who read earlier pieces of this work and provided feedback and discussion. In 2012, Rosio Barajas and Eduardo Mendoza at the Colegio de la Frontera Norte invited me to give a paper on the Eurozone Crisis and lessons from Mexico's experiences with debt and currency crises. I am thankful to them for their invitation and their spirit of collaboration. My colleague and friend Miguel Montoya at the Tecnológico de Monterrey, Campus Guadalajara, let me try out ideas as an invited lecturer in his Masters in Engineering Management program and the results became the genesis of the present work. The book took further shape when my friend Tom Passananti suggested we collaborate on an historical comparison of the financial sector policies of Mexico and Brazil in the 1890s. Tom later suggested we look at the impact of the Panic of 1907 on the Mexican Revolution.

I am grateful for these opportunities and for the friendship and support of my colleagues. Needless to say, I alone am responsible for the mistakes and errors of the current volume.

Academic colleagues and friends are essential but even more so is the support of my wife, Marion. For her patience, her enthusiasm, and her love, I am forever indebted.

1 Introduction

1.1 MORE FREQUENT, MORE EXPENSIVE, HARDER TO AVOID

Financial crises are a normal feature of contemporary market economies. They are analogous to diseases or natural disasters and, like some diseases and most natural disasters, are currently beyond the ability of science to prevent or to accurately predict. In part this because most of the preconditions of financial crises also occur in situations that do not develop into a crisis. Nevertheless, it is possible to minimize the risks of a crisis and to mitigate the damage when they do happen.

While financial crises usually do not kill people directly, the economic damage can lead to numerous indirect deaths, with monetary costs that are comparable to wars and that are far greater than the largest natural disasters. Compare the Subprime Crisis to recent natural disasters such as Hurricanes Katrina or Harvey. Estimates of the costs vary, but one estimate for Katrina is that it cost $160 billion, with Hurricane Harvey probably somewhat less (Dottle, King, and Koeze, 2017); conservative estimates from the International Monetary Fund (IMF) are that the United States lost output equivalent to more than 2.4 *trillion* dollars from 2008 to 2014, with proportionately similar estimates for other countries. And researchers at the Federal Reserve Bank of San Francisco estimated a persistent output loss from the Subprime Crisis of 7 percent of Gross Domestic Product (GDP) and a lifetime income loss of $70,000 for every US man, woman, and child.[1]

1 The IMF estimate is conservative because it lowers its estimates of potential output during a recession. In effect, it ignores the long run effect of the crisis in permanently lowering GDP. Researchers at the San Francisco Federal Reserve Bank capture the effect on GDP. Their estimates on lifetime income are in present discounted value terms (Barnichon, Matthes, and Ziegenbein, 2018).

Financial crises throw countries into recession or intensify pre-existing recessions, and lead to years of lost potential output. They can permanently lower economic growth rates through the impacts they have on laid-off workers and idle capital investments. They frequently cause governments to collapse and if contagious, which is often the case, they spread internationally. Unfortunately, financial crises are surprisingly common. Researchers at the IMF identify 219 balance of payments crises, sixty-seven debt crises, 147 banking crises, and 217 currency crises, all between 1970 and 2011, and with many of the different types of crises occurring simultaneously in the same country (Claessens and Kose, 2014: 33; Laeven and Valencia, 2014: 66). Clearly, the world would be better off if there were a way to eliminate crises, but unfortunately, they appear to be becoming more frequent rather than less so.

It is tempting to think that financial crises will never be completely eliminated given the constant evolution of finance and financial technology and the ever-changing stream of new challenges they generate for businesses, policymakers, and regulators. It is certainly true today that the elimination of crises is beyond our reach but it is perhaps too pessimistic to think they will never be eliminated. We once thought something similar about famines and disease, yet the historical record over the last two centuries is one of great advances in feeding a growing population and curing many intractable diseases. In the same way that a medieval peasant could not imagine a green revolution with modern machinery and satellite imaging of crops, so we cannot imagine how a world devoid of financial crises might operate. What would the financial system look like? How would macroeconomic policies work? What additional information would be available?

During a financial crisis, policy first responders are usually overwhelmed by a seemingly impossible and/or incomprehensible set of choices. During the recent Subprime Crisis (2007–2009), the fiscal stimulus response taught in every introductory economics course was limited in the United States by political disagreements, and was politically impossible in most of Europe. Traditional monetary policy was ineffective while non-traditional monetary policies were untested, and both fiscal and monetary stimuli were challenged by opponents of those in office. The choice between bailouts or doing nothing to help failing financial giants had no agreed answers, and at the scariest moment, as the investment bank Lehman Brothers collapsed in September, 2008, no one was quite sure what was going to happen next or how the spreading crisis might be contained.

Crisis response and crisis mitigation are two areas of ongoing research, along with crisis prevention. When a crisis occurs, it is followed by highly polarized debates and discussions of the potential causes and the weaknesses in the system. Mian, Sufi, and Trebbi (2014) show that political debate in the wake of a crisis usually becomes more polarized even though it frequently leads to legislation and new regulations. Regulation, however, necessarily focuses on the causes of the crisis, which are last year's problems, and cannot anticipate the next wave of financial innovation or macroeconomic shocks that will hit an economy. Regulations and statutes rarely evolve as fast as the economy changes and, consequently, become less effective with time. World events, such as spikes in oil prices, economic policy shifts, or currency appreciation and depreciation, alter international financial flows and create incentives for firms to adopt new strategies, invent new financial instruments, and develop new financial networks. Researchers are looking for ways to create a set of early warning indicators, but even if we had a reliable tool for predicting a crisis, its usefulness would be uncertain since the necessary steps to avoid a crisis might often be beyond the reach of policymakers. For example, we know that large inflows of foreign capital increase the probability of a crisis, but there is no consensus on the definition of "a large capital inflow" nor about the capacity of different countries to safely handle capital inflows. A factor in the Subprime Crisis was the collapse of a housing bubble that was partly fueled by large inflows of foreign capital, but even after the crisis there was no agreement about the role of those inflows, and even if there was, acting on that knowledge to successfully prevent a crisis would have been politically impossible.

Economists have recognized the need for regulations in banking and finance since the beginning of modern economics. Adam Smith wrote of the folly of unregulated banking (Smith, 1776 [1937]: 308) while more recent arguments stress the problems created by asymmetric or incomplete information. Both historical and current observers of financial crises recognize that the fallout from a collapse in banking or other parts of the financial system has consequences that spillover into the rest of the economy and hurt interests beyond the immediate source of the problems. The breakdown in the financial sector accelerates the collapse of normal economic transactions and occasionally turns ordinary recessions into Great Depressions. This idea, that the financial sector can accelerate an ordinary recession and turn it into something spectacularly destructive, is of relatively recent vintage but is widely agreed.[2] The financial accelerator explains why a recession coupled with a breakdown in finance has a much greater negative impact than the simple credit tightening that is often associated with a recession. It is a matter of degree, but the disappearance of normal credit flows severely affects market economies by limiting the ability of credit and finance to play their essential role in daily economic life. When lenders cannot or will not advance credit, firms have few options but to sell assets, layoff employees, cut output, and leave orders unfilled.

A textbook definition of a financial crisis is a "Major disruption in financial markets characterized by sharp declines in asset prices and firm failures" (Mishkin and Eakins, 2015: 164). This is as good a definition as any, although it makes crises sound somewhat less destructive than they actually are. Reinhart and Rogoff's (2009b) quantitative economic history of financial crisis lists three primary

2 For example, Nobel laureates that might be characterized as on the political right and left share this view (Lucas, 2012; Stiglitz, 2010). Former Chairman of the Federal Reserve, Ben Bernanke, has written extensively about the financial accelerator (Bernanke, 2000b and 2015: 35).

characteristics as a prolonged and deep collapse in asset prices, declines in employment and output, and a dramatic increase in government debt. This too may not convey a full sense of the destructive power of crises. Other researchers emphasize an increase in unemployment, increased poverty, longer recessions, and even an increase in suicides.[3]

1.2 ECONOMICS, FINANCE, AND HISTORY

This book examines financial crises since 1929 using the tools of economics, finance, and history.[4] The purpose of combing these particular fields is to avoid their individual limits and biases when looking at the complex phenomena of financial crises. Economics, for example, provides a great deal of insight about market forces and incentives, but its tendency to use the concept of equilibrium is sometimes an issue when addressing problems of disequilibria.[5] History provides insight about context and circumstances, but without models from economics and finance, it loses its ability to generalize beyond the specifics of a particular case. Finance is mostly about buying and selling financial instruments, but since the Subprime Crisis there is a general recognition that innovation in the purpose and function of financial institutions, together with

3 See Bordo, et al. (2001); Reinhart and Rogoff (2009a); Claessens, Kose and Terrones (2009); Claessens and Kose (2014); Laeven and Valencia (2014); and Stiglitz (2016).

4 This is not a particularly new approach; some of the best analyses of crises have adopted a similar perspective. For example, Kindleberger (1978); Eichengreen (2008, 2015); and Gorton (2012).

5 Standard economic analysis posits that economic systems tend towards an equilibrium level of activity and factors that interfere with the equilibrium are unusual, pathological, or representative of some type of interference (usually assumed to be governments) that prevents the equilibrium from materializing. Economists such as Hyman Minsky, who hypothesized that there is a natural tendency towards financial disequilibrium, are often rejected or at least ignored. Minsky wrote extensively about the natural tendency of market economies to encounter financial crises. His work was mostly ignored, partly perhaps because his writing was not as clear as it might have been. When the Subprime Crisis of 2007–2009 reached its most frightening phase in 2008, his books were mostly out of print, but used copies were selling on Amazon for hundreds of dollars. Since then, publishers have reprinted his work.

the design of financial instruments that are traded, matter a great deal.[6]

Economic models are powerful tools for understanding the forces that lead up to a crisis, how the crisis unfolds, and how societies ultimately escape from its grip. Economic models, however, are in their relative infancy in explaining how dysfunctional or harmful practices might be a normal part of an economic system. For example, when Charles Prince, CEO of Citigroup, was asked if he wasn't worried about taking on so much debt, he quipped that "... as long as the music is playing, you've got to get up and dance."[7] The relatively new field of behavioral economics identifies this as an example of herd behavior that can have large consequences on individual firms and the entire economy. If Citigroup did not "get up and dance" it would have stood out negatively from other firms since its short run rates of return would have been less than its competitors. So, it did what every other firm was doing. Another problem identified by behavioral economics is overconfidence bias. Overconfidence bias makes no sense if households and firms are completely rational in their behavior, so it is difficult to incorporate into economic models. The Citigroup case also reflects over confidence, but they were far from alone. In the lead up to the Subprime Crisis, many households and businesses took on more debt than they could handle, while believing they could manage any conceivable event that might be thrown at them.

A third problem of great relevance is that of deceptive practices. If an activity is legally permitted and leads to an increase in a firm's profits, or an household's enrichment, then economic theory says that some firms and households will engage in the activity even if it is deceptive. Such activities are possible only when information is

6 The Subprime Crisis largely occurred in shadow banking – a set of bank-like institutions that are technically not banks. Monetary economists were aware of the importance of financial institutions to general economic outcomes many years before the Subprime Crisis.

7 The quote is from an interview he gave to the *Financial Times*, July 7, 2007. Ultimately the large debt load of Citigroup caused it to fail. Prince resigned as CEO in November, 2007.

asymmetrically distributed. For example, buyers and sellers of complex financial instruments or insurance policies often have different information about the asset, with one side knowing something the other does not, and are able to take advantage of the information gap. Asymmetric information can be exploited for profit, particularly when it involves deceptive (but legal) practices. Economic models have begun to incorporate the possibilities for asymmetric information, but the range of possible outcomes is far greater than a simple, socially optimal, economic equilibrium.

Some of the factors that prevent a simple story of economic equilibrium are institutional and not necessarily individual. For example, it has long been recognized that there are forces that prevent prices and wages from easily falling during a recession. Most introductory economics textbooks propose a model of recessions that show rising unemployment leading to falling wages, and an adjustment back to full employment. This is a happy simple story that is easy to show in supply and demand format and even though reality does not happen in the way described, the elegance of the theory, its implication that government action is unnecessary, and the underlying emphasis on self-adjusting economic mechanisms are very attractive, particularly in comparison to a more complicated, messy, empirically accurate, but less elegant reality of wages that are asymmetric in their tendencies to fall or rise.

Historians have rarely worried about the need to explain complex phenomenon with a mathematical model or a geometric diagram. They may not have systematized the concept of asymmetric information, but they have long known about the roles of power and deception in human behavior and the ways that overconfidence and herd behaviors lead to deep crises. Among its many attributes, historical analysis often makes us wary of the idea of a single, unified model of human behavior. Different financial crises, for example, may have some similar patterns but the unique circumstances and characteristics of each one implies that there is no general theory applicable to all times and places. Each and every financial crisis is different and any attempt to fit them into a single analytical model only distorts the reality of the crisis by leaving out some important factors and exaggerating the roles of others. Even so, advances in our understanding of the causes and consequence of financial crises require us to look for common factors. Every crisis may be unique, but there are factors in common in each one. In particular, economic variables such as credit booms, exchange rates, current account balances, debt levels, and bank failures show up at critical moments. There may not yet be a general theory of crises and there may never be one, but economic analysis enables economic historians to work with the specific attributes of a particular time and place and to put them into a more general framework to highlight the risks and vulnerabilities that appear over and over.

The economic history of crises has always contained an implicit set of assumptions about the financial system even though the assumptions have not been formalized in meaningful ways, largely because the differences in financial instruments and institutions were not viewed as particularly important. More recent macroeconomic analysis has changed this view, however, and added a deeper understanding of financial institutions, financial instruments, and the roles they play in creating vulnerabilities and spreading a crisis once one starts. This is most visible in the ongoing debates over the causes of the Great Depression and in the Federal Reserve's response to the Subprime Crisis. What has emerged is widespread acknowledgement that the financial system is more than a passive actor, that financial institutions and instruments play an active role in determining the path a crisis takes, and in setting an agenda for policymakers concerned about prevention and mitigation of the damage. The Great Depression was as deep as it was partly because the entire financial system collapsed, while part of the reason the Great Recession did not become as destructive was because the Federal Reserve prevented a complete meltdown in the financial system. The Dodd–Frank reform package passed in 2010 is an attempt to reduce the vulnerabilities in the financial system and to create oversight with fewer gaps. Whether it will succeed as hoped is an entirely different issue.

1.3 PLAN OF THE BOOK

Throughout the book I try to find the consensus among economists. In some cases, there is no consensus even when the empirical analysis clearly supports a particular view. In these cases, the lack of consensus is, in my view, a result of ideological considerations. By ideology I mean not only a particular set of political preferences but also cases where a theoretical model is adopted because it has more internal consistency than an alternative, yet it leads to predicted outcomes that are not empirically supported. The world is deeply complicated and the assumption that theory should take precedence over actual measurements is, in my view, not only naive but also a step away from scientifically valid economic analysis. Hence, throughout the book, empirical analysis is given preference over theory when the two do not agree. It is also quite common that neither theory nor empirical analysis are clear in the answers they offer. There is much we do not know, and in those cases a skeptical attitude is most appropriate.

Part 1 is an introduction to financial crises. It provides a taxonomy of crises and describes the five main types that have been analyzed in the literature. While there is some disagreement about the taxonomy, it is not critical. After describing the main types of crises, Chapter 1 turns to a discussion of seven risk factors that appear over and over in the discussion of specific crises. A key point about the risk factors is worth emphasizing: They are risk factors and not determinants of crises. In that sense, they are similar to medical risk factors such as those associated with heart disease. We know that smoking and other behaviors are associated with an increased risk, but many people engage in risky behaviors without negative consequences. Similarly, countries may have asset bubbles, credit booms, excessive debt levels, or one of the other risk factors without experiencing a financial crisis. Given our current state of knowledge, we cannot put precise probabilities on particular risks. This is due in part to the fact that risk intensity depends on a large number of additional factors, such as the quality of a country's institutions, its role in the global economy, expectations about its future policies, and the ability to respond to changing circumstances, among many others. When crises occur, one or more of these risk factors discussed in Chapter 1 are usually cited as a significant causal factor.

Chapter 2 provides more background for readers unfamiliar with the economic history of globalization since the early nineteenth century. The chapter identifies the five main periods of world economic history since the onset of modern economic growth in the 1820s, and discusses the frequencies and types of financial crises in each period. The chapter largely passes over the first era of growth (1820–1870) in order to focus on the four later eras: the First Wave of Globalization (1870–1914); the Interwar Period (1914–1950); the Bretton Woods Era (1950–1973); and the Second Wave of Globalization (1973-present). While a later chapter discusses the Great Depression which expanded into much of the Interwar Period, this chapter presents the Bretton Woods era as a response to the Great Depression, and the Bretton Woods institutions, consisting of the IMF, the World Bank, and the Bretton Woods exchange rate mechanism, as having been designed with the intention of avoiding a repeat of the Great Depression and the crises of the Interwar Period.[8] The Bretton Woods era restricted international capital flows, fixed most countries' exchange rate to the US dollar, incrementally reduced trade barriers, and had fewer crises than any era since the onset of modern economic growth in the early nineteenth century. It is not an era we can return to, however, as international capital flows and flexible exchange rates, in particular, are too embedded in international economic relations, and the role of the United States as the undisputed world leader of market economies is no longer the case to the same extent it was in the aftermath and

[8] The General Agreement on Tariffs and Trade (GATT) can also be viewed as a creation of Bretton Woods although it came later. In 1995, the GATT was placed under the umbrella of the newly created World Trade Organization (WTO). All of the Bretton Woods institutions, including the GATT, were designed to increase international economic integration while, most importantly, decreasing international economic conflict.

first decades after World War II. The last era discussed in Chapter 2 is the current one, which many economic historians label the Second Wave of Globalization. It is an era of financial globalization, significantly lower trade barriers, and modern transportation and telecommunication systems. It also has more financial crises.

Part 2 of the book covers three important financial crises of the twentieth century, the Subprime Crisis of the early twenty-first century, and the mutation of the Subprime Crisis into a debt crisis in Europe. The three twentieth century crises are the Great Depression (Chapter 3), the Latin American Debt Crisis, 1982–1989 (Chapter 4), and the Asian Crisis, 1997–1999 (Chapter 5). Chapter 6 looks at the Subprime Crisis, 2007–2009, in the United States, while Chapter 7 examines its impact in Europe. The three twentieth century crises continue to shape our understanding of the mechanisms and causes of financial crises, as well as the types of policy responses that are more effective. The lessons of the Subprime Crisis are still debated but it promises to add insight and advance our understanding of crises. The Subprime Crisis began in the United States as a banking crisis but quickly spread to other parts of the world due in large part to our high degree of financial integration. As the crisis was winding down in the United States and some other affected countries, it morphed into a debt crisis in several countries in the European Union's Eurozone.[9] This added a second dimension to the Subprime Crisis and although all of the affected countries have begun to grow again (2018), several have real GDP levels that are significantly below their 2007 level.[10]

The crisis that for many decades shaped most of our understanding of financial crises is the Great Depression which is covered in Chapter 3. It is an important reference point and is foundational in the formation of contemporary economic policy. The Great Depression led to the development of modern macroeconomic

9 Note that Baldwin and Giavazzi reject the label "debt crisis" for the Eurozone Crisis, preferring instead to label it a "sudden stop crisis", or balance of payments crisis (Baldwin and Giavazzi, 2015b).

10 In particular, Cyprus, Finland, Italy, Greece, Latvia, and Portugal. Several more only recently (2015 or 2016) surpassed their 2007 level of output (IMF, 2017b).

analysis, created the modern social welfare state, ushered in a range of banking and financial market regulations, and remains a key moment for the creation of institutions and policies of contemporary industrial economies. The Great Depression continues to inspire debate in a number of important areas, including ideas about the stability of market economies, the optimal relationship between business and government, the efficacy of monetary and fiscal policies, and the problems of moral hazard and bank bailouts.

The Latin American Debt Crisis is the subject of Chapter 4. On the surface it seems like an ordinary case of unsustainable macroeconomic policies that led to a lost decade of economic growth. The debt crisis hit nearly every country in Latin America, except Colombia, and a few economies in Africa and Asia. It is remembered primarily for its stubborn persistence and for giving rise to a set of policy prescriptions, called the Washington Consensus, that were widely applied throughout the developing world in the 1990s and early 2000s. The lessons of the Latin American Debt Crisis extend beyond the mostly obvious ones about excess borrowing in foreign currencies and the need to pay attention to economic constraints. Prior to the crisis, several countries implemented extensive reforms in an attempt to free their financial systems from restrictions, many countries engaged in other economic reforms, and nearly all of Latin America borrowed excessively due to the easy availability of credit from banks in the United States and other advanced economies.[11] The obverse was that financial institutions, mostly in the United States but also in Europe and Japan, lent excessively. Lenders generally do not accept the symmetry of this view and try to present themselves as victims of reckless borrowing. In some respects the Latin American Debt Crisis may be the most complicated of the crises under consideration. Once it began, a toxic mix of domestic political conflicts in borrowing countries, fragile and overexposed banks in lending

11 Diaz-Alejandro (1985) describes the consequences of lifting financial constraints in the Southern Cone economies of Chile, Uruguay, and Argentina.

countries, and a rejection of mainstream economic theory by many indebted governments, made it difficult to escape.

Chapter 5 examines the Asian Crisis of 1997–1999. Unlike Latin America, the East Asian economies that fell into crisis were models of correct economic policy. Their growth rates were among the world's fastest, government budgets were sustainable, export sectors were strong and competitive, and for the most part, their institutions were in good shape. The sudden onset of a crisis in Thailand in July of 1997 was a shock to the world's system, especially as it spread to other fast growing countries of the region. The crisis threatened the United States and beyond, as it infected Russia and Turkey, before moving along to Brazil and Argentina and other countries. This historical example is unsettling to economists because the economic fundamentals of the countries involved did not make the crisis inevitable and it could have gone in a different direction if psychological expectations had been manageable. The long term fallout from the crisis was the push for new institutions in East Asia for managing the international economy, a reexamination of the IMF's role in crisis management, and a new dedication by some countries to ensuring a large supply of foreign reserves.

The Great Depression was the original lens through which economists and other analysts examined financial crises and their aftermaths, but the Latin American Debt Crisis, the Asian Crisis, and a number of smaller crises in one or two countries added to our understanding and expanded our perspective. Even so, the Subprime Crisis, which is the topic of Chapter 6, was a surprise. Economic forecasts missed it, popular risk management models failed to signal a warning, and regulators completely overlooked the systemic weaknesses of finance and the threats posed to the rest of the economy. Overconfidence and the mistaken belief that financial crises were a problem of developing countries, not high income countries with strong institutions, such as the United States, nearly caused another Great Depression. The systemic problems and near collapse of the world economy in 2008 and 2009 were not the end of the story, however. In 2010 and 2011, as most countries were in some stage of recovery, the crisis took a new and very deadly turn as it morphed from a banking crisis into a debt crisis in the Eurozone. This story is narrated in Chapter 7. Problems in the countries sharing the euro were compounded by fundamental policy mistakes and by conditions in the economic environment. The region that shares the common currency, the euro, is missing some of the institutions it needs to hold itself together when its member countries experience a profound divergence in economic conditions. Chapters 6 and 7 are chronological in their discussion of the crisis in the United States and Europe.

Part 3 addresses several of the lessons of the Subprime Crisis along with several additional lessons that were generally recognized before it occurred, but that were reenforced. Part 3 is a set of lessons from financial crises that are clearly warranted by both theory and data. I recognize, however, that they will not be universally accepted. In some cases, they conflict with political preferences, or with deeply held beliefs about the way economies would work if only some obstacles were removed. In thinking about these lessons, I have again tried to look for consensus and for empirical support without regard for other considerations such as politics or general philosophical concerns. I am not so naive as to believe that I am completely capable of that level of objectivity and I leave it to others to point out my mistakes. In the final analysis, the only certainty we can achieve is to know when we are wrong; certainty that we are right is not attainable.[12]

12 This point is made by Richard Feynman in his Messenger Lectures at Cornell University in 1964. According to the American philosopher John Kaag, Feynman learned this point from his friend, another American philosopher, Edward Hocking (Kaag, 2016: 182).

PART I Financial Crises

Chapter 1 offers a taxonomy of crises as identified by economists and economic historians, and a discussion of seven risk factors that increase the probability of a crisis. The risk factors are not deterministic and cannot be interpreted as predictors. Chapter 2 reviews the main eras of modern economic growth since 1820 and examines the frequency of crises in each era, along with the characteristics of economic institutions that increased or dampened the frequencies.

1 Categories and Risk Factors

1.1 AN INTRODUCTION TO FINANCIAL CRISES

Financial crises are rarely the result of a single causal factor or a single set of circumstances. In the lead-up to a crisis, economic, psychological, social, and other variables interact in ways that lead to vulnerabilities and increase the probability that a wrong turn of events will trigger a crisis in the financial system. Sometimes crises are triggered by recessions and related economic pressures, while at other times they are the causes of recessions. Crises sometimes involve fraud in a significant way, but most frequently and in very general terms, they are more likely to result from simple human errors compounded by well-intentioned but inadequate rules and organizations. During economic expansions, overconfidence bias expands and when reinforced by the social phenomena of herd behavior, the result can be too much risk, too much debt, and increasingly fragile economies.

In one of the classics of the financial crisis literature, Charles Kindleberger (1978) describes the entire process in the title of one of his best known works: *Manias, Panics, and Crashes*. The title reflects both a sense of irrationality – mania – in the lead-up, and a progression through stages – panic and crash. It seems to imply that if humans are wise enough and if we can keep our wits about us, particularly as everyone else seems to be doing the opposite in their scramble to get rich, then we should be able to avoid irrational exuberance and the seductive idea that this financial mania is different from others.[1]

[1] The term irrational exuberance was first used by Federal Reserve Chairman Alan Greenspan to describe the rise in stock prices in the 1990s. Subsequently, it was adopted as the title of Nobel Laureate Robert Shiller's work, *Irrational Exuberance* (2016, 3rd edition), which analyzes asset price booms from a behavioral finance

Kindleberger was among the group of economists that thought crises were an inherent part of market economies and would occasionally infect prosperous economies after a run of good times. Investment expands, caution is lulled by success, standards decline, and people take more risks in the expectation that they will make more money. The inherent stability or instability of market economies is an ongoing and ancient debate but since the Subprime Crisis of 2007–2009, the observation that market economies are prone to occasional financial crises has attracted more interest and analysis.

Until relatively recently, research on financial crises was mostly by economic historians, such as Kindleberger, or economic theorists such as Hyman Minsky. Minsky was not particularly influential during his life, even though Kindleberger incorporated his ideas into a widely read book.[2] Together, they might be considered the first generation of economists writing explicitly on financial crises using modern macroeconomic theories developed by J. M. Keynes and his followers. Limited by data availability and computing power, they developed their ideas before new information technologies made it possible to collect, organize, and analyze large datasets. Given these limitations, they did not try to create a set of tools to quantify features of crises or to measure differences over time, or across countries. The development of the study of crises with statistical techniques, particularly in the 1990s, moved the focus away from the choice between historical narratives or pure theory and toward a more explicitly quantitative analysis, even as history and theory continue to be centrally important in works on financial crises and, at their best, are well-informed by empirical analysis.

Quantification requires the construction of databases showing the start and stop dates of crises, the correlates, the policies used successfully and unsuccessfully to manage them, and other features

perspective. *This Time Is Different* is the title of the work by Reinhart and Rogoff (2009a) which analyzes several centuries of financial crises.

2 For example, Hyman Minsky's financial instability hypothesis (1977, 1986) was widely known but not taught in graduate programs or studied much by other economists. When Lehman Brothers collapsed in 2008 and the Subprime Crisis entered its most dangerous phase, he gained a level of posthumous fame.

that allow for more precise comparisons. Assembling a database requires a great deal of preliminary work. Most specifically, questions need to be answered about what, exactly, is being measured. Most observers probably know a financial crisis when they see one, but if they want to measure it, then there must be definite or at least reasonable markers of starting and ending points. Even this seemingly simple task turns out to be not so simple. To some extent it may not matter if the dating is off by a few months or more, but if we want to know, for example, how long a crisis lasts, we need to know when it started and when it ended. End points are also necessary if we want to measure how long an economy takes to recover its pre-crisis level of output and employment. Think about the most recent global crisis, the Subprime Crisis. Did it start in September, 2008, when the US investment bank Lehman Brothers collapsed? Or in March of 2008 when another US investment bank, Bear Stearns, teetered on the edge of collapse before the Federal Reserve engineered its takeover by JP Morgan Chase? Perhaps August, 2007, is a better start date since home prices were falling by then and the French bank BNP Paribas was forced to close two investment funds. According to some observers, the credit tightening in Europe that was triggered by BNP Paribas' troubles was the first event in the onset of the Subprime Crisis. Nevertheless, casual histories tend to pick the Lehman Brothers episode because that is the moment when the crisis intensified and reached its most dangerous panic phase. If the choice of a start date is difficult, dating the end of the crisis is even more so. If we were to ask citizens of Greece, they might respond that it is not yet over (July, 2018) since many banks are still insolvent, unemployment is over 20 percent and the economy is still 25 percent smaller than before the crisis began.

Finding the end dates is commonly difficult, but it is especially so when a crisis mutates from one set of characteristics into another. It is not uncommon for a crisis to become quiescent for a period of time, then to reignite with a different set of characteristics. The Latin American Debt Crisis is commonly dated as starting in 1982 and ending in 1989, yet Brazil, Argentina, and a number of other countries continued to experience varieties of financial crises after that, interspersed with near-normal periods. Were the reignited crises part of one long episode or should they be considered different crises? In the end, this is a judgment call.[3] It is necessary to decide if a period has one long crisis or several separate and distinct ones if we are to classify and categorize crises, but it should also give us pause as we try to draw statistical inferences about their effects based on a system of categorization that is not completely objective.

1.2 CATEGORIES OF FINANCIAL CRISES

The economics literature has settled into three main types of financial crises, with various subcategories and at least two contenders for additional main types. Claessens and Kose identify four main categories, as do Reinhart and Rogoff, but unfortunately they are not the same four (Claessens and Kose, 2014; Reinhart and Rogoff, 2009a: 8–14). Claessens and Kose's survey of the financial crisis literature defines banking, currency, debt, and sudden stop crises, while Reinhart and Rogoff's economic history defines banking, currency, debt, and inflation crises. Most research in this field is focused on one type of crisis, usually banking, currency, or debt crises the most popular, along with analysis of twin crises that occur simultaneously in banking and currency markets. Twin crises are relatively common and tend to be much more destructive than either banking or currency crises alone.

All of the crises in Table 1.1 except sovereign debt crises have subjective elements that require judgment on the part of the analyst to determine if a crisis is indeed a crisis. The main exception is a sovereign default crisis, when a government defaults on its loans. Currency and inflation crises are sometimes given

3 For example, Brazil in the 1890s experienced a series of crises, beginning in the banking sector, then passing into problems with its currency and high rates of inflation, a government default in 1898, and another banking crisis beginning in 1900 that lasted for five more years. In all, there were fifteen years of crisis. Was it one long crisis as Gerber and Passananti (2015) contend, or three separate crises as Bordo and Eichengreen (1999) and Reinhart and Rogoff (2009a) assume?

Table 1.1 *Types of financial crises*

Type	Main characteristics	Subcategories
Banking crisis	Significant number of bank defaults, forced mergers, or government support, including takeovers	Twin crisis: Simultaneous banking and currency crisis
Currency crisis	A significant and rapid decline in the value of a country's currency; precise thresholds are subjective and definitions vary.	Twin crisis: Simultaneous banking and currency crisis
Debt crisis	Sovereign default or a large number of private defaults	1. Sovereign debt crisis; 2. Private debt crisis; debt can be external or internal
Sudden stop	A sudden cessation of foreign capital inflows needed to finance a trade deficit	
Inflation crisis	A persistently high rate of inflation; some analysts use a standard of inflation exceeding 15–20 percent per year.	

Economists have identified five types of financial crises

a quantitative threshold for determining their existence but they too are judgment calls since there is no rule in economics that makes one level of inflation a crisis while a few percent less is not, or one level of depreciation a crisis and a few percent less not a crisis. Banking, private-debt default, and sudden stops are all somewhat arbitrary as to what level of disruption constitutes a crisis and what level does not, but as economic historians and researchers have begun to compile databases of crises, some agreements have emerged about the list of historical events that belong in the crisis category.

Debt crises are perhaps the easiest to observe but the most difficult to categorize since they have several sub-types. Economists distinguish internal from external debt, and private from public. Definitionally, external debt is owed to residents outside the country and internal debt is owed to residents inside. The significance of this distinction is that external debt is usually paid in a foreign currency and internal debt is usually paid in the domestic currency. The distinction between foreign and domestic currencies as defining features of external debt and internal debt are not always the case. For example, in March, 2018, Chinese residents (private and public combined) held $1.118 trillion in US government debt issued by the Treasury (US Department of Treasury, 2018b). Technically, this is an external debt of the US government, but is denominated in dollars. An additional distinction is the legal authority governing debt and disputes over repayment. External debt is usually subject to the rules and dispute processes in a foreign jurisdiction, while internal debt uses domestic rules and courts. Again, however, this is usually but not always the case as the US government's external debt, for example, is sold in New York and subject to adjudication in its courts. Debt is also either public or private, where public debt is debt issued by a public authority, and private debt is the debt of households and businesses. An intermediate version of the public/private categories arise when national governments provide guarantees to private borrowers who are then able to borrow in international markets at lower interest rates. In effect, this creates a public liability for private debt.

1.3 SEVEN RISK FACTORS

Given the high costs of financial crises, a great deal of effort has been expended to determine the conditions that lead up to a crisis. It seems reasonable to think that if we know what happens before a crisis, we might be able to prevent it or at least predict when one is coming. The problem with this approach is that although there are reoccurring conditions in the months before a crisis, they most often do not result in a crisis. For example, home prices and other asset prices frequently rise rapidly in the lead-up to a crisis, but most increases in home and asset prices do not end in a crisis.

Table 1.2 lists seven major risk factors associated with crises. It is useful to think of these as raising the probability of a crisis, much like the risk factors for heart disease or another medical condition. Each can interact with one or more of the others to increase the probability of a crisis, although we do not have precise measures of this. We have many examples, however, such as capital market liberalizations that generate credit booms and overvalued currencies that lead to excessive debt levels which, in turn, are much more dangerous when there are weak regulatory and supervisorial institutions. None of this makes a crisis certain, but the interaction of risk factors increases an economy's vulnerability.[4]

In the remainder of this chapter, each of the seven risk factors is discussed in more detail, with particular attention to the mechanisms leading from the risk factor to a financial crisis. As will be evident, there is a great deal of variation, particularly between countries with different levels of income. Many of the mechanisms through which one or more of the vulnerabilities adds to the probability of a crisis are known, but the precise increase in probability varies by the individual circumstance of each country.

4 There is an extensive literature on the causes of crises. See, for example the survey by Claessens and Kose (2014), and the historical treatment by Reinhart and Rogoff (2009a). Recent empirical work on the role of credit booms, financial liberalizations, trade imbalances, and institutional weaknesses can be found in, among others, Caprio and Klingebiel (1997); Demirgüç-Kunt and Detragiache (1997, 1999); Bordo and Meissner (2010); Jordà, Schularick, and Taylor (2011); Kose, Prasad, and Taylor (2011); Schularick and Taylor (2012); Jeanne, et al. (2012); Gorton (2012); Dell'Ariccia et al. (2014).

Table 1.2 *Common risk factors associated with financial crises*

Risk factor	Comments
Asset bubbles	A sustained rise in home prices appears to create more vulnerabilities than a sustained stock market increase; this is perhaps due to the association of housing bubbles with high debt levels.
Credit booms	A sudden increase in the supply of credit, whether from abroad or of domestic origin, increases debt and dependency on future credit inflows.
Weak institutions	The lack of adequate supervision and regulation of financial institutions leads to greater risk taking, moral hazards, and illegal activity.
Capital market liberalization	Open or liberalized capital markets permit large inflows of foreign capital which can be problematic if it suddenly reverses direction or leads to credit booms and a debt build up.
Overvalued currency	Currency overvaluation tends to create trade deficits and are is particularly worrying with fixed exchange rates since a correction through devaluation increases the real value of debt denominated in a foreign currency.
Large trade deficits	Trade deficits must be financed and usually require capital inflows; the adjustment required when capital is no longer flowing into a country can cause a deep recession and financial crisis.
Excessive debt levels	Debt can be public or private; defaults spread bankruptcies and cut off the supply of credit.

Common risk factors for financial crises discussed in the economics literature.

1.3.1 Asset Bubbles

It is usually impossible to know in advance when an asset bubble will collapse and turn into a financial crisis. Rising asset prices often lead to new higher plateaus that stabilize, or that hold for a while before continuing to rise again. A rapid increase in asset prices is not necessarily a sign of an impending crisis, and in stock markets at least, a crash is less likely than some other outcome

(Goetzmann, 2015).[5] This is one of the factors that make them hard to predict. When they do occur, other factors must be involved. Shiller (2005) emphasizes psychological factors that cause investors to feel overconfident, leading to overinvestment, rising asset prices, and a bubble if the overconfidence continues long enough. This process is propelled by emotional factors, such as the feeling of being left out of a new opportunity that seems to be making everyone else richer, and is subject to complex feedbacks that amplify the factors leading to asset bubbles. For example, an increase in asset prices often generates attention in the news media and leads to more activity and excitement as new investors try to take advantage of the moment.

A bubble can also be amplified if investors are subject to herd behavior. This common phenomenon is frequently observed in asset markets when individuals look for new information and base their decisions either wholly or in part on what others are doing. Bubbles can also be amplified by what Shiller (2005) calls "new era thinking" or what others have labeled "this time is different syndrome" (Reinhart and Rogoff, 2009a).[6] Former Secretary of the Treasury, Tim Geithner put it this way: "History suggests that financial crises are usually preceded by proclamations that crises are a thing of the past" (Geithner, 2014: 80). These psychological factors amplify bubbles by causing investors to believe that we have entered a new era of permanent prosperity where old truths no longer apply. Mania does not have to be pathological in order to be at work.

While some economists write about factors that cause asset bubbles, others think the concept of a bubble is not at all useful. Eugene Fama, who shared the 2013 Nobel Prize in Economics with Robert Shiller and Lars Hansen, prefers instead to think of the sudden

5 Goetzmann (2015) estimated that there is only about a 10 percent probability that a stock market will crash after a rapid doubling in prices. That is only slightly more than the probability (6 percent) of a crash when there is no boom in prices: "In simple terms, bubbles are booms that went bad. Not all booms are bad."

6 Shiller (2005) also discusses technological factors (including financial innovation), demographics, policies, and economic conditions.

increase in asset prices as a rational response to available information, and a collapse of asset prices as a reevaluation (Fama, 2010). Fama's goal is to force us to think more carefully about the meaning of the term "bubble," and highlights the underlying ambiguity of trying to determine if something is out of balance or not. Nevertheless, most observers agree that bubbles exist, even if they are difficult to precisely define or to anticipate when they might collapse.[7]

Regardless whether they are called sudden asset price increases or bubbles, they are sometimes, but not always, associated with financial crises when they burst. And if too little is known about the factors that set off a bubble, even less is known about those that cause it to burst, although Jordà and his colleagues note that bursting stock market bubbles are less often associated with financial crises than a collapse in a housing market bubble, most likely due to the greater use of debt in housing markets compared to stock markets (Jordà, Schularick and Taylor, 2016). Seemingly meaningless and random events, or some final accumulation of too much speculative investment, can lead to a sudden and precipitous panic that ends in collapsing prices as everyone rushes to sell their assets. This is the crash stage in Kindleberger's interpretation of Minsky's financial instability hypothesis.

The collapse of asset prices often spreads bankruptcies. If too many businesses or households are dependent on high asset prices as their source of positive net worth, and if their liabilities require payment at the same time as their assets are collapsing, bankruptcies can spread through the system. For example, during the Subprime Crisis of 2007–2009, households relied on rising house prices as a way to service their mortgage debts. When those prices stopped rising and started falling, homeowners defaulted in increasing numbers.

[7] Economists joke that their field is the only discipline where two people can share a Nobel Prize for saying exactly the opposite thing. In any case, bubbles do not have a precise definition. A common informal definition is asset prices that are not warranted by the present value of expected future earnings. The term "expected" introduces a degree of ambiguity and underlines Shiller's observation (Shiller, 2012: 178–179) that there is a large psychological component to bubbles.

The rise in defaults on home loans damaged bank balance sheets, cut off bank lending, and help set in motion a recessionary spiral.[8] Banks and other lenders tried to cover their losses in the mortgage market by selling off some of the assets they held, many of which had values that were tied to mortgages. When banks began to sell large quantities of their mortgage backed securities (MBS), their value in the market place declined.[9] The general outline of this problem was well-known long before the Subprime Crisis, although it probably seemed like an unlikely possibility in 2005. In the 1930s, the American economist Irving Fisher wrote about "debt deflation" as occurring when financial institutions sold large quantities of assets in order to shrink their debts, with the consequence that asset prices fell further due to the large quantity being sold, often under desperate circumstances (Fisher, 1933). Fisher described debt deflation as a major factor in the severity and prolongation of the Great Depression. The low prices can turn out to be too low to cover the short-term debts of financial institutions and will certainly depress prices even more, leading to further declines in profits, output, and confidence. Fisher was a pioneer in describing debt deflation and economists now recognize it as a contagion factor in the spread of crises and a key reason why the collapse of asset prices can turn into a recession or worse.

Collapsing asset prices can cause or intensify a crisis, but like most of the other factors discussed in this chapter, the outcome is not predetermined. For example, when the Dotcom Bubble burst in 2001, there were few defaults. In part this was because the bubble was in the stock market and was largely propelled by trading stocks back and forth and did not involve a large amount of debt financing. Consequently, when technology stocks collapsed in 2001, there were not nearly as many defaults on loans, credit markets remained

8 Bank assets include the loans they make to home buyers; if those loans are in default then bank assets are reduced and may fall below their liabilities, making them insolvent.

9 A mortgage backed security, or MBS, is similar to a bond but is backed by the payments on a group of mortgages that have been combined to form the security.

relatively healthy, and the economy was not dragged into a deep recession. The Dotcom Bubble episode shows why it is difficult to forecast a financial crisis. The bubble was a sudden collapse after several years of increasing prices, but it did not lead to a crisis since there was not a lot of debt involved. There was, however, a mild recession at the same time.[10]

1.3.2 Credit Booms

Credit booms are closely related to rising asset prices, since the later often depend on the former. Credit booms occur when there is a sustained increase in the supply of available funds for borrowing. The funds may be from domestic sources such as banks or the bond market, or they may come from outside through purchases of domestic securities or loans by foreign banks that may or may not be mediated through domestic banks. Credit booms lead to an increase in debt and rising vulnerabilities. If the economy suffers some kind of shock, a higher debt burden means that there is less flexibility to respond and that any decline in income makes debt service more difficult. For example, Spain and Ireland were two of the European countries most severely hurt by the spread of the Subprime Crisis from the United States to Europe. In the years leading up to the crisis, both countries received significant increases in credit from Germany, the Netherlands, and other European Union countries with savings surpluses and funds to lend. German banks and pension funds lent money to Spanish and Irish banks that in turn made loans for housing and local infrastructure projects such as airports. Germans earned higher rates of return than they would have if they invested only in Germany, while individuals and businesses in Spain and Ireland received

10 If we think of a crisis as a natural response by the economy to some sort of imbalance, then economists are relatively competent at pointing out when economies or markets are out of balance and in need of a reset. However, even if we are relatively certain that a crisis is likely, there is no certainty about the timing or the triggering event, or whether there might not be a last second intervention, either intentional or fortuitous, that prevents the crisis.

more funding for housing and other needs. Everyone won in the lead up to the crisis. Since this was a significant increase in the supply of credit, the buildup of debt was substantial, however. And when the economic downturn began in 2007, some borrowers defaulted on their loans from Spanish and Irish banks. As the dominoes began to fall, banks in Ireland and Spain were suddenly at risk of defaulting on the credit they had obtained from Germany, the Netherlands, and elsewhere. The crisis was in full bloom at that point and after a great deal of hand wringing and some discussion of the various options, governments stepped in to save the banks. This created another set of problems, discussed in Chapter 7.

While credit booms can be generated either domestically or from abroad, the source matters. A loan that must be paid back in a foreign currency can be disastrous if the domestic currency declines in value. Prior to the Subprime Crisis, for example, many home buyers in Hungary and other parts of Central Europe took advantage of low Swiss interest rates and the willingness of Swiss banks to lend abroad. A few years later, when the Swiss franc rose in value against the Hungarian forint, the burden of the mortgage debt increased for Hungarian borrowers who earned forint but were required to pay in francs.

Both quantitative and qualitative analysis support the linkages between credit booms and financial crises.[11] Quantitative analyses by macroeconomists and economic historians look at large groups of countries over long periods of time, while Kindleberger (1978) and Minsky (1977) are perhaps the most well-known qualitative analyses. Recent quantitative analysis support Minsky's fundamental point that capitalist economies have a natural tendency to expand credit and loosen lending standards when the economy is booming (Schularick and Taylor, 2012). This is a self-generating process that

11 For quantitative analysis, see Schularick and Steger (2010); Schularick and Taylor (2012); Dell'Aricca, et al. (2014). Qualitative studies are Minsky (1977); Kindleberger (1978).

ultimately leads to an overexpansion of credit followed by a collapse as borrowers reach a point where they cannot repay.

1.3.3 Weak Supervision and Regulation

Minsky's model implies that borrowers and lenders cannot help themselves in the late stages of the mania when credit flows freely, lending standards decline, debt levels grow, and everyone looks to make money in the boom. Regulators and supervisors are somehow missing in action in this model, or at least, ineffective at preventing overborrowing and a piling up of debt as the flow of credit rises higher and higher.[12] In the decades before the Subprime Crisis, for example, a growing segment of the economics profession became increasingly skeptical about the need for financial regulation, and as many barriers were removed in the 1980s and 1990s, there was a growing sense that regulations were unnecessary and possibly even counterproductive. This idea is examined in detail in Chapter 8.

The belief that regulations were unnecessary, or that they could at least be minimized, was an idea that developed in advanced, high income countries. In the United States, Western Europe, Japan, and other advanced economies, many business people, policy makers, and academics, accepted the idea that good contract enforcement, the rule of law, and well-defined property rights, created stable economic environments, where more specific and detailed regulatory measures for the financial system were less important and could even be counterproductive if they caused businesses to rely on government rules instead of using their own internal standards for oversight and due diligence.

Developing countries, by contrast, were known to need supervision and regulation of their financial systems. While it is true that emerging economies often have weaker contract enforcement and rule

12 See, for example, Gorton (2009); Financial Crisis Inquiry Commission (FCIC), (2011); Blinder (2013); Bernanke (2015). The Booth School of Business at the University of Chicago surveyed European and US economists about the main causes of the financial crisis. The most frequently cited reason was a lack of supervision (IGM Forum, October 17, 2017).

of law, along with less experience with regulatory oversight and supervision of the financial sector, it is also true that the assumptions about regulatory needs, and how they varied by the level of development, reflected a kind of myopic double standard that was not informed about the reality of financial crises in advanced economies. A common assumption was that advanced economies could outgrow financial crises and would be protected by general institutional developments in the areas of property rights, contract enforcement, and the rule of law. Many policymakers believed that cronyism, fraud, excessive risk-taking, and flawed incentive structures were problems for developing economies but not for advanced high income countries with strong laws and stable institutions. While it is undoubtedly true that there is a correlation between income per capita and institutional strengths, there is wide variation among high income countries, and "pretty good" may not mean "good enough" when it comes to regulating finance. Economic historians mostly did not share this double standard and tended to be skeptical about the ability of high income countries to avoid crises. The skepticism was supported by the empirical literature written before the crisis showing that advanced economies are crisis prone as well, particularly with respect to crises in the banking sector and often when financial liberalization and deregulation are put into place (Demirgüç-Kunt and Detragiache, 1997, 1999).

1.3.4 Capital Market Liberalization

Capital market liberalization refers to the dismantling of barriers to international capital flows. The new consensus is covered in Chapter 14 while this section is a general discussion of crises and capital market liberalization. There are a number of crises that can be traced to large inflows of financial capital, even though the relaxation of restrictions on capital flows can also be beneficial. For example, the first wave of globalization from approximately 1870 to 1914, had few legal restrictions on international capital movements yet rates of economic growth were good and there may have been fewer financial crises. Comparing the frequency of financial crises in different historical periods is somewhat problematic given that with the inclusion of more countries in regions with developed financial systems, we should see more crises, all else being equal, simply due to the existence of financial markets in places where they did not exist previously. Nevertheless, the first wave of globalization was the period when capital from Western Europe was used to build railroad networks in the Americas and European colonies, and incomes in many of those places rose significantly as transportation costs fell and more people were connected to markets beyond their own regions.

There are numerous potential problems with large capital inflows, but it is useful to distinguish the types of flows that were common in the first wave of globalization (1870–1913) from more recent types. Capital flows during the first wave were primarily for the construction of railroads and other utilities, or loans to government (Bordo, Eichengreen, and Irwin, 1999). Foreign capital inflows were usually in the form of bond financing and were used to invest in projects that generated revenue streams that were a source of funds for interest and principal payments. International capital flows today take many more forms and serve a wider range of purposes, including speculative ventures that do not have a guaranteed source of revenue. Furthermore, debt service may depend on additional future loans. For example, short-term international loans to a country's banking sector may be used to finance real estate projects. In the event of an economic downturn in the borrowing country, banks with short-term external debts are extremely vulnerable if they are cut off from their source of international finance. In a nutshell, this was one of the triggers of the Asian Crisis of 1997–1998, which is discussed in Chapter 5.

Open capital markets mean that the owners of both domestic and international assets are free to flee the country if such a move seems necessary. Capital flight often depends on an expected or actual decline in the value of the borrowing country's currency. If economic conditions warrant, investors and speculators sell their financial assets, convert the proceeds to dollars or another reserve currency, and relocate them outside the country. Capital flight drains the stock of international reserves that are available to convert the currency to dollars, increases the downward pressure on the value of the currency, increases the domestic currency value of external debts, and makes it impossible for banks and other firms to borrow in international capital markets. The ownership of financial assets, domestic or foreign, does not usually matter in scenarios of capital flight.

1.3.5 Overvalued Currencies

An overvalued currency is one that buys too much of another currency. There are various definitions of "too much" but in general, it is easiest to think of it as a quantity of foreign currency that lets you buy more goods and services abroad than at home when you convert to a foreign currency. A country's currency tends to rise in value with inflows of foreign capital, since they increase the demand for money in the receiving country. The increase in demand for the currency leads to an increase in its value, all else being equal, if there are floating exchange rates, or it puts pressure on the currency that must be countered by the monetary authority if exchange rates are fixed.

Fixed, or pegged, exchange rates have several other problems related to financial crises. Most countries with fixed exchange rates set them in terms of a major currency or a basket of currencies (IMF, 2014a). For example, Denmark pegs its currency, the krone, to the euro, and Saudi Arabia pegs the riyal to the dollar. With a fixed exchange rate, the monetary authorities must be able to convert their currency into the anchor currency at the set rate and vice versa. If the krone is worth 0.13 euro, then Denmark's National Bank will convert a krone into 13 cents (0.13 euro) or 13 euro cents into a krone whenever requested. Now, consider a hypothetical situation where Denmark has some inflation and the Eurozone has none. With a fixed exchange rate, the value of the krone continues to be worth 0.13 euro, but inflation reduces the purchasing power of the krone in Denmark while leaving it unaffected in the Eurozone. This is a real appreciation of the krone and reflects the fact that its weaker purchasing power at home and constant purchasing power in the Eurozone is a relative strengthening of the krone abroad. Real appreciation leads to fewer sales of Danish goods and services, higher sales for firms in the Eurozone, and imbalanced trade.

Real appreciation caused by fixed exchange rates and higher inflation at home is relatively common and, in the absence of an adjustment, leads to trade deficits. As long as the central bank has large enough stocks of foreign currency reserves, it can continue to convert domestic money for the purchase of imports, but at some point, declining foreign currency reserves are likely to undermine confidence. What happens next is completely unpredictable and depends on the reactions of individuals and firms. If people believe the problem is temporary and if the trade deficit country has sufficient foreign currency reserves to last, then nothing further may happen in the short run. If, on the other hand, people believe the reserves may run out if the fixed exchange rate is not devalued, there will be a strong incentive for everyone to convert to the currency of the surplus country. This intensifies the pressure on the deficit country's foreign exchange reserves and can precipitate a crisis. Since everyone has the same incentive, the goal is to be the first out the door of the trade deficit country. More money flows out and the central bank's reserves shrink faster.

The uncertainty about a future devaluation and the capital flight it sometimes provokes can have several negative consequences. First, the outward movement of capital results in a capital bust, the opposite of a boom discussed in the Section 1.3.4. Second, the devaluation of the home country currency increases the real value of debt, further intensifying bankruptcies. Note that this entire set of problems is due to two factors: a difference in inflation rates and fixed exchange rates. The relatively high inflation country experiences an overvaluation of its currency that enables it to buy relatively more goods abroad than at home, even though the exchange rate is fixed.[13] What happens after that is unpredictable and depends on the psychology of investors and businesses. Do they expect a devaluation, and therefore send their capital out of the country? Or do they expect nothing much in the way of changes, so they are content to leave things as they are? This pattern and the problems described are not rare events. Fixed exchange rates are often a source of currency instability and have been at the root of financial crises in Latin America, East Asia, and within the Eurozone.[14]

1.3.6 *Large Trade Deficits*

In the discussion of overvalued currencies, trade deficits played a significant role. It is worth a closer look since they are also frequently implicated as the cause of financial crises. In Section 1.3.5, an overvalued currency was the trigger for trade deficits and much of the blame for capital flight and the ensuing crisis. Trade deficits are caused by many other variables beyond overvalued currencies, however, and it would also be a mistake to think that deficits are always negative.

Trade deficits are, by definition, an excess of imports over exports. Another way to think of them is that they happen when a country buys more from the rest of the world than it sells. Countries are not households and the rules of households usually do not apply to entire nations, but one similarity between the two is that an excess of spending over income requires a source of financing. For households, it is a line of credit from a bank or a credit card company,

13 Exchange rate systems refer to the nominal exchange rate, or the number of units of one currency that exchanges for another. The real exchange rate is the nominal rate adjusted for price changes in the countries compared. In the example given, nominal rates are fixed, but the real rate changed due to the difference in inflation rates.

14 There are nineteen countries that share the euro (2018). Conceptually, the Eurozone is equivalent to each country having a fixed exchange rate with the other eighteen members, at a rate of one French euro equals one German euro equals one Spanish euro, etc. If inflation is higher in one country, then it has a real appreciation. The impossibility of devaluation is a substantial part of the reason for the prolonged recession in some Eurozone countries after the Subprime Crisis. See Chapters 7 and 13.

or dipping into the savings from previous years. For countries, a trade deficit has to be financed by selling stocks, bonds, real estate, bank loans, or another asset, or by dipping into the nation's reserves of foreign currency. Foreign currency reserves easily run out, however, so the most reliable way to finance a persistent trade deficit is to sell assets. The assets sold to foreigners lead to an accumulation of foreign exchange that can be used to purchase the excess of imports over exports. By way of illustration, consider the United States which typically runs a trade deficit of around 2–4 percent of GDP. Consequently, it must sell an equivalent amount of stocks, bonds, real estate, and other assets. Asset sales create a capital inflow from abroad, leading to the observation that a trade deficit is matched by a capital inflow and trade surpluses by capital outflows.

Suppose a nation has a persistent trade deficit and foreigners lose confidence in the its ability to manage the deficit. For example, foreigners might see something troubling about the economy and decide that they do not want to buy its assets. The cessation of domestic asset purchases by foreign interests means the country can no longer finance its trade deficit. In the economics literature, this is called a sudden stop, because the inflow of foreign capital often stops immediately when countries arrive at this point (Calvo, 1998). When capital inflows stop, policymakers must find ways to shrink the trade deficit. Cuts in spending, increased taxation, redirection of output toward exports and away from the domestic market, and other measures to reduce expenditures are elements of the standard recipe for reducing a trade deficit. A significant and sudden cut in expenditures frequently leads to a recession and if pressures are sudden and very strong, can lead to a financial crisis through sudden devaluation, capital flight, loss of access to foreign credit, or another of the mechanisms discussed.

Not all trade deficits end this way. The United States, for example, has been able to run substantial deficits since the early 1980s and has yet to experience this type of crisis. That does not mean that it will never have a financial crisis caused by its trade deficit, but it seems unlikely given the current state of world economic affairs. The US dollar is used in about 80 percent of all transactions worldwide, which makes for a strong and persistent demand for dollars. The US economy is one of the safest in the world for foreign investors – at least until recently – making it attractive to foreign capital in normal circumstances, and even more so when world events become tumultuous. This can change, but for the foreseeable future, the chances of a US financial crisis caused by a sudden stop of capital inflows seems unlikely. Other nations are not so lucky, and ones that run persistent and large trade deficits are much more vulnerable, although large deficits are not precisely defined but are generally considered to be above 4 percent of GDP. Factors that increase vulnerability are exchange rates that are fixed, reliance on a limited set of economic activities, such as copper mining or oil exports, and extensive short-term borrowing in international financial markets.

1.3.7 Excessive Debt Levels

Debt is sometimes useful, as most of us know. We take on debt to buy houses, cars, and, in some countries, college degrees. Debt allows us to do things that improve our lives. Businesses incur debt to expand their operations, to improve the products and services they offer, to explore new markets, and to manage their cash flows. Governments, too, incur debt because the taxes they collect are not sufficient to pay for the services they provide or the actions they take. Households, businesses, and government all use debt as a tool for accomplishing tasks they set for themselves. As a society, we worry more often about government debt, (which is more publicized and usually has better statistics), and we tend to think less about household and business debt. Nevertheless, excessive debt is associated with financial crises regardless who borrows.

The problem of debt is highly controversial. To a certain degree this is due to the issues surrounding government debt, but it is also probably due to the fact that we often do not know enough about private debt to understand the role it plays in creating financial crises.

While there are efforts by the IMF and others to fill this gap, private debt remains more opaque than public debt (Mbaye, Moreno Badia, and Chae, 2018). For example, many countries have much better measures of government debt than business or household debt. Government statistics related to borrowing and government bond sales are usually available, and if a country defaults on its government issued debt, there is generally a good set of measurements describing the size of the debt, who it is owed to, and how soon it must be paid back.

There are relatively good statistics on government defaults, from which it seems we should be able to make robust inferences about the amount of debt that is too much for a particular country. The problem is that government debt levels vary enormously for countries that default. In general, the higher the ratio of debt to GDP, the more likely is a default, but some countries default with relatively low levels of debt to GDP. Comparing debt levels of countries, we can say that a debt to GDP ratio of 30 percent is relatively low, while 100 percent is high. But defaults on debt are caused by many factors and Reinhart and Rogoff (2009a: 24) show that 20 percent of historical defaults are cases where debt was less than 40 percent of GDP.

Debt can be divided into private and public, where public debt is the debt of governments and private debt is that of households and businesses. Public debt is often divided into external and internal debt, where external debt is denominated in a foreign currency and subject to adjudication outside the national court system. For example, when the government of Argentina sold bonds in New York in the 1990s, it agreed to pay back dollars, and when it defaulted in 2001, the claims of its creditors were adjudicated in the New York court system, not in Argentina. These two characteristics of external debt make it riskier. Even so, many countries must resort to it because their domestic savings are insufficient to supply governments with the resources they want. Private debt, by contrast, is usually but not always internal debt.

It would useful to know how much debt is too much, but unfortunately, the answer depends on so many different variables that it is impossible to make any firm conclusions. We can say that when debt grows faster than the economy it is not sustainable, and conversely, debt that grows more slowly than the economy is sustainable, usually. We can also say that an indicator of potential debt problems is a rapid upward ratcheting of interest rates. If debt grows rapidly and interest rates are not moving, the signal from markets is that the debt can be absorbed without having to pay higher rates. On the other hand, debt problems can develop suddenly and without warning, which is why many people are leery of any size debt.

An important consideration is whether the debt is denominated in a nation's own currency. If so, then there is more flexibility since the debt is owed in a currency that only the national government can provide. It is hard to see how debt becomes excessive under these circumstances and indeed, Japan's large public debt (net) has been over 100 percent of its GDP since 2009 without an apparent problem. And the United Kingdom's public debt sometimes exceeded 200 percent of GDP and always exceeded 100 percent from 1756 to 1859, and again from 1918 to 1962, without triggering a crisis. (It did experience an industrial revolution during the first period – apparently the debt was not an obstacle.) Other nations appear to be very sensitive to debt, even at relatively low levels. Ecuador defaulted in 2008 with a debt to GDP ratio of only 20 percent, and Albania in 1990, shortly after the collapse of the Berlin Wall, with 16.6 percent (Reinhart and Rogoff, 2009a: 23).

Sovereign defaults often spread to the banking sector where they create additional solvency problems and sometimes become a banking crisis on top of the debt crisis. This occurs when banks hold large quantities of government bonds that are suddenly worth much less. Governments frequently require national banks to hold reserves in the form of government bonds, or to hold some percentage of their total assets as bonds, as a way to reduce the costs of financing government operations. During a crisis, this strategy becomes a major transmission channel of problems from the government sector to the banking sector.

1.4 WHAT DO WE REALLY KNOW?

Economists have been able to create a taxonomy of financial crises, and although it is not completely agreed, it does enjoy wide support for its general categories. That is helpful. If we think about the development of biology, the creation of a workable taxonomy was one key to its growth and maturation. A taxonomy enables researchers to define start and stop dates, and to compare the frequency and destructiveness of different types of crises, however imperfectly.

Economists have also developed a set of variables that are precursors to a crisis. Like medicine, however, the presence of a risk factor does not completely determine outcomes. Countries with similar initial conditions often have different outcomes with respect to the onset of a crisis. One goal of some researchers is to develop a set of early warning indicators. This goal is elusive, however, and seems far off, in part because of the complicated feedback effects a set of early warning indicators would generate. Using a medical metaphor again, we know the factors that increase the risk of heart disease, but we do not have a clear set of indicators that a heart attack is six months out, one month out, or even about to strike tomorrow. Similarly with risk factors for a financial crisis: When we observe the presence of a factor, the smart action would be to address it before a crisis sneaks up because there is no way to be certain when or even if it will occur.

One of the most useful developments in all of this research is the creation of datasets that combine information about historical crises, along with other important factors, such as policy responses and outcomes, time to recovery, and the behavior of variables such as debt, unemployment, GDP growth, and others. The creation of these datasets moves analysis out of a rarefied environment of theory, where economic assumptions often determine the expected outcomes, and into empirical economics where measurement can begin to untangle the uncertainties. This is a big step toward understanding financial crises because it allows economists to test hypotheses about causes and effects, about trade-offs between alternative approaches to crisis resolution, and about policies that might work. It is a beginning, not an end.

Economists cannot run laboratory experiments, except in a very limited way, and then usually at the level of individual decision making and not for macroeconomies. To the extent that the discipline of economics permits experiments, they are usually natural experiments, consisting of historical situations in which different conditions prevailed or different policies were implemented, and the outcomes are observed by posterity. For example, looking at the Great Depression of the 1930s, we know that countries that left the gold standard first, recovered first. This is not a perfect experiment because we do not know if leaving the gold standard was the key, or if the key was to leave the gold standard while some countries continued to stay on it. Theory helps to disentangle these two possibilities, but at a minimum the natural experiment gives a fundamental idea of where to look for further evidence. In this case, and supplemented with some theory, the natural experiment provides strong reasons for rejecting a return to a gold standard.[15]

Before turning to a set of key episodes that serve as natural experiments to provide insights into the actual causes and consequences of crises, it is helpful to briefly survey financial crises in economic history, beginning with the modern era of economic growth. This long period of two centuries saw the development of modern financial systems and contains most of the raw material for understanding financial crises. Many of the vulnerabilities discussed in this chapter are a consequence of the financial and

15 The role the gold standard played in delaying recovery from the Great Depression is explored in Chapter 3. See, for example, Eichengreen and Sachs (1985); Bernanke and James (1991); and Eichengreen (1992).

economic developments that occurred over this timespan, and many of the eventual lessons grow out of the experiences of countries with globalization and modern economic growth. We turn now to a brief survey of the patterns of financial crises during different periods in the development of the international economy.

2 Growth, Globalization, and Financial Crises

2.1 MODERN ECONOMIC GROWTH

The emergence of modern economic life with amenities such as electricity, sanitation and indoor plumbing, modern medicine, and transportation and communication networks, is a recent development in human history. In 1800, someone living in New York, London, or Shanghai experienced conditions that were closer to ancient Rome or Greece than to a mid-twentieth century city. Candles were the primary source of artificial light, modern medicines did not exist, food storage was primitive, and animals, wind, water, and humans supplied all the available power. The vast changes in living conditions since 1800 are the result of nearly two centuries of economic growth that came after several millennia of little or no cumulative progress in living standards. Significant changes did not begin until the 1800s and after approximately 1870 they accelerated further (Gordon, 2016: 1–18; Maddison, 2006: 29).

Economic historians divide modern economic growth into five separate periods since 1820. The dates are approximate but taken together they convey a remarkable historical pattern of economic growth and rates of improvement in living standards. The first period, from 1820 to 1870, represents a significant rise in economic growth rates after millennia of comparative stagnation. The beginning of sustained economic growth is characterized by the application of steam power, the beginning of modern transportation networks, and the beginning of large-scale multi-regional enterprises producing standardized goods in large batches. The growth of modern large-scale enterprises spread dramatically in the second period, from 1870 to the start of World War I in 1914. Modern management techniques developed for the management of giant industrial enterprises, and electricity, refrigeration, the telegraph, and telephone began to be deployed. Railroad networks were completed in the most advanced countries and the internal combustion engine appeared (Chandler, 1977, 1990). Chandler (1977) argues that the advent of modern management was as important as technology and a necessary complement to new technologies and scale economies that drove much of the growth. Gordon (2016) sets 1870 as the beginning of a century of high growth and most economic historians date the first wave of globalization from then as well. The interwar period came after the first wave of globalization and lasted from approximately 1914 to 1950. Economic growth was slower, yet still good by comparison to the first period (1820–1870) and very good compared to the centuries before 1820. Two world wars and a worldwide depression with banking and debt crises reversed most of the increases in international trade, capital flows, and migration that had occurred during the first wave of globalization. The fourth period lasted from approximately 1950 to 1973 and has been labeled the Golden Age of economic growth (Maddison, 1982, 1991). Economic growth reached its highest sustained level in human history, new international agreements helped manage economic relations, and national governments implemented demand management policies in the attempt to maintain full employment with high growth rates. The Golden Age was followed by the fifth and final period which began in 1973. Its outstanding feature is the second wave of globalization during which international migration, trade in goods and services, and flows of financial capital increased significantly. Economic growth, however, declined in nearly all countries from the rates attained during the Golden Age, with a few important exceptions, primarily in East Asia.

Each of the five periods has a different set of characteristics with respect to crisis frequency, severity, and crisis management policies. In particular, the last four are relevant for this book, since they include periods of extreme openness (1870–1914), financial collapse and depression (1914–1950), restricted capital flows (1950–1973), and

Table 2.1 *Estimated average annual growth of real per capita income*

	1820–1870	1870–1914	1914–1950	1950–1973	1973–2010
Regions (countries)					
Western Europe (30)	0.64	1.29	0.70	4.09	1.66
Eastern Europe (7)	0.67	1.39	0.52	3.89	1.49
Western offshoots (4)	1.25	1.81	1.56	2.45	1.64
Latin America (23)	0.42	1.63	1.30	2.60	1.10
East Asia (30)	−0.08	0.81	−0.17	2.39	2.55
West Asia (15)	0.30	0.87	1.22	4.47	1.08
Africa (6)	0.57	0.79	−0.06	1.95	1.04
World (115)	0.44	1.30	0.84	2.92	1.77

Growth in per capita income rises during the first wave of globalization, falls during the interwar period, and then reaches its highest rate during the postwar Golden Age. Western offshoots are Australia, Canada, New Zealand, and the United States. Source: Author's calculations based on data from Maddison Project Database, 2013.

a second wave of globalization (1973–present). Table 2.1 summarizes patterns of growth during the five periods with estimates based on data from the Maddison Project Database 2013 (Maddison Project Database, 2013; Bolt and van Zanden, 2014). Maddison was an early pioneer in the construction of comparable historical time series of economic variables and his data are among the first methodologically sound estimates of historical GDP, population, and GDP per person. Table 2.1 displays several patterns across the world's regions in average annual growth rates of per capita income. First, all regions had faster growth in the second period (1870–1914) than in the first period (1820–1870). Growth falls everywhere in the interwar period (1914–1950), with the exception of West Asia. During the Golden Age

(1950–1973) growth rises everywhere and reaches the highest historical rates experienced by every region. After 1973 and the break-up of the Bretton Woods system, growth declines in every region except East Asia. A few individual countries, namely China, India, Korea, and a few other smaller economies, are exceptions to the growth slowdown after the mid-1970s, but the pattern holds for the rest of the world.

2.2 MODERN GLOBALIZATION'S FIRST WAVE: 1914–1950

Nayan Chanda (2007: xiv) points out that globalization actually began in the late Ice Age when "a tiny group of our ancestors walked out of Africa in search of better food and security." From then on, an unending parade of "traders, preachers, adventurers and warriors" have spread their values, societies, and economies. It was not until the 1500s, however, that individual nations attained a global reach. Aided by disease and a few technological advantages, Europeans conquered the Americas and colonized parts of Asia and Africa. European expansion enabled a small number of highly valued commodities such as tea, spices, porcelain, silks, and silver, to trade internationally, but it was not until the 1800s that economic activity began to grow out of traditional, small scale, local enterprises confined to a single region.

The first wave of modern globalization (1870–1914) occurred during the industrial age and is notable for the rapid growth of trade, capital flows, and migration on an international scale. As countries built national transportation networks, largely consisting of railroads and canals, farmers and miners in the hinterlands could begin to move their products to a port city where ocean-going steamships provided transport to global markets. Prices in distant markets could be checked over the telegraph lines strung next to the railroads, and over cables that were laid across the Mediterranean Sea and the Atlantic Ocean by the late 1860s. Transportation and communication technologies in the second half of the 1800s facilitated the growth of international trade in agricultural products and the expanding export of manufactured goods, both of which would play major roles in twentieth century world trade.

2.2.1 *Open Capital Markets*

Agricultural products made up the bulk of international shipments during the first wave of globalization. Farmers in the United States, Australia, South America, the Crimea, and elsewhere produced for both local and international grain markets that were made possible by new financial systems facilitating trade. The Chicago Board of Trade opened in 1848 and by the mid-1860s, futures contracts were used to set a price for grain delivered at a future date, facilitating planning and reducing uncertainty about prices. In addition to commodity exchanges, new investments in transportation networks and urban infrastructure required enormous amounts of capital that necessitated the expansion of bond markets. The relative scarcity of savings coupled with the relative abundance of investment opportunities in the colonies and former colonies, caused much of the new investment in railroads and other large projects in the United States, South America, and elsewhere, to be financed by the savings of Europeans who lent significant shares of their national income outside their home countries. The system of international trade and finance was supported by transoceanic telegraphy, the legalization of joint stock companies with limited liability for individual investors, and a network of correspondent banks that worked together but were located in different regions. These institutional and technological developments, in the later part of the nineteenth century, made possible the development of giant enterprises that exceeded the limits of the informal family and socially based financial networks that were the norm prior to the growth of industry. Large-scale projects such as the transcontinental railroad in the United States; the Panama and Suez Canals in Central America and Africa; and a growing number of large industrial concerns that produced steel, farm equipment, and standardized consumer goods, needed vastly larger amounts of capital than family and friends could supply.

2.2.2 *The Gold Standard*

In addition to open capital markets, the first wave of globalization was also characterized by widespread use of the gold standard. During the 1870s, the gold standard was universalized in Western Europe and the United States (Kindleberger, 1984: 68; Eichengreen, 2008: 17). The frequency of banking crises during the gold standard undermines the idea of greater stability with gold standards, while the experiences of many countries during the Great Depression, including the United States and the United Kingdom, contradicts the common association of gold standards with prosperity. Gold standards usually perform adequately during periods of steady growth, but they are frequently inadequate during recessions. Economic downturns force governments to choose between protecting the gold standard by limiting the amount of money in circulation to curtail gold outflows, or combatting the recession by expanding the money supply at the potential cost of a loss of gold reserves. The conflict between external balance (keeping to the gold standard) and internal balance (adequate growth and employment) has been the most severe liability of gold as a monetary standard and exchange rate system.

The classical gold standard lasted until World War I when the hostilities and the collapse of international trade and capital flows led to its suspension. After the war, there were major attempts to return to gold, but new problems made it completely unworkable, as discussed below. Even during the period that is considered its zenith, from its adoption in most of Europe in the 1870s and its subsequent spread to most of the world during the remainder of the nineteenth century, up until its suspension in 1914, the tendency of the gold standard to impart a deflationary bias through the restrictions it placed on new money creation probably constrained economic activity. In addition, it did not provide a vaccine against financial crises as banking crises in particular were frequent.

2.2.3 *Financial Crises*

Financial crises were not uncommon during the first wave of globalization. In particular, banking crises were very common, while currency crises appear to be less so, at least in comparison to trends since 1973. Debt crises were also less common in the nineteenth century and early twentieth, but only in terms of the share of the world's GDP that was affected; in terms of the absolute number of countries, sovereign debt crises and defaults were about as common as they have been in the current period (Bordo and Eichengreen, 1999, 2002; Bordo, et al., 2001; Reinhart and Rogoff, 2009a: 72).

Reinhart and Rogoff (2009a: 156) show spikes in banking crises in the 1870s, 1890s, and the first decade of the twentieth century, particularly around the Panic of 1907. Jordà, Schularick and Taylor (2013) assert that the first wave of globalization experienced two periods in which crises rose to the level of global crises, one in 1890 and the other in 1907. The 1890 crisis, best known as the Baring Crisis, is named after the London merchant bank that nearly collapsed after the Buenos Aires Water Supply and Drainage Company defaulted on its debt. While the crisis in the United Kingdom was not large according to some estimates, banking distress also occurred in Argentina, Brazil, Paraguay, Chile, and the United States (Capie, 1992; Bordo and Eichengreen, 1999; Reinhart and Rogoff, 2009a: 344–347). The second global crisis was first identified in 1909 by the financial journalist, newspaper editor, and author, Alexander D. Noyes. Noyes wrote that the Panic of 1907 was a global crisis and not limited to New York which felt it intensely (Noyes, 1909). Noyes lacked databases and econometric techniques but recent work by economic historians supports his ideas, both with respect to the global nature of the crisis, and his observation that the panic had international as well as domestic origins (Reinhart and Rogoff, 2009a: 261; Jordà, Schularick, and Taylor, 2013; Rodgers and Payne, 2015).

One of the main reasons economic historians are interested in financial crises during the first wave of globalization is because the world economy of that period shares a number of characteristics with today. Financial markets were open and global capital flows were large by comparison to the size of national economies. Trade flows were also relatively free, although some countries such as the United States maintained high protective tariff walls. The second half of the nineteenth century experienced a dramatic growth in the number of banks, the size of the financial sector, and financial innovation. To be sure, there are also very significant differences between the second and first waves of globalization. International institutions such as the International Monetary Fund (IMF), the World Bank, and the World Trade Organization (WTO) did not exist in the first wave, nor did countries have the advantages that accrue from political commitments made by countries after World War II to keep their markets open when domestic political pressures push toward closure. Furthermore, there were not many bilateral trade agreements in the earlier period and most trade was in agricultural products whereas today it is manufactures.

It appears that banking crises in the two periods have about the same frequency and severity, although this is not completely certain. Currency crises, however, are more frequent today and perhaps more severe. The data are limited, particularly for the first wave, and are rife with problems of interpretation, making these conclusions tentative rather than definitive. In addition, nearly all of the quantitative comparisons of financial crises in the two waves of rapid globalization were carried out before the recent financial crisis (2007–2009). During the first wave of globalization, there were many fewer countries with independent banking systems and well-developed financial sectors, which may also make the comparison biased. One might expect there to be more banking crises today, compared to the earlier period of globalization, given that there are many more countries with their own centers of finance.

Differences in capital flows during the two waves of globalization are notable. By some estimates, the flow of financial capital across national boundaries was larger in the first wave of globalization than it is currently, although the first wave was mostly long-term lending with little in the way of short-term capital flows. Cross-border capital flows in the nineteenth century were almost exclusively bonds sold for the purpose of constructing infrastructure, particularly railroads, while lending to manufacturing, financial, or industrial firms was almost nonexistent (Bordo, Eichengreen, and Irwin, 1999). Railroads that borrowed internationally were not always successful, but the expectation was that they had a future stream of revenue they could use to pay their debts. Similarly, government debts were not always repaid, but again, the expectation was that government's ability to tax gave them a revenue source that could be used for interest and principal repayment.

2.3 INTERWAR INSTABILITY, 1914–1950

World War I brought an end to the first wave of globalization. The attempts to restore conditions after the war were hindered by the unworkable and punitive peace agreement signed at Versailles. The treaty created serious economic imbalances in Europe and led to violent conflict when French forces occupied the Ruhr Valley as part of their attempt to extract reparations from Germany. The financial, economic, and human costs of the war undermined the British economy and its ability to reestablish London as the world's financial center, while the country's long and misguided attempt to return to the gold standard at its prewar parity ultimately proved a failure. Wartime shortages pushed up prices for farm products and other commodities during and after the war but was followed by a sharp price drop, lasting from May of 1920 until October of 1921, as production was restored. Prices stabilized for a few years in the early 1920s, but then a long, grinding decline set in, from mid-decade until 1933 (NBER, 2016a, 2016b).

The interwar period was the most unstable of the five periods of modern economic growth. This is not surprising considering it spanned two world wars and a major world depression. Banking, currency, and debt crises were more frequent than in other periods and, by contrast, were more likely to occur in high income countries than in middle and low income countries. If there was any belief that financial crises were primarily a problem for developing countries, or that countries can outgrow the problem of financial crises, it is undermined by the history of the interwar period: banking and currency crises, in particular, were much more common at the center than at the periphery (Bordo, et al., 2001).

2.3.1 *Deflation*

Deflation was a persistent problem for economies during the interwar period. From the middle of the 1920s forward, prices trended down in many countries, including the United States, the United Kingdom, and Germany. Deflation in France came a bit later and did not start until the onset of the depression in 1929, but was as relentless as elsewhere (NBER, 2016c). Deflation implies goods are becoming cheaper and incomes will go farther, but those benefits were offset by slower growth, higher unemployment, and the decline in wages along with prices.

Another negative characteristic of deflation is that it increases the real value of debt. Farmers earned less for the crops they sold, but the amount they owed their banks did not change. Homeowners and other borrowers experienced the same effect, causing all borrowers to curtail spending in order to service the higher real debt. The expectation that goods will be cheaper in the future reinforces the reduction in spending by households and businesses as they postpone purchases and new investment declines in anticipation that output in the future will be worth less. Consequently, the effect of deflation is usually a decline in the demand for goods and services and a decline in production. The result is less income for everyone.[1]

1 The problem of deflation is generally accepted but not universally so. Recently some economists have argued that the historical record does not show a strong correlation between deflation and lower growth. That is, deflation may not be as big a problem as is often assumed by central banks and most economists (Borio, et al., 2015).

To be sure, with the major exception of Germany, the 1920s were much more prosperous than the 1930s. After the postwar recession, stock markets did well in many countries, electrical appliances and automobiles became widespread, and houses and cities began to offer many more modern conveniences. Nevertheless, between January, 1920, and August, 1929, when the Great Depression started, the US economy went through three recessions and spent forty-five months out of 116 (39 percent) in economic decline. The 1930s were worse, but the problems associated with widespread deflation, European economic and political instability, and harmful policies imposed by misguided attempts to return to the gold standard as if nothing had changed since 1914, made it impossible for countries to sustain rapid growth in the 1920s as well as the 1930s.

2.3.2 *Gold and the Great Depression*

After World War I, British leaders dedicated themselves to the restoration of the country's prewar glory. A central aspect of that project was to restore the gold standard and a gold value for the pound that was the same as its prewar value, £4.24 per ounce of gold. British leaders and economists understood that the pound was overvalued but they believed that a return to the prewar price of gold was necessary as a demonstration of stability and the strength of the British economy. The goal was to rebuild international confidence in UK financial markets and to ensure their position at the center of world finance.

An overvalued currency for a country on the gold standard implies that gold is too cheap and should cost more. In the British case, wartime inflation had reduced the purchasing power of the pound by an estimated 10–20 percent, or somewhere in the range of £4.66 to £5.08 per ounce of gold instead of the desired £4.24. Overvaluation hurt British exports, caused a persistent trade deficit, and made it difficult for the Bank of England to maintain adequate gold reserves. In order to make the overvalued pound work, British leaders understood that it was necessary for domestic prices to fall. Accordingly, deflation became official British policy, with all of its attendant problems. In particular, there were two major forces pushing Britain toward recession. First, the overvalued pound caused a decline in key export sectors such as shipbuilding, steel, cutlery, and other important manufactures. Second, policies intended to reduce prices and wages led to depressed spending and reinforced the decline in demand caused by the overvaluation. As a result, UK industrial production declined in 1925, the year the gold standard was restored, and especially in 1926, when British workers held a general strike to protest wage cuts and deflationary policies.

These conditions put severe pressure on Britain's status in the world economy. During the last half of the nineteenth century and the first decades of the twentieth, UK leadership played an important role in international commerce and finance. With a global empire, the world's strongest navy, and one of the world's largest economies, it had acted as a guarantor of open trade, open finance, and leadership. Its role included the ability to encourage cooperation among nations, with force if necessary. After the war, the United Kingdom's ability to fulfill its international leadership role was greatly diminished, and resulted in less cooperation among leading nations. The loss of British leadership was probably one of the key reasons for the disorganization, conflicting policies, and economic and political crosscurrents that caused the interwar period to be more chaotic and less prosperous (Kindleberger, 2013 [1973]; Eichengreen, 1992; Feinstein, Temin, and Toniolo, 2008).

Along with persistent global deflation, the loss of UK leadership, and political fights over war reparations, the gold standard was a liability during the interwar period. One of the obstacles it created was the straitjacket it put on monetary policy. To be sure, governments were not expected to cure recessions or depressions, or even to fight them, but the choice to return to the gold standard imposed a deflationary and recessionary bias. It is not a coincidence that the first countries to leave the gold standard were the first to begin a recovery from the Great Depression of the 1930s, and that there is an almost perfect correlation for all countries between economic recovery and termination of the gold standard (Eichengreen, 1992; Bernanke and James, 1991).[2]

As noted previously, during a recession, the gold standard imposes a choice between external balance and internal balance, or between staying on the standard (external balance in trade and exchange rates) or promoting prosperity at home (internal balance in employment and economic growth). When British prices were too high in the late 1920s into the first years of the 1930s, it caused trade deficits and gold outflows. Outflows were not sustainable, however, because the gold standard required the United Kingdom and other countries to maintain sufficient quantities of gold to be able to convert their currencies on demand. Too large a decline in gold reserves would remove the gold backing for the currency, so countries with trade deficits were forced to deflate their prices. That, in turn, requires high rates of unemployment, less demand for goods and services, and fewer purchases, all of which result in a recession or a period of slow growth. Anything policymakers might have done to arrest the recession would also have prevented prices from falling and would have led to continued gold outflows. Waiting out a recession and doing nothing to counteract it is not politically possible today, nor is it economically desirable.

2.4 BRETTON WOODS AND THE GOLDEN AGE, 1950–1973

Toward the end of World War II, the Allied powers met to arrange international affairs in favor of a liberal order with open economies. The goal was to avoid a return to the chaos, depression, and conflict of the previous decades, and to support the creation of a prosperous and peaceful world economy. Economic growth throughout the world reached its highest rates during the decades after the war, trade

2 Eric Rauchway (2015) discusses Roosevelt's ending of the gold standard in the United States in 1933, and the opposition's fears and uncertainties about the new policy. In part, no one could imagine how international finance could be organized without fixing currencies to gold or some other precious metal. It was not until the 1970s that flexible exchange rates began to be widely accepted, some twenty years after Milton Friedman (1953) published *The Case for Flexible Exchange Rates*.

barriers gradually came down, there were many fewer financial crises, and none reached global proportions. Banking crises disappeared altogether and debt crises were fewer than before or after, although currency crises were more numerous and continued to pose problems, particularly for countries with large trade imbalances and overvalued exchange rates (Reinhart and Rogoff, 2009a: 68–73; Bordo, et al., 2001).

The Bretton Woods regime imposed controls on capital flows, established a system of fixed exchange rates, and began a process of opening to trade. Forty-four allied countries participated in the Bretton Woods Conference, but the United States and the United Kingdom dominated. Together, they jointly designed an international system with three primary components, each with a role in reaching the goal of a more prosperous, stable, and a less depression-prone, global economy. One component of Bretton Woods was the creation of an international lender to provide finance in time of difficulties. The objective was to prevent liquidity crises from becoming solvency crises, and to arrange an orderly resolution when crises escalated into insolvency. This was the role for the IMF. A second component of the Bretton Woods system was targeted at keeping national markets open when countries come under pressure to close them. During the depressed years of the 1930s most countries enacted high tariffs in an attempt to keep production and jobs at home, or to retaliate against others. As a result, all countries lost export markets along with their reduction in imports, and most countries were worse off since the closure of markets caused them to be more concentrated in industries where they were less competitive. Keeping markets open occurred through a process of negotiating rounds and national commitments under the auspices of the GATT. In 1995, the GATT was subsumed under the umbrella of the newly created WTO.[3]

[3] The GATT is an agreement that mostly focuses on tariffs and quotas, as well as some basic rules for trade in merchandise goods. It omits several sectors, however, including agriculture and until recently, textiles and apparel. The GATT barely covered services trade which ultimately developed its own version of a GATT, called the General Agreement on Trade in Services or GATS.

A third component of the postwar system was designed to ensure an adequate flow of international lending for reconstruction and development purposes. This goal led to the formation of the International Bank for Reconstruction and Development, which eventually evolved into the World Bank. Initially, funding was intended primarily for rebuilding Europe, but as it became apparent that the needs were greater than the United States was willing to provide through a multilateral agency, the institutions of the World Bank reoriented toward the needs of non-European countries in the areas of technical advice and project funding for economic development.

2.4.1 *The Bretton Woods Exchange Rate System*

As important as the IMF, World Bank, and GATT, the Bretton Woods exchange rate system created a modified gold standard with the US dollar at the center and other currencies fixed in value to the dollar. The United States fixed the value of the dollar to gold at thirty-five dollars per ounce, other countries fixed to the dollar, and all countries could use dollars in place of gold when settling their international payments. This gave the United States a privileged position in international economic arrangements, although it was required to convert dollars into gold whenever requested by another country. A major benefit to the world economy from the use of the dollar was the expansion of the supply of international money which was no longer dependent on the amount of gold coming out of the world's mines. Bretton Woods planners correctly anticipated that incorporation of the dollar into the world's monetary standard would eliminate the deflationary tendency in the world economy by relaxing the restrictions imposed by a strict gold standard.

The new system created an obvious advantage for the United States, since its currency was in demand by all trading nations but it was the only country that could print more dollars. This was a necessary advantage, however, as countries needed a system for settling international payments that did not have side effects such as restricting economic activity. During the first years of the system,

US purchases of European goods with dollars were a welcome relief for war-torn countries short of gold and other assets. Trade was supported by new rules that allowed capital to cross national borders as long as it was in response to trade flows while financial stability was supported by rules in most countries that restricted or prohibited international capital flows for speculative or purely financial reasons. Restrictions on international capital flows made it nearly impossible to speculate against currencies when they were perceived as overvalued, and enabled national governments to use monetary policies for purposes other than defending the currency.

In the nineteenth century, no one expected the central bank (if a country had one) or the national government, to manage the macroeconomy. Economic fluctuations were largely viewed as natural phenomena, similar to tornadoes or forest fires, and beyond anyone's control (Friedman, 2013). In the middle of the twentieth century, this view was replaced by a deeper understanding of the economy and an ability to at least ameliorate recessions, if not avoid them altogether. In addition, the greater democratization of economic policy via the expansion of suffrage, the rise of unions, and increases in education levels, meant that governments could no longer ignore recessions and simply wait for them to end as they did in the nineteenth and early twentieth centuries (Ruggie, 1982). Since the Great Depression of the 1930s, a system that requires a country to surrender its monetary policy to the sole purpose of maintaining a fixed exchange rate system is not politically feasible in most democracies. The Bretton Woods solution to this problem was to close capital markets and thereby make it impossible to speculate against a currency.

2.4.2 *The End of Bretton Woods*

With the Bretton Woods exchange rate system, countries needed dollars as reserves. Consequently, most countries were content to let the United States run trade deficits since it was a way for them to accumulate dollars. This was particularly the case when dollars were scarce in the late 1940s and early 1950s. But by the 1960s, the supply of dollars had grown significantly and the ability of the United States to convert foreign dollar holdings into gold became more limited. One solution would have been to attract the dollars back into the United States with contractionary economic policies that raised interest rates and reduced imports, but this would have been unpopular and few politicians would have been willing to attempt it. Instead, as gold supplies shrank, President Nixon suspended dollar conversions in 1971. Two years later he took the United States completely off the Bretton Woods exchange rate system.

The end of the Bretton Woods system lines up closely with changes in a number of long-term economic trends. Most importantly, world economic growth began to slow after this period. There is no consensus as to the cause, nor is it likely to be due to a single reason, but beyond the growth slowdown, many advanced economies in the 1970s began to shift the priority of their economic management policies away from maintaining low unemployment and toward controlling inflation. This was particularly important as inflation began a long run increase in the 1960s so that by the late 1970s it was becoming a serious problem. Economic inequality in the United States also appears to have begun a long run increase around 1973, and the oil shortages of the 1970s led directly (1974–1975) and indirectly (1980, 1981–1982) to painful recessions in the United States and elsewhere. The end of Bretton Woods led to a new wave of international finance as capital markets became more open and countries adopted flexible exchange rates in place of fixed ones. One of the first waves of new international finance was a large volume of direct bank loans from the United States, Europe, and Japan to governments and businesses in Latin America, Asia, and Africa. The bank loans would ultimately form the basis for the Latin American Debt Crisis, the first great financial crisis after the Great Depression.

The Bretton Woods era's record of economic growth and financial crises was one of the best. Not only were rates of economic growth higher in that era, but banking crises and debt crises were rarer than in any other period of modern economic growth. Currency crises, however, continued as before and perhaps became even more frequent. The growth record is measurable, as are the absence of banking and debt crises. What are not measurable are the determinants of those things, particularly growth. Many hypotheses have been advanced for the causes of the growth slowdown after Bretton Woods, most have some salience, and most observers probably agree that economic growth did not slow for one reason alone. Our understanding of this issue is complicated by the fact that it did not slow everywhere, and that the two most populous countries in the world, China and India, had growth accelerations.

The absence of banking crises and the decline in debt crises during Bretton Woods must be related in some degree to the policy of closed capital markets. Countries were dependent on their own level of savings and in cases where foreign investment entered, it was most often channeled into infrastructure projects as with World Bank loans, manufacturing enterprises, or other productive activities. The flow of speculative, short-term, financial capital was very limited by comparison to the present era, and consequently, most foreign loans and investments were less liquid and unable to suddenly flee. Even without the presence of large, speculative, and highly volatile financial flows, currency crises continued to be a problem. Their higher frequency during the Bretton Woods era indicates that some countries had trouble managing their fixed exchange rates and were forced into sudden large devaluations when they began to run out of reserves.

The end of Bretton Woods was inevitable given the excess of US dollars, together with the recovery of Europe and Asia from the war and the growing pressures to open financial markets. The key institutions created at Bretton Woods, including the IMF, the World Bank, and the GATT which is now managed by the WTO, remain vital today, albeit not without enormous controversy and considerable pressure from new populist movements. What is gone is the exchange rate system, the least sustainable part of the Bretton Woods system.

In its place, many countries have selected something nearly unimaginable in the 1950s and before: flexible exchange rates. Flexible exchange rate systems are still in the minority, however, as a majority of the world's nations (126 of 191) operate some type of fixed exchange rate, often fixing to the dollar, the euro, or a basket of currencies (IMF, 2014a).

2.5 THE SECOND GLOBALIZATION WAVE, 1973 TO THE PRESENT

Not surprisingly, the current period is the most intensely studied and has the greatest quantity of available information. This is the first period in which a majority of countries have national data collection systems, often supported with technical assistance from the United Nations, the IMF, and other agencies, and it overlaps the explosion in electronic information gathering, storage, and distribution. In addition to the quantity and quality of information, international agencies, national institutions, and academics have begun to analyze patterns of financial crises. In order to accomplish that goal, it is necessary to compile extensive datasets of crises, along with their correlates such as debt levels, growth rates, trade balances, currency movements, and other variables hypothesized to be relevant to the onset of a crisis, or that show the crisis' progression as it takes hold, intensifies, and eventually dissipates. Consequently, there are many databases of crises, often building on each other, and covering a time period from around 1960 or 1970 until a year or two before the database was published.

What the data show are a large number of crises of every variety. As noted in the Introduction, researchers at the IMF have cataloged 219 balance of payments crises, 67 debt crises, 147 banking crises, and 217 currency crises, between 1970 and 2011 (Claessens and Kose, 2014: 33; Laeven and Valencia, 2014: 66). This is a lot of financial crises and the fact that the rise in the number coincides with the onset and growth of financial globalization is not a coincidence. Not only does it feel like there are more crises now, the data show that they actually are more frequent. At the same time, improvements in data gathering and availability mean that the higher number of crises may be partially a result of information availability. Even taking into account data availability, the frequency of crises is greater, no doubt, due in part to the growth of finance in countries that did not have financial systems of any size or importance prior to the 1950s or later. Countries that were colonies or relied on foreign banks, as many did early in their initial period of industrial growth, usually had less developed financial systems and smaller probabilities of financial crises.

2.5.1 *Factors Behind the Increase in Financial Crises*

Several developments in international trade and finance have contributed to the increase in financial crises. First, more countries have received international flows of financial capital. The attraction of emerging markets for various kinds of financial assets along with outsourcing of manufacturing and some services to developing countries, and the growth of international financial conglomerates, have created a global financial market where funds move much more easily across national boundaries. Secondly, international trade has grown dramatically over the last fifty years, and along with it, cross-border investment in manufacturing, finance, real estate, retail, and other commercial activities has taken off. Transportation and communication revolutions enable multinational firms to do business in many countries simultaneously, increasing the breadth and depth of cross-border ties, including financial ties. The result of all these changes is an increase in the possibility for problems in one region or country to spill over into a completely different part of the world, as happened when the Asian Crisis of 1997–1998 began in Thailand, then spread to other East Asian export economies, and eventually into Argentina, Brazil, and Russia, before it brought down a giant US hedge fund with the potential to cause major damage. The transmission mechanism of the crisis across these countries was a dense web of trade and financial ties, unlike anything that existed in the nineteenth century or, indeed, before the second wave of globalization.

A third factor that has increased the frequency of financial crises is the growth of short-term international lending. In earlier periods, most lending was long-term. We do not have good measures of the breakdown of short versus long-term lending in, say, 1900, but we do know that it was significantly less than today. The Bank for International Settlements estimates, for example, that $5.1 trillion dollars of foreign exchange was traded on a daily basis in 2016. This was actually down from the $5.4 trillion they estimated for 2013, but still represents daily global currency trades equal to more than one-fourth of the annual US economy (Bank for International Settlements, 2016). There are many reasons for this enormous amount of trading, including the desire to protect against the risk of currency fluctuations, to engage in short-term speculation, or to finance trade when payments or receipts are in a different currency. With so much money trading hands every day, it is not surprising if things occasionally go awry, particularly when there are many examples of financial flows invested in extremely liquid speculative assets that allow the investor to sell their stake and leave the country with the push of a couple of computer keys.

A fourth factor that has increased the frequency of crises is a result of the intense pressure that was put on countries to open their financial markets and to allow freer flows of funds in and out. This was promoted by the IMF, the United States Treasury and Commerce Departments, Wall Street, and many academic economists beginning in the 1970s and intensifying up to the Asian Crisis of 1997–1998. Some arguments for the benefits of foreign capital inflows are valid and point to the fact that foreign capital adds to the supply of domestic savings, making it possible for countries to invest more than they could if they relied only on their own savings. High savings rates in Germany, Japan, Singapore, and Taiwan can find more productive uses in Poland, Thailand, Spain and the United States, than they have at home, and the receiving countries are able to invest more in their productive capacity than they would be able to otherwise. The reality is tempered by the fact that not all foreign savings are put to productive uses when invested abroad. German savings, for example, were invested in US subprime mortgages with few benefits for either Germany or the United States. What we have learned since the breakdown of the Bretton Woods agreement is that there are degrees of openness, and countries must prepare for international capital flows if they are to avoid the worst of the potential problems. Regulatory oversight, high quality institutions to implement regulations, and avoidance of macroeconomic imbalances and overvalued currencies are key (Demirgüç-Kunt and Detragiache, 1997; Caprio, 1998; Caprio and Klingebiel, 2002). This issue is examined in greater detail in Chapter 14.

A fifth factor contributing to an increased frequency of financial crises was the increasing inadequacy of regulation and supervision of financial services. While there were many examples of regulations that were rolled back, the increasing complexity of finance and the adoption of new financial innovations led simultaneously to many new rules. On balance, it is impossible to say if on the eve of the Subprime Crisis there were more rules or fewer rules than in, say, 1970. Regardless of the quantity of rules, the quality of regulation and supervision was completely inadequate for the economy of the twenty-first century. When a group of European and US economists were polled as to the most important causes of the Subprime Crisis, the top choice was "Flawed financial sector regulation and supervision" (IGM Forum, 2017). Needless to say, the flaws did not suddenly appear but instead developed over time, both in legislative omissions and commissions, and in expert opinion that came to view regulations as increasingly onerous and decreasingly necessary.

2.6 CONCLUSION

Over the entire period of modern economic growth from 1820 to the present, there has been a surprising amount of correlation in the growth rates of the world's national economies. Considering that the correlation was across very disparate countries, economic historians have been able to identify five main periods since 1820, each with its own set of characteristics. The five growth periods differed with respect to the frequency and severity of crises, and the groups of countries most affected by crises. For example, the interwar period had very high levels of instability that, unlike the other periods, most severely affected the leading economies of the time. The Bretton Woods Period saw no banking crises, most likely due to the restrictions of international capital flows, but it did have a significant increase in currency crises, no doubt in part due to the problems created by the period's quasi-gold standard and the difficulties countries experienced when their fixed exchange rates needed adjustment. The most recent period has seen the highest frequency of crises in any period, most likely due to several causes. Among them are the commitment of many countries to allow the free movement of capital and the adoption of fixed exchange rate systems that slowly but not infrequently became overvalued. In addition, as trade and finance have encountered fewer restrictions across international boundaries, and incentives have increased for firms to operate in many countries simultaneously, the opportunities for transmitting the effects of spending imbalances and economic shocks has grown as well. These economic forces have been intensified by a general tendency for regulations and supervision to fall behind changes in finance.

Prior to the Subprime Crisis of 2007 to 2009, it was tempting to believe that financial crises were mainly a problem of institutions and that once countries developed sufficiently, they might leave crises behind. Perhaps surprisingly in the wake of the Subprime Crisis, there is some indication that this does happen, but only to a degree (Bordo, 2008; Bordo, et al., 2001). Flexible exchange rates and more mature government finance seem to help countries "graduate" from debt crises as income rises, but Reinhart and Rogoff (2009a: 150–155) show that countries with money centers such as New York and London have more banking crises, not fewer. Overall, the lessons of history seem to be that financial crises will be a permanent feature of the economic landscape until we know much more than we do currently and until effective systems of crisis prevention are in place. If crisis elimination is currently beyond our reach, the next best goal is polices to reduce their frequency and to manage them better when they occur so they might become shorter and less severe.

PART II Five Case Studies

Five cases studies drawn from the twentieth and twenty-first centuries illustrate how historical conditions gave rise to many of the risk factors described in Chapter 1, and the role of financial institutions and economic conditions in generating financial crises. These are among the most important crises, both in terms of their global effects and in terms of what they tell us about economic policies and financial regulations.

3 The Great Depression, 1929–1939

3.1 WHY STUDY THE GREAT DEPRESSION?

The Great Depression has an outsized hold on the imagination of economists. Former Chair of the Federal Reserve, Ben Bernanke, once began an academic paper with the line "To understand the Great Depression is the Holy Grail of macroeconomics" (Bernanke, 1995). His sentiment reflects the importance of the Great Depression and a sense of mystery that is perhaps beyond our ability to completely understand. Many other economists have tried their hand at the Great Depression and many more have chosen careers in economics partly so they could develop a deeper understanding of the causes of that seminal event in world history.

The importance of the Great Depression cannot be overstated. At a practical level, the experience of the 1930s led to the creation of new social programs and regulatory institutions that millions of Americans rely on today. The Great Depression and its aftermath dramatically changed how we view the economy and the expectations we hold about government's role in ensuring prosperity. The experience of the 1930s led straight to an intellectual revolution in economic thought and laid the foundation for the development of the field of macroeconomics. Twentieth-first century citizens of advanced economies may disagree about the details of economic regulations and safeguards, but most of us take for granted that we need oversight and controls such as insurance on bank deposits, rules for trading assets, and other regulations on financial institutions. Research on the Great Depression led to a clearer understanding of the purposes and limits of monetary policy and to the development of tools for fighting depressions with fiscal policies.

In the field of economics, the Great Depression led to a number of breakthroughs in our understanding of economic forces. Perhaps most importantly, economists learned that government spending was not zero sum during a depression and it did not crowd out or replace private spending. This led to a revolution in fiscal policy and to the perception that government demand management policies can lessen the effects of recessions and depressions. Military expenditures during World War II clarified the efficacy of fiscal policy, and after the war it came to play a prominent role in presidential administrations up to and through the Nixon years and again when President Obama took office at the height of the Subprime Crisis. The Obama administration's passage of a large fiscal stimulus in 2009 was controversial, but most economists believe it lowered unemployment rates and that its benefits outweighed the costs (IGM Forum, 2014a).

The Great Depression, like all depressions, was a complex, puzzling, and devastating event, but it is overly agnostic to call it a mystery. Contemporary scholars still debate some facets and we do not understand the precise cause or effect of every move in the economy at the time, but the general outlines are relatively well understood. There is a large amount of first rate scholarship on the Great Depression and several generations of economic historians have increased our understanding of the period.[1]

Even with the progress made by the many scholars who have studied the Great Depression, there is still a fair amount of uncertainty, however. This, I would argue, is partly because the Great Depression is a dramatic historical event that is easily converted into a lesson for favored political ideologies. Interpretations of the Great Depression span a wide range of economic ideologies and political agendas. It has been simultaneously interpreted as an excuse for both large and small

1 Some of the highlights from economists include books and articles by Irving Fischer (1933), John Kenneth Galbraith (1955), Milton Friedman and Anna Schwartz (1963, Chapter 7), Charles Kindleberger (2013 [1973]), Peter Temin (1976,1989), Hyman Minsky (1975), Cristina Romer (1990, 1993), Ben Bernanke (1995, 2000b), Barry Eichengreen (1992, 2015), and Keynes' magnum opus *The General Theory of Employment, Interest, and Money* (1936).

government, more and fewer economic regulations, and both more and less government intervention into labor and product markets. It has been used to promote large-scale government employment programs and Keynesian demand management policies as a way to bring the recession to a quicker conclusion, and to argue for laissez faire, free market policies as a way to do the same. Some observers argue that it shows the costs of an incompetent Federal Reserve, while others point out that the US central bank acted as expected given the requirements of a gold standard. Some argue that it illustrates the dangers of economic policy coordination with other nations, and others offer it as an object lesson in the dangers of a leaderless world economy. All of these views can find some support in the historical narrative, but obviously, they cannot all be completely correct.

In spite of the temptation to use the Great Depression to prove one point or another, our understanding of what went wrong has expanded and clarified. Several generations of economic historians have produced a growing body of scholarship rooted in empirical analysis and informed by economic theory. Ideologues still argue about fundamental issues that are mostly settled, but we have a much better idea about what went wrong than we did in the 1930s or the 1970s. There is a fairly clear explanation for how the depression started, how and why it spread, and why recovery began when it did. A test of this body of knowledge came during the Subprime Crisis when we might very well have fallen into another Great Depression if the state of knowledge or the speed of policy responses had been as they were in the years 1929 to 1932. Policymakers did not prevent the Subprime Crisis, but even in a divided political environment that quarreled over the need for government actions, politicians and policymakers were able to marshal knowledge about the Great Depression and apply some of the lessons in order to prevent the recent crisis from becoming much more catastrophic.[2]

2 This is implicit in the alternative name for the Subprime Crisis as the Great Recession. The use of a name that evokes the Great Depression, but refers to it as a recession rather than a depression implies that it could have been similar to the 1930s if policies had been as they were at that earlier time.

3.2 FACTORS LEADING UP TO THE DEPRESSION

The 1920s are embedded in the historical imagination of most Americans as a relatively prosperous time. Electrical appliances turned American homes into something much closer to their current form, cars and car culture took hold, radios, jazz and movies brought new forms of entertainment to the city, and telephones came into common usage. According to most estimates, overall growth rates for the economy were relatively good with rates of per capita income growth that would be very acceptable today.[3] The 1920s, however, were like most other periods in American history in the sense that there were good times and bad. Between January, 1920, and August, 1929, when the Great Depression began, the country went through three separate recessions but fortunately, only the first recession, from January, 1920 to July, 1921, was considered severe, even if investors that lost their savings when a Florida real estate bubble burst in 1925 felt otherwise.

While the US economy did relatively well in the 1920s, the same could not be said about Europe. The legacy of World War I and the punitive settlement imposed on Germany by the Allied powers disrupted capital markets and strained international economic relations. These problems were compounded by the return to the gold standard, steep declines in agricultural and other commodity prices, and economic uncertainty resulting from the changing leadership status of the UK. All of these problems during the 1920s – volatile international capital markets, the gold standard, falling commodity prices, and the changes in international leadership –have been emphasized as sources of instability leading up to the Great Depression.

One area where there is less agreement and more debate is over the relative roles of international versus domestic (US) events in the creation of the Great Depression. It is beyond dispute that the Great Depression was an international event, but it is not so clear whether

3 GDP per person rose at the annual rate of 2.4 percent per year from 1920 to 1929 (Maddison-Project, 2013 version).

international events intensified or prolonged the Great Depression in the United States. Romer (1993), for example has argued that we do not need to use international conditions in order to explain the onset of the Great Depression, while Kindleberger (1978) and Temin and Vines (2013) view the lack of leadership in the global economy as a major source of instability. This debate over the relative roles of domestic versus international forces is a perennial one and is not limited to discussion of the Great Depression. For example, it is also part of the debate over the Subprime Crisis, with Federal Reserve Chairman Bernanke and others pointing to a "global savings glut" as at least partly responsible, and others emphasizing purely domestic US issues such as regulatory laxness, excessive risk-taking, and distorted incentives in the housing market.

Most analysts would probably agree that the United States would have suffered a Great Depression in the 1930s even if the international economy had been calmer. The fact that it was in turmoil, however, surely made contagion a danger once a depression began in the United States, and probably contributed to its prolongation since foreign markets for US goods were not in good shape. Furthermore, the neat division of events into domestic or international fails to explain some of the complexity of the circumstances that confronted countries around the globe. Consider for example the role of the gold standard. The UK and the US both returned to the gold standard in 1925 after having suspended it during World War I. Britain's determination to restore the same gold price for its currency as before the war was partially driven by national pride, but even if nationalist sentiments played a role, many bankers and politicians thought it was a necessary step for the restoration of UK leadership in international finance. Although it was not recognized at the time, Britain had in fact lost that role to the US and was not going to get it back even though the latter was neither prepared nor desirous of assuming Britain's place in international financial relations. Britain's loss of empire and its relative economic decline had not yet registered in the thinking of financial and political leaders, and the

US was not yet interested in asserting its economic power on the world stage.

Policy in the United States during this period was closely aligned with the United Kingdom. The New York Federal Reserve actively held down interest rates in the United States in order to avoid becoming a magnet for British gold outflows.[4] The close personal ties between the heads of the Bank of England, Ashley Montague, and the New York Fed, Benjamin Strong, were supplemented by a sense that Britain's return to the gold standard was an important step toward restoring pre-World War I conditions to the world economy. The United States had the military strength to prevail in the World War I, but it lacked the institutional and political capacity to assume a role of word leadership, as it would after World War II. Hence, the United Kingdom was viewed by US interests as the best guarantor of world stability and peaceful economic relations. Consequently, the Federal Reserve maintained a policy of relatively low interest rates in order to avoid attracting gold from the United Kingdom and to support Britain's attempt to stay on the gold standard at the prewar parity for gold and the pound sterling. Low interest rates in the US avoided a large outflow of gold from British reserves, but at the cost of fueling speculation on Wall Street by making loans for speculation cheaper than otherwise. By 1928, when the Federal Reserve Bank of New York reversed course and began raising interest rates in order to calm the speculation on Wall Street, stock prices had reached new levels and the speculative mania had its own momentum.

Britain's exchange rate problems and the spillover into US policy was not the only instability in the world economy. Countries in Latin America had increased their agricultural production when European output fell during the war. This was matched by increases in US and European agricultural output after the war as soldiers returned to their farms and land was put back into production. Higher levels of

4 The New York Federal Reserve was the most important of the Federal Reserve banks. In the 1930s, power over monetary policy was centralized with the Board of Governors of the Federal Reserve.

production in the Americas and the gradual return of European producers to world markets contributed to a period of plentiful supply and falling prices. Agricultural prices in the US peaked in June of 1925 after which they began a downward trend. By 1929, crop prices were 19 percent below their 1925 peak, and from there they fell another 63 percent by the time Roosevelt was inaugurated in March, 1933 (NBER, 2016a).

How important was the decline in agricultural prices? It is hard to put a precise estimate on it, but through the early 1930s, as the US spiraled deeper into the depression, several waves of bank failures in agricultural regions of the US were provoked by bankrupt farmers and undoubtedly contributed to the problems of the US national economy. Nor was this only a US problem. Agricultural trade was still a mainstay of international trade and had a relative importance that it no longer has in our age of manufactures and services trade. As agricultural prices fell, countries devalued their currencies in order to make their products more competitive, but this only fed the decline in prices and contributed to rounds of competitive devaluations (Kindleberger, 2013 [1973]: Chapter 4).

Problems caused by exchange rate devaluations and falling agricultural prices were compounded by several additional factors. A private credit boom in the United States during the 1920s enabled households to finance the purchase of cars and electrical appliances that were beginning to fill middle class homes (Olney, 1991). Credit was helpful to families, but it led to a significant buildup in private household debt. Businesses too were able to expand their access to credit as corporate bond financing more than doubled between 1920 and 1929 (NBER, 2016d). Credit was also more plentiful for investing in the stock market and as investors took out loans to buy stocks, equity prices rose. Between 1924 and the stock market crash in October, 1929, prices expanded 240 percent. The steady increase, seemingly without interruption, caused many investors to view positive returns on the stock market as a near certainty (Shiller, 2012). Outside the US, credit markets also expanded, particularly after 1924 when the US temporarily resolved the problem of German reparation payments with new loans and easier terms under the Dawes Plan. Those steps set off a wave of loans to Germany and other countries in Europe (Kindleberger, 2013 [1973]: pp. 38–44.)

Looking back at Chapter 1's list of factors that increase vulnerabilities to a financial crisis, nearly all were present. In the 1920s, particularly the second half, the US stock market saw a major increase in prices. Dramatically higher levels of credit were offered to households wanting to buy cars and appliances, and to businesses that were able to borrow in the bond market. There were few supervisorial or regulatory institutions before the Great Depression, and entities such as the Securities and Exchange Commission (SEC) or the Federal Deposit Insurance Corporation (FDIC) would not be created until the mid-1930s. Capital markets had few controls, and if the US dollar was not overvalued, the traditional leader of the world's financial system struggled with serious overvaluation. And finally, we can say that debt levels increased in the private economy, if not for governments, outside of Germany. None of this means a recession was inevitable, let alone a Great Depression. Nevertheless, we can read signs of vulnerability in the data from our vantage point of nearly a century of hindsight. These weaknesses did not cause the Great Depression, but they did increase countries' vulnerabilities and some factors made it harder to escape a depression once it began.

3.3 WHAT CAUSED THE GREAT DEPRESSION?

The Great Depression in the United States was actually two separate recessions. The first began in August, 1929, and lasted until March, 1933. Real GDP bounced back rapidly after hitting bottom, as is common in the recovery from a severe recession. The second recession began in 1937 and lasted until mid-1938. Popular views of the Great Depression tend to see it as one long painful event that lasted throughout the 1930s, but real GDP growth was 10.8 percent in 1934, 8.9 percent in 1935, and 12.9 percent in 1936. While annual growth for 1937 overall was still positive, the economy fell back into recession in May, and remained there until June, 1938. Since the 1929–1932 recession was so deep and long-lasting, the growth years between March, 1933, and May, 1937, were not enough to bring unemployment down to normal levels and when the second recession began in 1937, it was still over 11 percent. By the middle of 1938 the unemployment rate was back up to 20 percent and did not fall below 6 percent until the middle of 1941. Hence, in the United States we call the Great Depression the period from the middle of 1929 until sometime around 1939 or 1940 (NBER, 2016e, 2016f).

Early interpretations of the Great Depression agreed that there was a relatively sudden decline in the consumer and business demand for goods and services. The decline began in August, 1929, and continued until March, 1933, the same month that Roosevelt entered the White House. The decline in total aggregate economic demand sent a signal to businesses that they should cut back production and layoff workers. Most business analysts and economists in the 1930s understood that the collapse in demand for goods and services was a central fact about the onset of the Great Depression. What was not well understood then, and still forms the basis of many debates about the Great Depression, is the cause of the collapse in demand.

Given the dramatic events on Wall Street and the collapse of the stock market in the fall of 1929 at about the same time as economic conditions began to deteriorate, it seems natural to connect the two events. Probably most economic historians would agree that the Great Depression was aggravated by the Wall Street crash to some degree, but few view it as a decisive factor. The Standard & Poor (S&P) composite index of stock prices reached 31.3 in September, 1929, approximately one month after the recession began. By November, it was down 34 percent, to 20.58. The reason that many economists do not place a great deal of weight on the stock market for an explanation of the Great Depression, even though the uncertainty it created must have had a negative effect on spending, is that many expert observers at the time thought that falling stock prices were a healthy development since they would get rid of the excess speculation and put shares on a more realistic footing. It was a hard but necessary correction that would return the market to a more stable basis after the "lunatic fringe" had been shaken out. By April, 1930, the market had recovered about half of its losses and the predictions of a return to more reasonable prices seemed to be holding steady. Nevertheless, from that point forward, stock prices began a grinding, painful decline that did not come to a stop until they hit bottom in June, 1932, at a S&P composite index of 4.77. Cumulatively, the decline from the peak to the bottom was nearly 85 percent (Shiller, 2013). Toward the end of 1930, the decline in the stock market and growing economic distress were intensified by the first of what would be several waves of bank failures. The collapse of some important and high profile banks led directly into a period of greater pessimism and a growing recognition that the downturn was more than just another brief recession. The stock market decline, however, was more of a symptom of the spreading distress, not a cause.

The main question confronting early analysts of the Great Depression was about the causes of the large decline in GDP and the concomitant rise in unemployment. In price adjusted terms, GDP fell by more than 26 percent from its peak in 1929 to its bottom in 1933, while unemployment exceeded 25 percent (NBER, 2016e, 2016f).[5] A stock market crash may depress spending and expectations about the future, but it seems unlikely to cause such a severe collapse in overall economic activity.[6] There must have been other factors in play as well.

While most analysts thought that the answer had something to do with the end of the boom in consumer credit and the fall in spending on new household items such as cars and electrical appliances, the search for reasons for consumer pessimism led to many hypotheses.[7] Among the more common explanations were the

5 By contrast, US real GDP fell 4.2 percent from its peak before the financial crisis (fourth quarter, 2007) to its bottom (second quarter, 2009), and civilian unemployment peaked at 9.9 percent in December, 2009.

6 For example, the all-time largest one-day decline in the Dow Jones Industrial Average was a loss of 22.61 percent on October 19, 1987. By comparison, October 28, 1929, decline was 12.8 percent. No recession resulted from the 1987 crash.

7 Olney (1991) discusses the economic history of consumer credit in the 1920s.

markets saturation of consumer demand for newly introduced electrical household appliances, housing construction cycles, the fall of investment from unsustainable predepression levels, the adoption of protectionist trade policies, and normal business sector dynamics that suddenly turned deadly. Nor did economists neglect the fact that the depression was international. Great Britain had struggled in the late-1920s (although the year 1929 was better), agricultural prices depressed the farm economies of most countries, and the German economy suffered for several years under the heavy debt burden of war reparations and ultimately imposed onerous austerity programs. As European and the US industrial economies fell into recession, primary commodity suppliers in Latin America followed.

While most postdepression economic analysis agreed about the lack of demand and the problems it created, the underlying causes of diminished demand lacked consensus for many years. Furthermore, the possibility that spending would remain depressed for a long period of time seemed unlikely, both to contemporaries and to economists who would later try to understand the causes of the Great Depression. Economic theory before Keynes' work of the 1930s favored the idea that economies self-adjust and that any deviation away from full employment will be corrected by falling wages and prices that pull it back toward a long run equilibrium closer to, or at, full employment. As the depression dragged on, the lack of adjustment and the failure to return to normalcy were mysteries that defied traditional explanations.

3.4 THE KEYNESIAN IDEA

The explanation developed by Keynes over the course of the 1930s and published in 1936 in his most cited work, *The General Theory of Employment, Interest and Money*, overturned traditional economic theory with an alternative that put more emphasis on the role of uncertainty in economic decision-making. In Keynes' model, economies could fall into a relatively long-lasting equilibrium level of output that involved high levels of unemployment and low levels of output: Depressions can last for extended periods of time and economies do not necessarily self-correct quickly. Keynes understood that periods of high uncertainty cause households to save rather than spend as they worry about the security of their income and jobs, and opt to pay off existing debts rather than accumulate additional ones. At the same time, businesses will withhold spending on new investments until they have a clearer picture of future economic activity and will also choose to reduce their debt loads rather than take on new obligations. The lack of spending in the private sector only increases the intensity of the falloff in production and raises even higher the level of uncertainty about the future.

According to Keynes, if private spending was absent, then government could substitute for it with increased public spending to raise the level of demand for goods and services. This new theory did not sit well with proponents of laissez faire and with the traditional view that any increase in government spending would necessarily come at the expense of decreased private spending. Proponents of laissez faire disliked the idea of an increased governmental role in economic management, while traditionalists assumed that increased public spending would always crowd out private spending. Both groups preferred to believe that market economies are stable and will right themselves relatively quickly when they are disturbed, just as long as government interventions do not make conditions worse. In addition to his counter-arguments that idle resources in the form of massive unemployment created space for an overall increase in spending and production, and the visible fact that the Great Depression was lingering and was not ending of its own accord, Keynes and the economists who extended his work offered a theoretical explanation for an increase in government spending during a depression as a complement to private spending and as a means to increase overall demand. This was a revolution in economic thought. Governments which had been considered bystanders in the ebb and flow of economic activity now had a positive role in economic management and perhaps even more importantly, a responsibility. At the right time and place, government spending could actually shorten economic recessions.

The alternative to Keynesian analysis never disappeared. It continues to believe that private market economies are inherently stable and when disturbed they will move relatively quickly back toward full employment and normal growth. That is, unless they are blocked by interventions into the economy. During the presidency of Herbert Hoover, this view was expressed most forcefully by his Secretary of Treasury, Andrew Mellon, who believed that the solution was for the depression to burn itself out with temporarily high unemployment and lost production. Depressions in this view are quickly followed by a return to normal levels of output as businesses take advantage of the lower costs of production that result from the reduced prices and wages created by the depression. In Mellon and his follower's view, government actions to shorten the length of the depression were likely to undermine confidence and prolong the pain.

From the Great Depression on, most economists accepted the idea that market-based economies have a long run tendency to move toward normal growth and something close to full employment, if not actual full employment. Since Keynes, the debate has been over the length of time required. Proponents of laissez faire with markets free from government interventions view the time as relatively short, while economists in the tradition of Keynes see the possibility for prolonged recessions and slow recoveries. This issue about the stability of market-based economies and their inherent tendency for self-adjustment remains one of the main divides in economic thought.

3.5 THE MONETARIST RESPONSE

After World War II, as analysis of the Great Depression developed, the idea that it was caused and prolonged by failed government policies received a boost from two influential economists. In 1963, Milton Freidman and Anna Schwartz published their *A Monetary History of the United States* and suddenly there was an historically consistent, theory-based explanation for the depression's onset, depth, and duration. Before the publication of the *Monetary History,* Friedman had worked assiduously for many years to restore monetarism as an economic school of thought. His work with Schwartz provided an empirically verifiable, historically grounded, explanation for the ups and downs of major macroeconomic variables such as nominal GDP growth, unemployment, and inflation, all of which were framed by the monetarist vision of the economy.

Friedman and Schwartz argued that the primary cause of the Great Depression was a failure on the part of the Federal Reserve to maintain the money supply after several waves of bank failures that began in late 1930. In their view, a garden variety recession of no particular severity became the Great Depression after waves of bank failures led to a precipitous decline in the stock of money in circulation. Bank failures began in late 1930 (November, December), then had a second wave in March 1931, and a third wave in late 1932 and early 1933 (NBER, 2016g). After Roosevelt declared a bank holiday and closed all banks in March, 1933, as one of his first acts as president, 2,000 banks never reopened. In total, between 1929 and 1933, over 11,000 banks failed (out of a population of approximately 24,000 banks). Deposit insurance did not yet exist and the effects of so many bank failures were severe. Monetarists put the weight of their explanation on the decline in the money supply that occurs when banks shut their doors. In normal times, banks expand the money supply by making new loans: the depositor has their money in the bank, and the borrower has their loans, so a dollar of deposits supports many times that amount of money. In bad times, particularly without deposit insurance, the system works in reverse as bank closures destroy both deposits and the availability of funds that the borrower had on credit.

Friedman and Schwartz's influential critique is based on their observation that the Federal Reserve did not properly exercise its function as a lender of last resort. As banks came under pressure to provide cash to their frightened depositors, the Fed should have been ready and willing to make funds available, at least to those banks that were illiquid but still solvent. This is the position first advocated by the nineteenth century British journalist Walter Bagehot who proposed a set of rules for dealing with a banking crisis. Bagehot wrote that central banks should lend freely during a crisis to banks that were solvent but short of cash, that they should charge high interest rates to discourage similar problems in the future, and they should demand adequate collateral (Bagehot, 1873: Chapter 7).[8]

The Freidman–Schwartz hypothesis lays blame for the Great Depression at the feet of the Federal Reserve and points to their failure to exercise their lender of last resort function for solvent banks, and their failure to offset the decline in the money supply as insolvent banks failed. It is an influential critique for several reasons, including the fact that their critics did not have as clear a way to explain the sudden drop in spending that led to the declines in production, output, and employment. In the Friedman–Schwartz model, spending fell because the Federal Reserve allowed the money supply to shrink. This grounded their explanation for the Great Depression in monetarist theory and provided a direct explanation for the importance of the large number of bank failures. Alternative theories continued to be influential after the publication of the *Monetary History*, but the re-emergence of monetarism in the late 1960s and 1970s as a mainstream school of thought lent significant prestige and credibility to Friedman–Schwartz hypothesis.

3.6 TWO COMPLICATIONS TO THE MONETARIST STORY

Over time, two significant layers of complexity have been added to the simple monetarist story blaming the Fed. One, the work of Bernanke (2000b) and others has shown that the bank failures cause

8 Bagehot's Dictum or Bagehot's Rule is conventional wisdom today, but has become somewhat less clear in the age of megabanks and systemically important financial institutions. At the start of the Subprime Crisis, after Lehman Brothers investment bank was allowed to fail, Bernanke and others argued that it had no good collateral and that the Fed could not lend (Bernanke, 2015: Chapter 12). Ultimately, however, the Federal Reserve and the Treasury felt compelled to lend to systemically important institutions whose failure might bring down the entire system.

far more damage than can be explained by a decline in the money supply. When banks fail and there is no insurance on deposits, everyone loses their savings. A sudden loss of savings depresses spending, both by those who are suddenly poorer and by others who face increased uncertainty about the future. A second effect of the banking collapse is that there are fewer banks to extend credit to businesses and farmers, hurting both new and existing enterprises. And a third effect is that those banks that do not fail become much more cautious about taking risks, such as extending credit. Their caution is compounded by the fact that they must gather additional information about businesses no longer served by functioning banks, and the increase in the cost of credit intermediation adds to their reluctance to take on new customers. Not only in the United States, but in many countries, the entire financial system ceased to function normally as banks collapsed. Credit dried up, nonbanking firms in different sectors of the economy could not get the financing they needed to manage temporary cash shortages or to finance their day-to-day operations, and avoiding a shutdown of operations became a major challenge.

This view of the effects of a collapse in credit markets does not contradict Friedman and Schwartz but rather provides a different mechanism for the depression in the form of a collapse of the credit system rather than simply a decline in the money supply. When a country's banks are hit by a crisis and many fail, the money supply will shrink unless that tendency is counteracted by central bank policies. Nevertheless, a fall in the money supply is an indicator and a rule of thumb for tight credit, not a direct cause of an economic collapse. The most important impact of a banking crisis is not the effect it has on the money supply, but rather the fact that it can destroy a significant part of the financial system and through those impacts it becomes more difficult to maintain normal business operations that rely on finance and credit. All of this adds to overall economic uncertainty and causes households and businesses to hold back on any unnecessary expenditure.

In the Friedman and Schwartz story, the Federal Reserve receives a great deal of criticism for its policies in the early 1930s. They argue that the Fed should have loosened the money supply and provided liquidity to illiquid banks facing withdrawals by frightened depositors and that it should have made open market purchases of government bills in order to counteract the contraction in the money supply. Putting more emphasis on the financial system and less on the physical quantity of money gives a more complete picture of the mechanisms at work when an economy enters a recession or depression. As with the Subprime Crisis of 2007–2009, keeping credit flowing was the key to avoiding a much more severe downturn. By itself, adding to the money supply will not be effective policy if banks are unwilling to lend and choose to sit on their reserves instead of putting them to work.

A second complication that has changed our understanding of the Fed's actions during the onset of the Great Depression is a greater appreciation for the limits imposed by the gold standard. As long as financial resources were free to move in and out of the country, monetary policy was limited in its choices. Inevitably, it is not uncommon with any type of fixed exchange rate, whether a gold standard or some other, that there are moments when policy must choose between supporting the value of the currency or supporting the domestic economy. The first years of the Great Depression were one of those moments, and the Fed chose to support the currency.

In 1931, the United Kingdom finally decided that its ever-shrinking reserves of gold and the constant need to exert deflationary pressures on prices made it more sensible to give up on its struggle to maintain the gold standard. After the United Kingdom left the gold standard, speculators assumed that it was only a matter of time before the United States would join it and leave gold as well. Looking back, we know that as speculation turned from the pound to speculating against the US dollar, the Federal Reserve could have chosen between raising interest rates to attract foreign capital inflows and protect US gold reserves, or cutting rates to try to encourage some additional spending and some support for the domestic economy. Any signal that the Federal Reserve was not going to protect US gold reserves and was instead going to provide lower interest rates for domestic economic purposes, would have supported speculation against the dollar. Such a move would have increased the tendency for gold to leave the US and put added pressures on the Fed to act in defense of the dollar and its dwindling gold reserves.

The roles of the gold standard and increased cost of credit intermediation are two of the complications of the Great Depression not explored by the Friedman–Schwartz hypothesis of monetary contraction. If the collapse of credit markets were the key mechanism for transmitting the negative effects of the depression from one region to another and from one enterprise to another, then it adds a refinement to the monetary story. And if the Federal Reserve was acting as expected in placing its highest priority on defending the US dollar, then the story about the Federal Reserve's incompetence as the primary cause of the deepening and spreading of the Great Depression is questionable. Certainly a wiser Federal Reserve would have acted differently and would not have allowed interest rates to rise as the economy spiraled into depression, but it is not the case that it completely ignored the charge it had been given when its charter was created.

Debates over the causes of the Great Depression have clarified two critical issues. One is the role of a smooth and well-functioning financial system for maintaining the overall health of an advanced industrial economy, and two is the tension between the management of a fixed exchange rate system and the needs of the domestic economy. Both of these issues point toward a larger reality, first hypothesized by Keynes, that it is essential to maintain aggregate demand for goods and services when the economy is falling into recession. This is perhaps Keynes' greatest contribution to economic science and one that has been forgotten and relearned, sometimes poorly, by subsequent generations. It is a lesson that was not fully understood until after the Great Depression ended with a sudden worldwide increase in public spending. Unfortunately, the spending was for military purposes as countries prepared for war.

3.7 ECONOMIC RECOVERY AND RELAPSE

There are two questions about the chronology of economic recovery and relapse. One, what explains the timing of the recovery that began in 1933? And two, what were the causes of the second recession in 1937? Looking at the question of recovery in 1933, it may be a coincidence that the worst part of the Great Depression ended just as Roosevelt took office, but there are reasons to think it was the result of deliberate actions taken by the newly elected president. One of Roosevelt's first actions was to declare a bank holiday and temporarily close the nation's banks. That move stopped the waves of bank failures that periodically ravaged the banking sector during Hoover's presidency and effectively ended the banking crisis that had been playing out since late in1930. When banks reopened, the fact that only solvent ones were allowed back into operation had a positive impact on depositor's beliefs about the credit-worthiness of the banking system. Banks that reopened had been vetted and were determined to be solvent and, therefore, could be trusted with deposits. This was quickly followed in 1934 with legislation setting up the FDIC, which guaranteed bank deposits and further increased confidence in the banking system.

The end of bank panics and banking crises were a significant part of the change in household and business expectations about the future direction of the economy. Beyond the bank holiday, Roosevelt's monetary policies were a second set of fundamental changes that altered economic relations and expectations. Specifically, Roosevelt immediately but somewhat opaquely took the US off the gold standard. This was done by freezing payments that were contractually obligated to be in gold and devaluing the gold value of the dollar. Technically, this was a government default since the gold value of contracted payments were reduced. Out of their fear of adverse reactions in financial markets and political opposition by the business community, the president and his advisors presented the policy as a temporary suspension of the convertibility of the dollar into gold rather than a permanent termination of the gold standard.[9] Effectively, the United States had followed the United Kingdom off gold with a lag of two years. The impact of the suspension of convertibility was to give the Federal Reserve greater freedom in its conduct of monetary policy since it no longer had to defend the gold value of the dollar by ensuring adequate gold reserves. As a result, monetary policy became more expansionary than it had been up until then, and the long deflation in prices that began with the onset of the depression in 1929 came to an end (NBER, 2016h).

Policies that ended the banking crisis and that allowed for an expansionary monetary policy played major roles in bringing the first recession to an end. Given these specific policy changes, it seems unlikely that it is only a coincidence that the recovery began in 1933, more or less simultaneously with the inauguration of Roosevelt and the implementation of these new policies. Not uncommonly for an economic recovery after a long period of recession, the recovery that began with the new president's inauguration was spectacular. As mentioned earlier, real GDP grew 10.8 percent in 1934, 8.9 percent in 1935, and 12.9 in 1936 (NBER, 2016e). With so many workers unemployed in 1933, and so much idle factory capacity, a rapid recovery was possible.

The recovery was not long-lived, however, and in May, 1937, the country fell back into a recession that it did not escape until June, 1938, by which time the unemployment rate was on its way up to 20 percent. There is a strong candidate for the main cause of the relapse: fiscal policy. This may seem strange given that the two most prominent images of the Roosevelt Administration are its success in the war against Nazism and the New Deal. Both the war effort and the New Deal involved large government expenditures, but the

[9] Rauchway (2015) argues that this was a deliberate strategy by Roosevelt, in consultation with J.M. Keynes, to loosen the grip of the gold standard on economic policy and to devalue the dollar.

former dwarfed the latter. There is little doubt that the vast expenditures on military preparations for war fulfilled the Keynesian role of substituting government spending for the missing private spending and finally put an end to Great Depression. In purely fiscal terms, the New Deal was another matter. In spite of its great accomplishments in poverty alleviation, job creation, and public infrastructure, its net contribution to total domestic spending was a tiny fraction of the war effort and not nearly enough to pull the country out of depression.

A major obstacle that stood between New Deal spending and recovery from the depression was economic orthodoxy from the period before the Great Depression and Keynes' writings. Predepression orthodoxy held that government budgets must be in balance at all times and that spending should never exceed revenues. This idea posed a problem for both Hoover and Roosevelt since depressions usually cause a steep decline in government revenues due to joblessness and the overall lack of spending. Tax collections decline precipitously and expenditures rise by amounts that depend on the social safety net, although in the 1930s, government programs did not exist in their modern form. Nevertheless, even without a recession-induced automatic increase in social safety net expenditures, the decline in federal revenues threw federal and state budgets into deficit. Both Hoover and Roosevelt were concerned that the deficits would undermine business confidence, reflect badly on the president's management abilities, hurt the party in power, and delay recovery. Both presidents struggled to balance the federal budget during the Great Depression.

In 1932 the federal government passed the Tax Revenue Act of 1932 which raised tax rates on everyone, but especially low and middle income groups. This was followed in 1937 by the newly enacted social security tax which was intended to pay for the new benefit passed by Congress and signed by the president. These new taxes partially offset the increases in federal expenditures that commenced in 1933 with Roosevelt's Administration. While the overall federal budget was expansionary despite the tax increases, it was marginally so and not enough to offset increasingly contractionary state and local government budgets. An influential study in the 1950s noted, "Fiscal policy, then, seems to have been an unsuccessful recovery device in the 'thirties—not because it did not work, but because it was not tried" (Brown, 1956). It was not until after the war that policy makers began to understand Keynes' ideas about government spending during a recession as a supplement for inadequate private spending caused by a lack of aggregate demand. Through the 1930s, macroeconomic management was still a foreign concept, even if poverty alleviation and humanitarian spending were not.

3.8 CONCLUSIONS

The Great Depression changed the way economists and most politicians think about the economy. Its legacy was permanent and far reaching as it led to the development of some of the first social welfare programs in the United States and elsewhere, to new and lasting regulatory agencies such as the SEC and the FDIC, and to a new role for the state in managing the economy. Since the 1930s, conservatives and progressives alike have assumed that governments share a responsibility with the private sector for maintaining employment and adequate economic growth.

In the lead up to the Great Depression, the United States exhibited many of the vulnerabilities that are associated with financial crises such as debt accumulation, large international capital flows, a lack of supervisorial institutions in finance and banking, and a bubble in the stock market. Nevertheless, at its onset, the Great Depression appeared to be little more than a regular economic downturn. But it was a downturn that became deadly once the recession spread to the banking sector and developed into waves of banking crises beginning in late 1930. At that moment, a more active Federal Reserve might have avoided the worst of the crisis by ensuring that credit markets did not freeze and that banks had sufficient liquidity to stop withdrawals by panicked depositors. It lacked the insight of the Fed of 2008, however, and was working without the FDIC and other regulatory supports. Perhaps most importantly, it also lacked the tools and ideas of postwar macroeconomics. The Fed also faced the obstacle of the gold standard which required policies that contributed to the crisis and prevented it from taking a more expansionary policy position. It was not until 1933, with the inauguration of Roosevelt, that the restrictions of the gold standard were abandoned and monetary policy could turn expansionary. Yet Roosevelt and many of his advisors still lacked the tools of fiscal policy and, as a consequence, were not able to implement expansionary policies until the build up for World War II forced them to prioritize spending over budget balancing. At that point, the US finally escaped the Great Depression for good.

Economists and policy makers learned from the experience of the Great Depression. When the Subprime Crisis began in 2007, both the Federal Reserve and the federal government had many more options than in 1929 or 1933. Even so, while the Subprime Crisis came to a relatively rapid conclusion in 2009, the effects of the Great Recession lingered for years, perhaps in part due to the lessons of the Great Depression. By 2008, policymakers knew enough to avoid a repeat of that historical episode. But success in avoiding the Great Depression allowed politics to interfere with the application of policies that might have ended the recession sooner and promoted a faster recovery.

4 The Latin American Debt Crisis, 1982–1989

4.1 CONDITIONS LEADING UP TO THE CRISIS

On Thursday, August 12, 1982, Mexico's Secretary of Finance, Jesús Silva Herzog, sent a letter to the country's creditors telling them that Mexico did not have adequate foreign currency reserves to make interest payments on its national debt due the following Monday. In anticipation of the reaction in Mexico and abroad, Silva Herzog closed the foreign exchange markets in Mexico and phoned the heads of the (IMF), the Federal Reserve, and the US Treasury Department, before flying to Washington, DC, to negotiate assistance (Boughton, 2001: 289–90). So began the worst financial crisis since the Great Depression.[1]

In the run up to the crisis, no one sounded an alarm. Official observers at the IMF and World Bank were confident in the direction of the world economy even though debt levels were rising and a few countries were in default (Edwards, 1995; Ffrench-Davis,1998; Thorp, 1998). Bolivia had defaulted on its sovereign debt in 1980, and Peru had a string of defaults in 1976, 1978, and 1980, but all of these were easily absorbed by world financial markets (Reinhart and Rogoff, 2009a: 96). Mexico, however, was different. It was a major oil exporter with the world's tenth largest economy. Banks in the US, Western Europe and Japan were more exposed than they were in Bolivia or Peru, having lent generously when Mexico's new oil fields began pumping in 1978. Five years prior to the Mexican oil boom,

1 The Debt Crisis was not limited to Latin America, but two-thirds of the largest debtors were Latin American, and nearly all the countries of Central and South America succumbed to the crisis, with the exception of Colombia. Other large debtors included Ivory Coast, Morocco, Nigeria, Philippines, and Yugoslavia. See Sachs (1989).

political events in the Middle East caused dramatic jumps in the world price of oil and turned Mexico's oil reserves into a near guarantee of repayment on foreign loans. After another round of oil price increases in 1979, prices were not expected to come back down and Mexican President Lopez Portillo famously announced that the challenge for his country was to "manage the abundance." The possibility that a country with large oil reserves would not be able to pay its debt was not given serious consideration inside or outside of Mexico.

The long Golden Age of postwar economic growth touched most countries in the world, including Mexico and the rest of Latin America. By the early 1970s, Latin American incomes were significantly higher than after the war, the region was more urban than rural, and industry and services were the key drivers of economic growth. Traditional commodity exports of agricultural and mineral products continued to be important, particularly as a source of foreign exchange, but the postwar migration of people from the countryside to the city had turned most countries in Latin America into urbanized economies. According to the World Bank (2017a), more than 60 percent of the population of Latin America and the Caribbean lived in urban areas by 1975.

After the breakdown of the Bretton Woods exchange rate system, international financial markets also began to adjust. More markets opening in many parts of the world meant that savings in one country could be lent abroad as a portfolio investment, a bank loan, or a direct investment in businesses. Countries debated the type of exchange rates they would adopt and in many high income countries the arguments of Milton Friedman and others favoring flexible exchange rates were persuasive and gradually won over policymakers (Friedman, 1953). A majority of the world's nations preferred the certainty of a fixed exchange rate, however, and adopted a variety of hard and soft pegs, often choosing to tie their currency to the dollar, the French franc, the British pound, or another major trading partner. Pegged currencies continue today to be far more common than flexible (IMF, 2014a).

On paper, the new era had some advantages in dealing with financial crises that economies in the Great Depression era lacked. One was the postwar organization of international economic relations. The end of World War II and the beginning of the Cold War led to the creation of a set of intergovernmental organizations that served as forums for discussion and research, provided resources for addressing some economic problems, and offered technical and financial assistance. The World Bank, but especially the IMF, were designated to play important roles in crisis resolution and to provide mechanisms for addressing economic emergencies in developing countries. The policies of the new international organizations were shaped by the division of the world into US and Soviet blocs and the requirement that the financial and technical assistance meet the needs of the United States and its Western allies in the furtherance of liberal democratic systems and the containment of the USSR.[2] In contrast to the 1920s, after World War II the United States was committed to a leadership role in global economic affairs and was willing to provide support for countries that were not aligned with the Soviet Union.

4.2 THE IMF'S FIRST GLOBAL CRISIS

The debt crisis that began in Mexico and spread through Latin America and other middle and low income countries was the first large-scale financial crisis since the Great Depression. As with the Great Depression, the Latin American Debt Crisis defied easy solutions or even any solution at all, it often seemed. In the early stages, the severity of the crisis was not well understood by leaders in the United States, Western Europe, and the IMF, who all assumed that

2 Nearly all relevant organizations had Cold War objectives as a part of their mission. Organizationally, they were dominated by the United States and the other major market-oriented economies. See Joyce (2013) for a comprehensive analysis of the performance of the IMF in handling crises during the second half of the twentieth century. The literature on the goals and efficacy of these organizations is voluminous. See Easterly (2013) for a critique by an insider of the advice given by development economists and IMF staff.

more short-term capital flows would restart economic growth and enable countries to begin repayment. It took several years for politicians and technocrats in the United States and other high income countries to realize that the solution to the crisis was more elusive and far more complicated than originally thought.[3] From the beginning and for several years, the problem was viewed as one of illiquidity and not insolvency (Cline, 1984). That view led to several efforts by the IMF and the US Treasury to provide loans and to coordinate lending by private banks. While these efforts had modest success in generating some new capital flows, they failed to restart growth or to address the growing problems caused by the increasingly widespread macroeconomic imbalances.

The view that an easy solution to the Latin American Debt Crisis involved more lending so countries could outgrow their debt burdens, was gradually replaced with another oversimplification, one that the crisis was caused by failed government policies – often imposed by military governments – in which populist leaders made politically easy but economically costly choices in order to stay in power (Dornbusch and Edwards, 1990).[4] When the United States and other industrial economies entered a period of two recessions in 1980 and 1981–1982, Latin American economies were unable to obtain the financing they needed to maintain public spending and to pay for their trade deficits. Governments were economically overwhelmed by the depth of the crisis, while their own political turmoil stymied their ability to form a coherent response. Hence the crisis dragged on for many years until the United States and other high income countries were able to formulate a coordinated strategy that involved internal reforms in the indebted countries.

3 Lindert and Morton (1989) make the point that the twenty three party negotiations between debtors, creditor banks, and the IMF (with the support of the US government), was actually more complicated and created higher costs than earlier historical debt crises that only engaged debtor governments and creditor banks.

4 The Dornbusch and Edwards (1990) political economy model of economic populism is a good description of some of the tendencies then and now, in Latin America and elsewhere. It does not fully describe the incentives in countries where there was a debt crisis without populist leaders.

There is some truth in the view just expressed, and most observers agree that the policy choices of many Latin American governments were symptomatic of political turmoil and weak political institutions that made them vulnerable to a debt crisis (Sachs, 1988, 1989:31). Nevertheless, Latin American governments and international agencies such as the IMF were in uncharted economic terrain in the years before the crisis began. Traditional state-led development policies that were advised by the UN's Economic Commission on Latin America (ECLA) had served countries relatively well during the Bretton Woods era of rapid economic growth, but were no longer as effective in the decade before the crisis (Bértola and Ocampo, 2012: 138–97). In the late 1960s, the ECLA began to encourage countries to pay greater attention to exports and to modify the inward orientation of their policies. But many attempts at reform were unsuccessful or were undermined by easy access to direct loans from foreign banks that became available in the mid-1970s.[5] Several Southern Cone countries liberalized their financial sectors by removing controls on international capital flows, only to experience dramatic accumulation of private debt (Diaz-Alejandro, 1985). When the debt crisis began, the lack of dynamic, productive export sectors meant that it was nearly impossible to earn dollars or other foreign currencies without major economic reforms, and those were severely complicated by the depth of the crisis.

Prior to the debt crisis, the IMF had not yet been tested by a crisis that threatened to bring down the global financial system. The IMF's

5 The UN commission was headed by an influential economist, Raúl Prebisch, who provided theoretical and empirical reasons for an inwardly focused set of policies called import substitution industrialization (ISI). See Gerber (2007) for a review of the economics of ISI. By the late 1960s, Prebisch recognized that many countries were too inwardly focused and began to advocate for export promotion policies and regional trade agreements that were expected to capture economies of scale. The regional trade agreements did not significantly increase trade flows and Thorp (1998) notes that many other early reform efforts were undermined by the inflows of private lending, which gave governments the foreign exchange and spending power they needed to maintain and even increase their investment levels. Ffrench-Davis (1998) describes the reasons for the resistance to expenditure cuts and tax increases that some viewed as necessary to avoid future problems.

involvement with countries in distress had been focused mainly on helping individual countries deal with budget and trade imbalances or overvalued exchange rates. It had never encountered a situation where many countries simultaneously experienced every type of financial crisis, from debt to banking, to currency, to inflation, to sudden stops.

4.3 THE CREDIT BOOM

The credit boom in developing countries began in the 1970s. It was a direct result of recycling the profits earned by oil producing countries after the oil price increases began in 1973. Middle Eastern producers with relatively small populations and limited financial sectors had little capacity to absorb all their earnings at home and chose instead to recycle their petrodollars through New York, London, Tokyo, and other financial centers. The increased openness of world financial markets eventually turned these funds into loans from financial center banks to sovereign governments and foreign firms, many of the latter with government guarantees. In theory, Latin American governments used the loans for development purposes, but in practice they were often spent on military equipment, failed investment projects, and consumption. Country-level experiences varied but many of the nations that eventually defaulted used their access to foreign bank loans to support their state-led economic development strategies, including government-controlled or government-directed investment. In other countries, for example Chile, the military dictatorship implemented reforms that reduced the economic role of the state and, as a consequence, allowed private interests to borrow abroad as much as they were able.

In Mexico, the new oil reserves led to a change in its credit worthiness. In 1978, when its new fields began production, oil resources were perhaps the best possible collateral against default, particularly when it was controlled by the national government. Venezuela and Ecuador also had large oil reserves while Peru's problems were partly a result of an expectation of oil discoveries that did not materialize. Given that the demand for oil was expected to increase indefinitely and that the world's supply of oil was considered fixed, most analysts thought oil prices could not fall significantly and would increase in real terms over the long run. Consequently, loans to oil rich countries were viewed as nearly risk free. Today, this view seems naive since it assumed that there would be no significant new discoveries, no technological breakthroughs in exploration and recovery, no significant developments in conservation or oil efficiency, and no meaningful development of alternative energies. Even if those assumptions had not been made, however, changes in technology, usage, and resource supply were medium to long run, and uncertain at best.

If we consider the general outline of the international economy in the years leading up to the debt crisis, it is apparent that most of the vulnerabilities listed in Chapter 1 were present. The two oil crises in 1973 and 1979 caused oil prices to shoot up and created windfall profits for oil producers. In Shiller's terminology, there was a great deal of "new era thinking" that the scarcity of oil was now a permanent feature of economic life. The bubble in oil prices produced an unusual credit boom in international financial markets as banks in countries with deep financial sectors suddenly received large deposits from oil producers in developing countries, mainly Middle Eastern, where there were insufficient financial markets to absorb the windfall profits. Citibank, Bank of America, and other large financial firms in the US and Europe needed to recycle their petrodollar deposits, which they did by lending directly to developing countries. Given that this was a relatively new form of financial activity, one in which governments took loans from banks in high income countries rather than selling bonds in international capital markets, there was less oversight and fewer regulatory controls in either the lending or borrowing countries. Many countries had persistently overvalued exchange rates, with growing trade deficits and a lack of competitive exports other than primary commodities.

4.4 VARIETIES OF CRISES

The crisis was devastating for wages, employment, and social conditions such as educational attainment, food availability, health care, and others (Lustig, 1990, 1998). It began a "Lost Decade" in Latin America during which incomes fell, often by a considerable amount.[6] Economic conditions worsened throughout the 1980s as the debt crisis spread to more countries and then beyond government debt into the banking sector. Sovereign defaults led to recessions and banking crises, which led to inflation and currency crises, all on top of the sudden cessation in foreign lending and the drastic decline in imports.

Latin American vulnerabilities were exposed when US monetary policy changed in order to address a growing problem of inflation. Beginning in the 1960s and continuing through the 1970s, inflation in the United States gradually accelerated to a maximum of 14.4 percent in May, 1980 (Bureau of Labor Statistics, 2016), causing the newly appointed Chairman of the Federal Reserve, Paul Volcker, to implement an anti-inflation strategy (Medley, 2013). Volcker's disinflation policy was successful, but the consequences included higher and more variable interest rates, a mild recession in 1980, and a more severe one in 1981–1982. Rising interest rates and recession in the United States were harmful to many Latin American economies, particularly given the vulnerabilities that were building. Many of their loans in the 1970s were short-term, variable rate loans, denominated in dollars and requiring repayment in dollars. The two US recessions reduced the demand for Latin American products and made dollars harder to obtain, while the short maturities and rising interest rates required finance that was no longer available. Mexico and Venezuela and other oil producing

6 Real income per person measured in the national currency was nearly 24 percent lower in 1990 than in 1980 in Argentina, 5.6 percent in Brazil, 4.1 percent in Mexico, 27.6 percent in Peru, and 19 percent in Venezuela. These five countries were more than 75 percent of the total population of Latin America. Among the larger countries, only Colombia avoided the debt crisis, although it did have a mild recession in 1982–1983 (IMF, 2016).

countries were also hit by steep declines in oil prices that began in 1981. From Mexico, defaults spread across Latin America. Lenders in the United States, Europe, and Japan turned cautious and took closer looks at countries where there were the same or similar economic fundamentals as Mexico. Argentina, Ecuador, and the Dominican Republic also defaulted in 1982 and were followed by Brazil, Chile, Costa Rica, Panama, Uruguay, and Venezuela in 1983, and Peru and Costa Rica in 1984 (Reinhart and Rogoff, 2009a: table 6.4).

Early diagnoses of the crisis viewed it as temporary and a problem of liquidity (Cline, 1984). Banks exposed to the bad loans formed a creditor cartel that worked separately with each country and blocked the formation of a similar debtor cartel that might have been able to bargain collectively with the creditors. The creditor cartel encouraged governments to publicly guarantee private debts that had been contracted without guarantees and worked with the US and other governments to pressure less exposed banks to participate in making new loans, and pushed economic restructuring programs designed to open markets. Debtor governments made serious and relatively successful efforts to cut spending in order to direct more resources toward debt service, but deficits in government accounts increased in many countries due to the recession-caused decline in tax revenues (Edwards, 1995: 26). The recessions also pushed the banking sector into crisis as economic activity declined.[7]

The disappearance of external financing forced governments to seek new sources of revenue, even as they were cutting expenditures. Borrowing was impossible and tax revenues were down (and tax compliance was low in many countries). The remaining option was the inflation tax. In the 1980s, most central banks in Latin America were not independent but were branches of government. Elected leaders

7 Reinhart and Rogoff (2009, appendix A.4.1) show banking crises through most of the 1980s in many countries, and one or two years of banking crises in several others. Few countries escaped, and none of the six largest economies (Argentina, Brazil, Colombia, Mexico, Peru, and Venezuela). Many banks were also holding government debt as part of their asset base. When governments defaulted, bank balance sheets were hit with a decline in the value of those assets and the potential for insolvency.

could request the central banks to put newly created reserves in the government's account where they were available for spending. This was a stop gap policy that remained in place for many years in some countries, but nearly all countries resorted to one degree or another to printing money as a solution to inadequate tax revenues.[8] One consequence was an escalation of inflation rates and, in some cases, severe inflation crises. Argentina, Bolivia, Brazil, and Peru had rates above 1,000 percent in some years, and averaged over 300 percent between 1982 and 1989. Mexico averaged 80 percent during that period and was above 100 percent in 1983 (World Bank, 2017a).

Every government with its own currency derives some of its revenue from printing money, called seigniorage. For example, in the 1980s, the United States made revenue equal to about 1.6 percent of the federal budget from the printing of money (Neumann, 1992). Using seigniorage as a source of government revenue creates negative feedback effects, however, and actually increases the size of the deficit and the need to print more money. This is known as the Olivera–Tanzi effect (Olivera, 1967). High inflation causes taxpayers to delay payments in order to let the real value of the tax payment decline. This reduces tax collection in real terms and increases the size of the deficit, all else equal. If inflation is running at several hundred or several thousand percent per year, the tax bill might end up as a rounding error if taxpayers delay payment. The Olivera–Tanzi effect shows that when seigniorage is used to finance government budgets, the monetary authority has to keep increasing the amount of money in circulation, which of course increases the rate of inflation and requires more seigniorage.

Depending on the type of exchange rate system in use, an inflation crisis can cause real appreciation in the currency which often leads to a sudden and severe devaluation. Latin American external

8 Many countries resorted to printing money in the 1970s, before the debt crisis began, as a way to compensate for inadequate revenue. In a number of countries, money creation accounted for between 15 percent and 25 percent of government spending (Edwards, 1995, 83).

economic relations were heavily oriented toward the United States and many countries fixed their currency to the dollar. Inflation, however, upsets this arrangement by causing real appreciation as the domestic purchasing power of the currency falls relative to its foreign purchasing power. To compensate, countries need to devalue their currencies. If they do not, the trade deficit will continue to increase until they run out of reserves and the crisis intensifies. Policymakers in many countries, however, sought to use the fixed exchange rate as a check on inflation. They reasoned that if they devalued by an amount that was slightly less than the inflation differences, then producers of domestic goods would lose a little competitiveness but not too much, and would be forced to limit their price increases in order to stay competitive. In order to compensate for their higher rates of inflation, Mexican officials and those in a number of other countries began to devalue on a regular basis by an amount that was slightly less than the differences in inflation rates at home and in the United States. The hope was that they would force their own producers to hold back on price increases, but at the same time, not let the slight real appreciation cause the trade deficit to balloon.

Foreign and domestic speculators saw that there were several countries with high inflation, growing trade deficits, and exchange rates that adjusted, but not enough to offset the effects of inflation. They knew these conditions were unsustainable and would almost certainly lead to major devaluations at some point in the future. Owners of assets denominated in a currency with high inflation, wanted to sell their assets and convert to dollars or another international reserve currency before the large devaluation came. This put pressure on governments to come up with the dollars demanded by speculators or others that expected a devaluation, and led to a decline in reserves that was often followed by a sudden radical devaluation.

Currency collapses and a constant rate of unexpectedly high devaluations became common throughout the 1980s. Argentina's currency depreciated 142 percent per year from 1980 to 1982, then after a reform it depreciated 153 percent from 1983 to 1984, then after a second reform in 1985, it depreciated 348 percent per year until the end of the decade. Brazil's experience was similar and also included several reforms and an escalating rate of depreciation. Mexico did somewhat better but its currency still depreciated 55 percent per year over the decade with no reforms until 1992.[9]

By the mid-1980s, it seems that every type of crisis was happening at once, from debt to banking to inflation to sudden stops to currency crises. Recession was the norm across the region, and the actions of the IMF and the US were completely ineffective at bringing an end to the crisis. The US faced a serious problem of its own due to the fact that several large banks had more bad loans to Latin American countries than the value of their capital base. If they were to acknowledge that the loans would not be repaid, a number of banks would have been insolvent. Consequently, the strategy was to avoid marking down the value of the loans until they accumulated sufficient reserves against loan losses and could value them at their real value without causing bankruptcies.[10] US strategy included pressure on Latin American governments not to sell their debt in secondary markets since that would have established a valid market price for the value of the loans on the balance sheets of US banks.

4.5 THE SEARCH FOR SOLUTIONS

In the initial phase of the Latin American Debt Crisis, the US government, the IMF, and commercial banks tried to restore capital flows to indebted countries. They were partially successful in this effort, although the new loans were less than the interest payments of the debtor countries and could be viewed as indirect subsidies to US and other banks. In this first phase, debts were restructured, but

9 Argentina finally got control of inflation and currency devaluation in 1991; Brazil in 1994 (Montevideo–Oxford Latin American Economic History Database, 2016).

10 US banking regulations required banks to take losses on loans that fell behind in interest payments, so the strategy was to ensure that debtor governments at least kept paying interest. Sachs (1989: 10) and Cline (1995: 74–75) show that the nine largest US banks' exposure to Latin American debt was more than 175 percent of their capital in 1982.

not written down. The repayment of principal was lengthened, but interest rates were increased so the real value of the debt did not change. This was intended as a means to give the debtor countries some breathing space in paying off their debts, but mainly it helped the creditor banks who did not have to take losses on their loans. Debtor governments were expected to stay current in their interest payments and to stabilize their domestic economies by reducing their budget and trade deficits. The hope was that macroeconomic austerity and some new lending would let debtor governments direct their scarce revenues toward repayment of debt.

Key economic variables were out of balance in many countries before the onset of the crisis. After the crisis began, both the policy advice of the IMF and the conditions for rescheduling debt dictated that government spending had to be cut, deficits reduced, and exchange rates devalued. As the crisis developed, several of the largest debtors such as Mexico, Argentina, Venezuela, and others, cut government spending by more than 20 percent in the first few years (Edwards, 1989: 170). Yet budget deficits still grew for three basic reasons. Higher interest rates that were part of the debt rescheduling increased the interest payments governments had to make; the loss of tax revenue from the deep recessions, which were exacerbated by the spending cuts; and the exchange rate devaluations increased the real value of the debt and, consequently, the burden of interest payments.

Throughout the 1980s, a secondary market for government debt developed despite the US attempts to discourage banks from selling their loans. Banks sold the debt of national governments and private firms with government guarantees at discounted prices reflecting an estimate of the real value of the debt. In several cases, state-owned enterprises and private enterprises repurchased their own debt at discounted prices. This became more and more feasible over the course of the 1980s, as the crisis dragged on and estimates of the likelihood of repayment declined and caused a decline in the secondary market price of debt (Cline, 1995: 187, 224).

The central question seemed to turn on whether economic growth could be restored without some form of debt relief. Could both creditors and debtors be better off if creditors forgave some or all of the debt? Creditors would lose their claims on Latin American governments, but perhaps they would increase the chances that they would recover more of the face value of the debt than if refusal to offer any relief caused countries to default on the entire amount. Others reasoned that no debt relief was necessary since several countries, including Chile, Colombia (which never defaulted but did suffer a recession), and several countries outside Latin America, eventually managed to resolve the crisis without receiving debt forgiveness.

The economic history of sovereign debt defaults in the nineteenth and twentieth centuries is a record of crises that are only resolved when debt forgiveness is part of the solution. Prior to the Latin American Debt Crisis, countries in default negotiated with creditors who were ultimately willing to accept debt write downs in exchange for partial repayments (Lindert and Morton, 1989; Eichengreen and Portes, 1989). Both sides were forced to recognize that debt that cannot be paid will not be paid, and partial payment was better for everyone. The alternative was continued conflict with international lenders and greater difficulties in obtaining foreign capital in indebted countries.

Several East Asian economies also borrowed heavily in the 1970s and found themselves in trouble toward the end of the decade and at the start of the 1980s. South Korea's ratio of debt to GDP was nearly the same as Argentina's in 1980, indicating that the burden of debt was approximately the same. Brazil and Mexico both had debt ratios that were significantly less than Korea's in 1980, but the latter escaped the debt crisis, while Argentina, Brazil, Mexico, and most of the rest of Latin America did not. The difference between Latin American economies and South Korea was in the ability to service their debts, and that difference stemmed from their relative export strengths. Korean exports were a much larger share of its economy and its ratio of debt to exports was only about 60 percent of the level of Argentina and Mexico, and less than half the level of Brazil.[11]

From approximately the end of World War II, Latin American economies pursued ISI policies that were inward looking and protected domestic industries behind high tariff walls and import restrictions. The goal was to use the domestic production of goods that substitute for imports as an industrialization strategy that would meet existing demand and also conserve on the use of scarce foreign currency by producing goods domestically rather than importing them. The preferences given to industries that produce import substitutes was an implicit bias against export industries, since the former were made more profitable at the margin. Import substituting industries were favored with a variety of industrial policies such as trade protection, credit subsidies, tax breaks, and others. There were attempts to encourage export promotion in the 1960s, but they were relatively unsuccessful and manufacturing remained focused on domestic markets and untested by world markets. When the debt crisis began, Latin American exporters of manufactured goods were relatively undeveloped. Some observers have blamed ISI for the debt crisis, but that is a mistake and confuses causes of the crisis with policies that made the crisis difficult to escape. ISI did not cause the debt crisis, but it did contribute to the weakened ability of Latin American economies to respond.

While ISI was the standard development strategy after World War II and was promoted by development experts and institutions, some ISI countries outside Latin America began to alter their policies in the 1960s at approximately the same time that ECLA was encouraging reforms in Latin America that were ultimately less successful. South Korea, for example, began to favor more explicit export promotion while keeping some of the elements of ISI. By the late 1970s, its

11 In 1980, the ratio of debt-to-GDP was 51 percent in Argentina, 29 percent in Brazil, 32 percent in Mexico, and 49 percent in South Korea. But the ratio of debt-to-exports was 131 percent in Korea compared to 242 percent in Argentina, 301 percent in Brazil, and 233 percent in Mexico (World Bank, 1987).

export sector was strong enough to reduce the burden associated with debt service.[12] In addition to moving away from relying on inward looking ISI policies, South Korea and other East Asian economies also had greater policy flexibility. Korea's economic policy in the 1970s targeted six industries it believed were important to its future growth and development. When those policies began to drain the national budget at the same time that interest rates were rising and the debt service burden was escalating, the country shifted away from supporting industries that were not doing well, implemented a currency devaluation, and opened it markets wider to imports (Westphal, 1990). Its ability to act when confronted with adverse economic conditions was central to its success in avoiding a crisis. By contrast, political turmoil, political party fragmentation, and class conflict prevented the same quick, decisive action in Latin America.

Lacking the export industries needed to earn sufficient revenue, and shackled by recessions which made it difficult to invest in industries that might have produced competitive exports, it became increasingly clear that the solution would require some form of debt forgiveness. Debtor country governments, commercial bank lenders, the IMF, and the US government, began negotiating partial debt forgiveness in return for economic reforms. The first set of reforms included efforts to stabilize economies through a reduction in budget deficits, along with curtailment of money creation, and devaluation of the currency. A second group of reforms focused on structural adjustments intended to increase overall economic efficiency. The main components included privatization of state-owned enterprises, reform and greater opening of the financial system, and a general opening of markets to foreign competition.

Stabilization plus structural adjustment became the mantra of reformers in high income countries. Countries that wanted debt relief had first to show they were complying with the general intent of the reform policies before they would qualify for a menu of debt relief

12 The ratio of exports to GDP in Korea in 1980 was 30 percent. By comparison, Argentina was 5 percent, Brazil was 9 percent, and Mexico was 11 percent (World Bank, 2014).

options. By the late 1980s, several countries were moving toward compliance, and in 1989, the first debt relief package was given to Mexico, the country where the debt crisis began, and one of the first to implement economic reforms. A number of countries eventually received debt relief packages, including Argentina, Brazil, Peru, Venezuela, and others, both in Latin America and elsewhere.

4.6 THE RETURN OF CAPITAL FLOWS

The timing, speed, and extent of the reforms varied considerably across Latin America. In addition to gaining control of budget deficits and money creation, most reform programs also included trade openings, exchange rate adjustments, tax reforms, financial reforms, and privatization and reform of public enterprises (Edwards, 1995; Stallings and Peres, 2000). In the end, nearly every economy engaged in some reforms, and some economies in all or nearly all. It is hard to overemphasize the importance of these reforms because even in cases where they were not effective at restarting growth, they were a significant shift in economic policy away from state-led economic development.

The adoption of economic reforms together with the signing of a debt reduction agreement was a signal to the international financial community that it was safe to invest again in Latin America. Beginning in the early 1990s there was a sharp increase in capital inflows but unlike the 1970s bank loans, the composition was a combination of portfolio investment (stocks and bonds) and foreign direct investment (the establishment of new businesses and the purchase of existing ones). In the short to medium run, this loosened constraints on investment by providing outside capital. In the long run, however, it contributed to another round of increased trade deficits and overvalued currencies (Ffrench-Davis and Griffith-Jones, 2011).

By the early 1990s, the Latin American Debt Crisis was mostly over and countries began to grow again. The fact that growth remained volatile and mediocre gave rise to a number of debates about the economic reforms undertaken, the role of the IMF in crisis management, and the lessons to be learned. Economists agree that the large budget deficits and overvalued exchange rates of the 1970s and early 1980s, together with the bank loans that made the deficits possible, were major vulnerabilities. Yet the prescription that countries remove those obvious imbalances proved to be harder than expected. In many countries, local and state governments had direct access to central bank financing so that balanced budgets at the federal level could be undone by spending at the sub-national level. This made it hard to even know what the deficits were, in some cases (Sachs, 1989, 22.). Furthermore, cutting government expenditures was complicated by politics and class divisions that manifested themselves as mass mobilizations, extremism of various sorts, and political violence in some cases. It was not simple to navigate a cut in spending or a tax increase. Some outside observers argued that the budget and other reforms required countries to elect a nontraditional group of technically skilled politicians, labeled "tecnopols," who understood technical economics from a market perspective and at the same time were capable of navigating the rough currents of the political process (Williamson, 1994).

4.7 LESSONS

The policy of austerity in the face of severe recessions and debt overhangs made things worse. This is one of the first instances on a grand scale of the failure of austerity and the inability of the world's leaders to find a more effective and humane way to address fundamental imbalances in the macroeconomy. There were no clear alternatives to austerity other than debt forgiveness, but that seemed to be ruled out by arguments of moral hazard and the desire to punish incompetent and profligate politicians. Many argued that if complete or partial debt forgiveness was granted, it would reward poorly managed countries and perhaps remove the incentive to find better economic managers. In the end, however, indebted countries conformed to the pattern of previous debt crises and did not start to recover until their debts were partially forgiven. It may not be an ideal outcome, but it was reality and after more than six years trying to avoid debt forgiveness, it was finally accepted as part of the solution.

There are several additional lessons from this episode of large-scale financial crisis. The first set applies to avoiding a crisis. The second set concerns the steps countries have to take to get out of a sovereign debt crisis and the role of the IMF and other international actors, such as the US government. And the third set applies to the policies that become necessary if countries are unable to escape.

In retrospect, it is obvious that the large-scale capital flows from money center banks to governments and enterprises in Latin America created vulnerabilities that, in an ideal world, would have been guarded against. The normal response is to blame the borrowers for accepting loans that ultimately proved to be beyond their capacity to repay, but the responsibility of lenders must also be considered. Money center banks were anxious to earn a return on the money deposited by oil rich economies and looked for new ways to lend. The CEO of Citibank, Walter Wriston, declared that countries do not go out of business and as such, they were a great place to lend petrodollar deposits.[13] It is impossible to know if this was a superficial quip, meant to justify risky but lucrative investments, or if it is meant to be taken literally. In either case, the history of lending to sovereign governments is littered with defaults and was well known in Wriston's time. As in the case of the later Subprime Crisis, Wriston and other bankers probably felt that when the music is playing, you either have to dance or explain to your shareholders why you missed an opportunity.

Overlending is rarely considered a problem on par with overborrowing even though both sides are responsible. From the

13 Wriston expanded on his view in a 1987 article in *Institutional Investor* and a later interview: "And the facts are – if anybody reads that article, which, of course, nobody does – what I said was that the infrastructure doesn't go away, the productivity of the people doesn't go away, the natural resources don't go away. And so their assets always exceed their liabilities, which is the technical reason for bankruptcy. And that's very different from a company" (Wriston, 2007).

borrower's standpoint, the worst would have been avoided if they had been more cautious. Caution in this case would have meant an avoidance of relying on external financing, particularly in the form of bank loans, and a greater effort to ensure capital inflows were put to productive use. Fewer bank loans and more foreign direct investment would have helped reduce the problem of unproductive borrowing, while avoidance of external financing altogether would have required more savings domestically, both private and public. At a minimum, the avoidance of large budget deficits would have provided more public savings and improved fiscal conditions. Consequently, the main lesson that many have taken away from this episode is that Latin American governments needed more stability in their macroeconomic policies: smaller budget deficits, competitively valued currencies, and sound tax policies to avoid seigniorage as a source of financing. This is undoubtedly correct.

During and immediately after the Latin American Debt Crisis, the positions of borrowing nations and lending banks were viewed asymmetrically. Borrowers were vulnerable to sudden shifts in capital flows which created problems that were intensified by recessions and by the concerted efforts of lenders to avoid debt forgiveness. Lenders faced insolvency and would generate spillover effects into the global financial system if the debts were not repaid. Consequently, lenders were treated more carefully in order to avoid contagion outside Latin America. On the borrower side, the crisis was a painful lesson in the need to develop better fiscal management policies. Lenders, however, were given implicit protections which meant that no similar lessons emerged. Banks took losses on many loans, and some had an existential threat when their exposure to Latin American debt was revealed, but there were no banking reforms and no attempts to reign in lending. Furthermore, the 1980s began a period of deregulation in the financial services industry and consequently cautionary tales and potential lessons for banks were lost.

The lessons for debtor countries were also less clear than it seemed at first. No one argues against the need to maintain a country's fiscal accounts in good shape, but other elements of the reform packages were less clearly of benefit. Labor market reforms that make it easier to hire and fire workers, privatization of state-owned enterprises, opening of capital markets to foreigners, and free trade, may have benefits, but the complexity of real world economies enmeshed in unique historical conditions and country-specific political processes means that reforms must have a high degree of tailoring to individual country needs. Those characteristics require local knowledge at a minimum, which is often lacking in the urgency of reform, particularly when it is promoted by outside experts. Furthermore, the assumption that economists or others know enough to be able to reform a national economy and put it on a stable growth path is questionable at best and deeply destructive at worst.

As governments implemented reforms and gained access to debt restructuring, the crisis eased and growth returned. But the rate of growth was disappointing and still highly volatile. Debates developed over the extent of reforms, the kind of reforms, and the order of reforms. Relatively quickly, the argument turned toward a discussion of institutions, the capacity for real reforms, and new institutional issues such as corruption, the rule of law, the ease of doing business, and other elements of institutional quality. Meanwhile, disappointing growth rates and a lack of reforms focused on issues of inequality led some governments to turn back toward a stronger role for the state and explicitly state-led development.[14]

The interconnectedness of different types of crises made escape from the Latin American Debt Crisis extremely difficult as policies for correcting one type of problem often made another worse. Devaluations made economies more competitive, but they also increased the domestic currency value of debt that was denominated in dollars. Open markets enabled foreign goods to put competitive pressures on

14 See, for example, Edwards, 2010 and Weitzman, 2012. These movements have mostly failed as well. Chavez's Venezuela became extremely vulnerable to oil price declines, and Brazil, Argentina, and Ecuador, have also suffered from declining commodity prices.

domestic producers and helped hold down inflation, but also widened the trade deficit and increased the need for foreign financing. Tax increases and cuts in spending helped reduce deficits, but they also hurt growth and eventually resulted in greater deficits. The opposite policy, increases in spending or cuts in taxes, might stimulate growth but at the cost of larger deficits and a greater needs for external financing. Untangling all these issues remains an extremely complicated and uncertain process.

Specifically, Latin American economies needed to earn foreign exchange and the primary way to do this is through exports. This brings us to the second set of lessons, beyond the obvious need to avoid large macroeconomic imbalances. Import substitution industrialization policies did not cause the debt crisis but their implicit bias against exports made escape more difficult. When Latin American economies needed to sell products in the world market to earn revenue to pay their debts, they had few competitive products other than traditional agricultural and mineral commodities. Manufacturing grew significantly during the ISI years, but it mostly produced for a highly protected domestic economy and did not penetrate into international markets. Mexico, the country where the crisis began, clearly illustrates this point. In 1982, Mexico relied on oil and tourism for a majority of its exports. When oil prices fell and recessions in the United States reduced the supply of tourists, its vulnerability was exposed and the crisis was triggered. Over the second half of the 1980s, Mexico remade its economy so that by 1994, when the North American Free Trade Agreement was implemented, it had a vibrantly strong manufacturing sector. And when a currency crisis hit the country at the end of 1994, it experienced another painful recession with a large devaluation, but rather than a six or seven year crisis, it returned to growth by the end of 1995. Mexico's makeover gave it the ability to export manufactured goods in large quantities and to avoid another prolonged crisis (Lustig, 1998). Plenty of problems remained inside the country, but the basic ability to export manufactured goods added a resiliency that was lacking in 1982.

Prior to the Latin American Debt Crisis, the need for manufactured exports and the advantages they confer was observed by a number of countries outside of Latin America. As mentioned earlier, Korea began its economic development after the Korean War with a set of economic policies that were very similar to ISI, but it began to develop complementary and effective export promotion policies in the 1960s. In many respects they were following the lead of Japan. Other export oriented economies developed, primarily in East Asia, and experienced very high rates of growth which were sustained over long periods. While exports of manufactured goods do not solve all problems or insure against a crisis, they do create resiliency and would have solved many of the ills afflicting Latin America in the 1980s.

The last lesson is the previously discussed point that the historical record and the history of this financial crisis show that debt crises are rarely resolved without some form of partial or complete debt forgiveness. The search for alternatives is part of the reason why the Latin American Debt Crisis became the Lost Decade instead of the Lost Year or the Lost Two Years. The initial insistence that the problem was simply one of liquidity was followed by a recognition that it had many other elements, but both views included searches for alternatives to debt forgiveness that ultimately failed. In the end, debt forgiveness was granted, albeit in limited amounts and under the condition of economic reforms.

4.8 FROM LATIN AMERICA TO EAST ASIA

The crisis in Latin America ended gradually and unevenly across the region. The most commonly cited end date is 1989, not because the crisis was resolved but rather because that is when the US-initiated Brady Plan began to offer a menu of debt restructuring and modest debt forgiveness for selected countries and because Mexico immediately qualified as the first country with access to the plan. As noted, Mexico embarked on a wide range of economic reforms beginning in the middle of the decade, including reduced budget deficits, lower trade barriers with GATT membership, fewer subsidies for industry and agriculture, privatization of hundreds of state-owned enterprises, and most dramatically, the announcement that it was seeking a free trade agreement with the United States. Mexican reforms were consistent with IMF and US proposals for stabilization and structural adjustment and its qualification for debt restructuring elicited a positive response from international capital markets. The groundwork seemed to be in place for a new "Mexican economic miracle" as foreign capital moved to take advantage of the opportunities created by the sale of government assets, more open trade, closer economic ties to the US economy, and the fundamental change in Mexican economic policy that moved the country away from a state-led development strategy and toward a market-oriented, liberal economic order.

In the background of Mexican reforms and qualification for debt relief, investors worldwide were discovering "emerging markets." Google's Ngram Viewer for the English language shows the first usage of the term "emerging market" in 1950 but very infrequent usage until it slowly begins to be adopted in the 1970s and 1980s. There is a sharp upturn in1989 and usage grows significantly thereafter (Google, 2018). In the late 1980s and early 1990s, firms in emerging markets began listing their shares more frequently on US stock exchanges, US-based mutual funds began to offer emerging market funds, and advances in telecommunications created new opportunities in a range of high-growth middle-income countries for multinational corporations and other investors.

Mexico's qualification for debt restructuring under the Brady Plan was a seal of approval from the IMF and the US Treasury Department, and the fact that it was embedding its economic reforms in an international agreement with the United States and Canada provided a degree of certainty that the reforms would last. Capital poured into the country but, unlike the bank loans of the 1970s, was more foreign direct investment and portfolio investment. Between 1988 and 1994, when the free trade agreement with the United States and Canada was implemented, inward foreign direct investment increased 300 percent (UNCTAD, 2018).

Capital inflows were positive for growth and investment but two problems appeared. The inflows created new demands for the peso and caused real appreciation, as described earlier, and led to a rising current account deficit. Mexico used a crawling peg exchange rate policy that fixed the currency to the US dollar with regular adjustments for its slightly higher rates of inflation than in the United States. Mexico's crawling peg did not completely offset its higher rate of domestic inflation, however, and by the summer of 1994, analysts outside Mexico were warning that the peso was overvalued by about 20 percent (Dornbusch and Werner, 1994). One consequence was a growing current account deficit and, by early 1994, a steady loss of reserves as investors began to suspect a future large devaluation. The problems of an overvalued exchange rate and a current account deficit were potentially manageable, depending on the responses of investors and speculators. The 20 percent overvaluation of the peso was not a certain fact, as there are multiple ways to determine the equilibrium value of an exchange rate, and the Mexican government insisted that the actual overvaluation was much smaller, if it existed at all. A sizable number of investors and speculators, both domestic and foreign, thought differently, however, and chose to convert pesos to dollars and take them out of the country. While the political context was completely different, the economics and psychology of the situation were similar to what was to play out in East Asia less than five years later. If owners of financial capital had been convinced by the frequent statements of the Mexican president that the peso would not be devalued, they might have left their funds inside the country and no crisis would have occurred.

Mexico's international reserves fell dramatically in the first quarter of 1994, then stabilized until the fourth quarter when they fell again. By mid-December, 1994, the country's ability to defend its currency was exhausted and, after a false start with a small devaluation on December 15, the government announced on December 22 that it would let the currency float. The peso fell immediately and continued to fall for several months, provoking a steep recession and requiring a package of loans and lines of credit from a consortium of the IMF, the United States, Canada, and the Bank for International Settlements.

Mexico's peso crisis of 1994–1995 was a harbinger of the Asian Crisis in several respects. First, Mexico enacted a series of reforms in the years leading up to the crisis that turned it into an emerging market model economy with open trade and market-driven policies. Second, its successes in enacting economic reforms encouraged international optimism and led to large inflows of portfolio and direct investments. Third, once it was revealed that the currency was overvalued, the country's leaders fought to maintain the existing exchange rate, largely for noneconomic reasons. And fourthly, uncertainty about the peso's overvaluation and Mexico's ability to adjust smoothly created two possible equilibriums: one good equilibrium in which the country manages its currency and current account imbalances without any major shocks; one bad equilibrium in which the currency collapses due to the loss of reserves and a continuing high level of demand for the dollar. Ultimately, the bad equilibrium proved to be stronger.

5 The Asian Crisis, 1997–1999

5.1 STABLE ECONOMIES AND RAPID GROWTH

Perhaps the most surprising fact about the financial crisis that engulfed several East Asian countries in 1997 and 1998 was that it happened. Their long-run economic successes and stability did not place them on anyone's list of countries likely to suffer major financial crises. The focus of East Asian specialists was on the reasons for the region's economic growth and when or if it might slowdown. Sometimes the debate was heated, particularly about the longevity of high growth rates and whether there was a new Asian model of economic success, but no one was thinking that a major financial meltdown would begin in East Asia and spill over into other parts of the world.

The worst hit countries were a subset of the nations that the World Bank had labeled "High Performance Asian Economies" (HPAE), and included Indonesia, Korea, Malaysia, and Thailand (World Bank, 1993). While the World Bank's label was not universally accepted, it became widely used in the 1990s, probably at least in part because of the economic successes achieved by countries given the label. Regardless of the label's deficiencies, there is no doubt about the rapid economic development from the 1960s forward, or that the countries were frequently cited as role models for developing countries. Anointed with nicknames such as the Little Dragons or the Four Tigers, these countries had such extraordinary high rates of growth of GDP and GDP per person that it was hard to believe they were on any trajectory other than a steady march toward ever higher material prosperity. To be sure, there were debates about what would happen when they approached the same level of income as the world's leaders, and how growth must inevitably slowdown as they reached the limits of technological borrowing and began their own research and development processes.[1] But the rapid transition from low- to middle- to high-income was relatively smooth and so well managed that the notion of a financial crisis was not part of anyone's thinking.

The World Bank's study, *The East Asian Miracle,* singled out seven countries for their high rates of growth and economic transformation: Hong Kong (still independent of China until 1997), Indonesia, Korea, Malaysia, Singapore, Taiwan, and Thailand. China was not included in this group since its transformation from a centrally planned, socialist system posed a different set of issues, and Japan had been a high-income, market economy for some decades. Of the seven countries labeled HPAE, four were deeply ensnared in the financial crisis that began in 1997 (Indonesia, Korea, Malaysia, and Thailand). Taiwan escaped the crisis altogether, and Singapore and Hong Kong felt the effects of speculation and the decline in regional trade, but were shielded against the worst of the crisis by strong macroeconomic fundamentals and large currency reserves.

Table 5.1 shows the rates of growth in GDP from 1980 to 1997, separately for 1998 which is the depth of the crisis, and 1999 which was a year of strong recovery in all countries except Indonesia. The first column shows why these were labeled high performance economies: average annual real GDP growth varied from 6–9 percent over this period. Due to compound growth, an average annual growth rate of 6 percent implies that GDP doubles in twelve years, and at 9 percent in eight years. The following year, 1998, was disastrous in all but Taiwan, which maintained a positive rate of growth, and Singapore, which had a milder recession than the others. In contrast to the Latin American Debt Crisis, all of the Asian Crisis countries quickly rebounded, with the partial exception of Indonesia, which continued to feel the effects of the crisis for several years.

1 When Paul Krugman (1996) wrote an essay exploring the consequences of diminishing returns to capital in East Asia, he was loudly criticized for having supposedly undermined the East Asian achievement and for having a Western bias that did not appreciate the new growth model in Asia. Asian exceptionalism is discussed in section 5.2 below.

Table 5.1 *Annual average rates of real GDP growth*

	1980–1997	1998	1999
Hong Kong	6.06	−5.88	2.51
Indonesia	6.81	−13.13	0.79
Korea	9.09	−5.47	11.31
Malaysia	7.32	−7.36	6.13
Singapore	8.01	−2.23	6.09
Taiwan	6.76	4.21	6.72
Thailand	7.28	−7.63	4.57

High average annual rates of growth were followed in 1998 by steep recessions caused by a financial crisis that started in Thailand in 1997. Except Indonesia, countries quickly rebounded in 1999.
Source: Author's calculations and IMF, 2016.

Table 5.1 raises several questions. First, why were growth rates so high in these countries and were they related in any way to the crisis that begin in mid-1997? Second, what triggered the crisis? Given that the individual countries had mostly avoided financial problems throughout their recent economic history, and had barely registered any years of negative growth, why did they fall into such a deep crisis in 1997–1998?[2] Third, why was the recovery so quick compared to crises elsewhere? Latin America remained mired in its crisis throughout most of the 1980s (and beyond in the case of some countries), the Great Depression lasted a decade, and the recent Subprime Crisis at least two years in the countries with the quickest recoveries and much longer in the slowest recovering.

5.2 EXPLANATIONS FOR RAPID GROWTH

There is no single explanation for the rapid rates of growth over a long period of time, but there are several characteristics that countries shared to varying degrees. Nobel Laureate Amartya Sen sums them up thusly:

2 Between 1980 and 1997, Malaysia, Singapore, and Taiwan, each had one year of negative GDP growth. The four remaining countries had none.

> While different empirical studies have varied in emphasis, there is by now a fairly well-accepted general list of "helpful policies," among them openness to competition, the use of international markets, a high level of literacy and school education, successful land reforms, and public provision of incentives for investment, exporting, and industrialization (Sen, 1997).

Sen's list is fairly comprehensive, but might be extended to include strong institutions and avoidance of large macroeconomic imbalances, such as the budget deficits, inflation, and currency misalignments that plagued Latin American economies in the 1970s and 1980s.

Sen and others explicitly dismiss authoritarianism and the lack of democracy in several of the countries, including Korea and Singapore, as factors that contributed to growth. The casual observer may believe that authoritarian states seem to have an advantage over democratic ones when it comes to promoting economic development since they can command resources and have greater control over the use of inputs. Fortunately, there is a relatively large empirical literature on the relationship between economic development and political freedoms and the general conclusion is that the correlation between the two is so close to zero that it is hard to infer any systematic relationship. The ability of authoritarian governments to command resources also means that there are fewer checks and balances and a higher risk of harmful or disruptive policies persisting over longer periods of time. The world is full of authoritarian systems that have failed to achieve sustained economic growth.

A related set of questions focuses on the idea of Asian values and whether they were at least partially responsible, as some observers claim, for the high growth rates and the quick escape from the crisis.[3] The status of this view is beyond this chapter, but it should be stressed that most scholars disagree with the idea that uniquely

3 Not just outside observers made this point; Lee Kuan Yew, the former Prime Minister of Singapore and the chief architect of its economic policies made this argument repeatedly in a wide range of forums. Barr (2000) supports Prime Minister Yew's view and Sen (1997) is critical.

Asian values played an important role, or that the concept can even be defined. The countries included in Table 5.1 are far from a monolithic cultural region and the range of thought found in their contemporary and historical texts makes it impossible to offer meaningful generalizations that can be contrasted to an imagined set of Western values. A further technical economic problem with the values argument is that if something called "Asian values" played a significant and independent role in East Asian economic success, it would be measurable indirectly. Economists conceptualize growth in economic output as a result of an increase in one or more of several factors, or inputs: an increase in the labor supply, an improvement in labor skills, an increase in the amount of physical capital (equipment and machines), and an improvement in the way things are done. The last factor is a catchall term for various possibilities, including values as well as more traditional factors such as technological improvements, reorganizations of production, improved management, or one of a number of additional possibilities. Economists routinely measure labor and capital inputs along with improvements in labor skills, but have a hard time directly observing improvements in the way things are done since it includes hard-to-measure variables such as technological advances, management and organizational improvements, and other intangibles. Improvements in the way things are done can be measured as a residual, however, so that after we subtract from output the increase that is caused by increases in labor supply, improvements in labor quality, and increases in the physical amount of capital used, whatever remains of new output that is not explained by those inputs can be attributed to a better way of doing things, whether it be caused by organizational, technological, managerial, or some other variable such as values. In the East Asian example, if values played a different role than they did in the growth of non-Asian economies, then the increase in output that cannot be explained by labor and capital inputs, would be larger than elsewhere.

What we find in the East Asian case is as Sen describes. Households, businesses, and governments in the fast growing countries saved and invested at high rates (capital increases), made high school education standard (improvements in labor quality), and went through demographic transitions that increased the supply of labor while reducing the number of young children. Technological progress was rapid, as well, but not so rapid as to cause observers to believe that a new kind of economic model had been discovered. In the end, economic growth in East Asia as in North America, Western Europe, and everywhere else, is about working and saving and investing.

The fact that East Asian economies were successful without having discovered a new key to economic growth does not diminish the accomplishment. What they achieved was remarkable and would not have been possible unless there were the right incentives to work, save, and invest. For that to be the case, another feature of East Asian economies has to be recognized, namely the quality of their institutions. To be sure, institutional quality was not uniformly high across all countries, and there is a strong correlation between institutional quality and income per capita, with the lower income countries ranking below the higher income ones in institutional quality indexes. For example, the Worldwide Governance Indicators measures key institutions such as regulatory quality, overall governmental effectiveness, the rule of law, and others.[4] The four highest income countries of Table 5.1 (Hong Kong, Korea, Singapore, and Taiwan) score very well and often near the top of the world rankings. The three countries with somewhat lower incomes (Indonesia, Malaysia, and Thailand) all

4 The indicators measure six components of a country's institutional quality, all of which affect economic performance. These are the following: 1. Rule of law: The confidence of individuals and businesses in the fairness and impartiality of the law, police, and the courts. 2. Control of corruption: The ability of governments to prevent the use of state power for individual gain. 3. Voice and accountability: The ability of citizens to participate in government and to express themselves freely. 4. Government effectiveness: A measure of the quality of public services and the civil service. 5. Political stability and the absence of violence/terrorism: A measure of the absence of political instability, violence, and terrorism. 6. Regulatory quality: A measure of government's ability to implement effective and necessary regulations (Kauffman, Kray, and Mastruzzi, 2010).

score below the best performers, but with the exception of Indonesia, usually in the top half of the world's countries.

In addition to institutional factors that supported the incentives to work, save, and invest, macroeconomic conditions in all of the countries were also supportive, at least up until the onset of the crisis in 1997. Inflation rates were kept low, budget deficits were under control, and currencies were valued competitively. Furthermore, firms were encouraged to enter foreign markets, so their growth was not constrained by the size of the national economy. Technology imports and inward foreign investment ensured that new techniques were available, while export incentives in several countries made it profitable to seek out foreign markets for domestic products.

Conditions in global financial markets were also supportive. As described in the Chapter 4, a key development of the 1990s was the growth of emerging market investment opportunities. After the problems of bank-led investments of the 1970s and 1980s, equity investments appeared to be a way to avoid excessive debt and the problems that froze Latin American economies for a decade. Stock funds, hedge funds, and other investors added to the flow of foreign direct investment and portfolio investment, making it easier for retail investors in the United States and Europe to invest abroad and outside the world of financial markets in high income countries. The new concept of emerging markets implied that many developing countries were hungry for capital to support their takeoff into sustained economic growth and, theoretically at least, offered higher rates of return than more capital abundant countries in the developed world. In East Asia, investors found a group of countries that seemed stable, with good institutions (or at least ones that were biased in favor of economic growth), strong macroeconomic fundamentals, and relatively open markets.

5.3 THE ONSET OF THE CRISIS IN THAILAND

The Asian Crisis began as a currency crisis in Thailand in July, 1997. Throughout most of the 1990s, Thailand tied its currency, the baht, to the dollar at just over 25 baht per dollar. The exchange rate varied a bit but stayed within a relatively narrow band around that level. In the first few days of July, 1997, as the crisis began to unfold, the baht moved from 24.52 to 30.18 per dollar, a devaluation of 23 percent. It continued to slide in value through the year, falling to 46.80 baht per dollar in December, and to 54.20 in January, 1998 (Board of Governors of the Federal Reserve, 2017a).[5]

Thailand's devaluations came after years of relative stability and were a surprise to investors. The buildup of problems that led to the devaluation developed slowly, causing most observers to assume the problems were manageable. Throughout the early 1990s, Thailand's inflation rate was slightly higher than the rate in the United States, but as the baht appreciated in real terms, observers did not worry about the loss of competitiveness or fear a crisis caused by a large and relatively sudden devaluation. By the end of 1995, two years before the crisis, the baht had appreciated 12 percent higher in real terms compared to 1990, but it seemed manageable and was not a major concern.

Thailand's situation was complicated by the fact that China also pegged to the dollar, so a change in value of the yuan affected not just its dollar value, but also its baht value. In the early 1990s, China engaged in a series of gradual devaluations as it tried to offset its higher rate of inflation and keep its currency competitive. Gradual devaluations against the dollar were not enough, however, to prevent the yuan from appreciating in real terms. To correct its perceived imbalance, China implemented a large nominal devaluation of approximately 34 percent against the dollar. Since the Thai baht was tied to the dollar, this was also a nominal devaluation of the yuan against the baht. And since Thailand was not the only country pegged to the

5 By the end of 1998, Thailand's exchange rate had partially recovered, to 36.5 baht per dollar. This is a typical case of exchange rate overshooting, where an overvalued exchange rate is devalued more than is necessary, then recovers some of the value it lost during the (excessive) devaluation.

dollar, other countries in the region experienced the same effects from the Chinese devaluation.[6]

The real appreciation of Thailand's currency was not unmanageable. Appreciation made exports less competitive and increased the country's already large trade deficit, but as long as Thailand could attract sufficient capital inflows, the trade deficit was not a problem. In addition, two other factors were in Thailand's favor. One, its economy was growing rapidly, even after China's devaluation, and growth gave foreign investors little reason to think that investment opportunities would suddenly disappear.[7] And two, Thailand's financial sector had developed significantly and was able to obtain financing from many new sources in the international economy.

Thailand could have gradually devalued its currency and thereby eliminated or significantly reduced its real appreciation. In part, it did not do that because one of its strengths was also one of its weaknesses. The development of Bangkok as a regional financial center, with aspirations of something even more important, led to the inflow of large amounts of foreign capital, a significant part of which was in the form of short term dollar-denominated loans from international banks. Devaluation would have increased the real baht value of debt denominated in dollars and might also have undermined the faith of foreign lenders in Thailand's economy and economic management which, in turn, would have reduced the inflow of funds. Since many of the loans obtained by Thai banks were invested domestically in real estate and property development, there was a maturity mismatch between the assets and liabilities of Thai banks. Bank liabilities were short term loans from international banks, but assets were in the form of long term real estate projects. Banking, by definition, is the process of borrowing short term in order to lend long term, and all

6 An additional pressure was exerted by the depreciation of the Japanese yen. The yen appreciated through the early 1990s, rising in value from around 150 per dollar in early 1990 to below 100 in 1994. After that, however, it begins to fall in value, reaching 140 per dollar in 1998.

7 Real GDP grew 8 percent in 1994, 8.1 percent in 1995, and 5.6 percent in 1996, the year before the crisis began.

banks must manage the mismatch in maturities between their assets and their liabilities. However, in the international economy there are no lenders of last resort and a sudden cessation of international lending can be disastrous since there is no institution to support a bank until it can sell off its assets or find an alternative source of financing to cover its short term payments.

Thailand's currency and capital flow problems might still have been managed in a way that avoided a crisis if economic conditions and financial markets had been able to convince currency speculators that the problems would pass. As with the Mexican peso crisis in 1994–1995, there was a large psychological element as outsiders tried to decide whether the baht was going to fall significantly, or whether it would find enough support in international markets to keep its demand relatively steady. The question was whether investors and speculators saw the devaluation as inevitable, or whether they might decide that it would be avoided.

The central role of psychological expectations about the future movement of the currency and the indeterminacy of the direction that the baht would move were new features of a currency crisis (Eichengreen, Rose, Wyplosz 1995; Krugman, 1996; Obstfeld, 1996; Kaminsky and Reinhart, 1999). This new type of crisis was interpreted as offering a new lesson for emerging market governments that an effective way to deter speculators was to maintain large pools of international reserves. If only Thailand had had a large pool of reserves (which it would have obtained through export surpluses instead of trade deficits), it could have provided speculators with ample supplies of dollars when they sold Thai baht and would have neutralized the downward pressures on the currency. Use of reserves was how Taiwan and Singapore either avoided the crisis altogether or minimized its effects. Their large pools of foreign reserves were accumulated through years of large current account surpluses and were a lesson absorbed by several countries.

The guesses by speculators that the baht was going to lose value led them to sell the currency and, ultimately, caused its devaluation.

Guesses that devaluation was inevitable were reinforced by Thailand's relatively large trade deficits. Between 1990 and 1996 (inclusive), current account deficits averaged nearly 7 percent of GDP, and in the year before the crisis, they were 8 percent. While other fundamentals such as GDP growth, budget deficits, and inflation, were healthy, anyone looking at the trade balance and trying to decide whether it was sustainable or not, was likely to conclude that Thailand would have a hard time attracting sufficient inflows of capital to finance the deficit, particularly if there were questions about the value of its currency. The decision to speculate against the baht at its current level of twenty-five to the dollar in mid-1997, seemed like the better choice.

The devaluation of the baht beginning in July, 1997, led to additional problems, including an increase in the real value of dollar-denominated debt owed by Thai banks to foreign lenders. The rise in their debt burdens made it harder for them to obtain the short-term funding they had relied on to finance real estate and other long-term lending and spread the crisis beyond currency markets into the financial economy, and from there into the real economy. Real estate lending stopped, projects were terminated in midstream, construction workers were laid off, and the economy began a severe decline in the second half of 1997. In 1998, growth fell to its lowest point, at -7.6 percent.

5.4 CONTAGION AND COMMON FUNDAMENTALS

When financial crises occur simultaneously in two or more countries, it is the result of either common fundamentals or international contagion, or both (Reinhart and Rogoff, 2009a: 241–6). Common fundamentals were at play in the Latin American Debt Crisis when multiple countries experienced similar conditions that made debt service impossible and macroeconomic imbalances made them more vulnerable to external shocks. By comparison, the East Asian economies with the most severe recessions had fewer similarities and fewer macroeconomic imbalances. Rather, uncertainty about the abilities of individual countries to maintain their exchange rate pegs caused speculative attacks that they could not fend off. Contagion effects spread a crisis when the economic linkages of countries via trade and financial flows are large enough so that events in one are felt in another. In the case of East Asia, these are a better explanation for the spread of the crisis outside the region than they are for its spread inside. A set of financial linkages pushed the crisis out from East Asia into Russia, Turkey, Argentina, and the United States, as Asian defaults spread to institutions in other parts of the world.[8]

The IMF was the primary responder to the crisis in East Asia. The role of speculative attacks as a crisis trigger was not fully incorporated into the IMF's analysis, however, and it responded as if East Asia was another instance of problems with economic fundamentals, as in the case of Latin America. In East Asia, however, government budgets were in surplus in all four of the main crisis countries in 1995 and 1996, the years before the crisis. And while current account deficits in Thailand played a central role, it was somewhat different from the other countries in this regard. Thailand's deficits were not sustainable, at more than 8 percent 1996, but Indonesia's deficits were relatively small and Korea's even smaller. Only Malaysia had current account deficits comparable to Thailand's.[9]

All four countries' currencies appreciated in real terms through the 1990s, but the subsequent crisis and GDP decline were out of proportion to the problems created by relatively small appreciations. As noted, Thailand's exchange rate underwent a real appreciation of about 12 percent between 1990 and 1996, but that is relatively mild, and was not matched by any other country except Malaysia. It would be unusual for an exchange rate appreciation of that size to cause

8 The United States felt the effects when the hedge fund, Long Term Capital Management, collapsed and required a bailout by a consortium of financial firms. The firm was large enough to create turmoil in US financial markets. Since the Subprime Crisis, we would refer to the firm as a structurally important financial institution, or a SIFI. See Lowenstein (2001).

9 Indonesia averaged 2 percent during the 1990s before the crisis; Korea's average was 1.5 percent; Malaysia's was 5.2 percent and rising (IMF, 2017b).

a decline in GDP of over 7 percent. Real appreciations in Indonesia and Korea were much smaller and cannot begin to explain the large GDP decline they both suffered.[10] The relatively greater appreciation against the Chinese yuan may explain some of the ensuing problems, but is an unlikely source of major depressions in all four economies.

In general, macroeconomic variables such as budget and trade balances, exchange rates and inflation, cannot explain the Asian Crisis in the way they explain the Latin American Debt Crisis. The common fundamentals are not found in the macroeconomy. Where they can be found, however, is in the interaction between domestic financial sectors of the four economies and the international economy. During the 1990s, all four countries moved to open their financial markets to international flows and removed many of the regulations that limited the activities of banks and other financial firms. For example, Korea made it easier for banks to lend, decontrolled interest rates, and cut many of the ties between banks and large industrial firms and between banks and the government, making banks more independent. Korea also opened its capital market to foreign flows and lifted restrictions on foreign investment and borrowing from abroad. Thailand, Indonesia, and Malaysia implemented policies that differed in details but all went a long way toward the same goals that gave the financial sector greater freedom of action along with access to foreign lending and borrowing (Furman and Stiglitz, 1998).

Capital market opening and the removal of many restrictions on domestic financial institutions were also goals of the IMF and the US Treasury throughout the 1990s and into the 2000s. The IMF and Treasury reflected a widely supported but still controversial opinion that open capital markets and less financial regulation would provide more funds for investment purposes and more efficient financial services. The timing of the regulatory and policy changes coincided with a dramatic increase in international capital flows. Financial services

10 The Korean won appreciated 4 percent and the Indonesia rupiah 7 percent. Real exchange rates are calculated using the Consumer Price Index for each country and 1990 as a base year. Rates are calculated using data from the IMF (2017a and 2017b).

firms, government officials, economists, and others added emerging markets to their vocabularies while technological changes in communications and transportation reduced the transaction costs of investing abroad. As a result, capital inflows to East Asia were a significant part of the overall increase in global capital flows, and in particular both private long-term capital and short-term debt saw large increases (Furman and Stiglitz, 1998: 21, 54).

The second country to fall after Thailand was Indonesia. As with the others, it had a strong growth record and had achieved some economic reforms by 1997. The government of Indonesia was widely known to intervene aggressively in support of the economic interests of politicians and their family members, but its macroeconomic performance and stability were considered more important than the problems of nepotism and corruption, and the resulting economic inefficiencies. In July, 1997, after Thailand's problems surfaced, speculators began to attack the Indonesian rupiah. In August, Indonesia decided to let the currency float rather than defend it, but by October it had lost 30 percent of its value. The worst was yet to come: Six months after the Thai problem surfaced, Indonesia's rupiah was down 74 percent (OECD, 2017).

Korea was in a much stronger position than either Thailand or Indonesia. Its average growth in per capita output was more than 8 percent from 1980 to 1997, a rate that doubled per capita income every nine years. Industrial leaders such as Samsung, LG, Hyundai, and others had penetrated foreign markets in a variety of industrial and consumer goods, and it had deftly handled a macroeconomic crisis in the 1980s. Beginning in mid-1996, Korean authorities started compensating for the slightly higher inflation at home with small devaluations that held the real value of the won nearly constant. In October, 1997, speculation against the won increased and the currency began to fall more rapidly. By January of 1998, it had lost 45 percent of its value (Board of Governors, 2017b and 2017c).

Malaysia's experience paralleled the other three countries, both in timing and in scope. Its currency began to depreciate at an accelerating pace from July, 1997, and continued through January, 1998. By that time, it had lost 41.4 percent of its value. As with the other three, its economic conditions reflected a set of unique circumstances that in aggregate produced a similar outcome: speculative attacks, a rapidly depreciating exchange rate, and all of the attendant problems that come with a sudden collapse in the currency.

As noted, the common fundamentals of Thailand, Indonesia, Korea, and Malaysia that made them vulnerable to speculative attacks against their currencies were not related to their macroeconomic balances, as in the case of Latin America, but were shared experiences in the international economy. All had opened significantly to international financial flows with the effect that their influence over the amount of capital flowing in and out was diminished. The lifting of financial sector regulations made it easier for banks and other firms to seek international loans and other sources of foreign financing and increased the use of short-term international debt. And finally, their stellar growth records attracted a disproportionately large share of international capital seeking the potentially higher returns offered by emerging markets.

5.5 CRISIS RESOLUTION

The IMF's role in international financial affairs is to serve as a lender of last resort when asked by countries in crisis. Assistance comes at the cost of IMF imposed conditions that must be met if countries are to receive its help. The standard conditions have evolved over time, but in the 1990s, and particularly after the Latin American Debt Crisis of the 1980s, the two categories of demands were (and still are) for improvements in macroeconomic stability (stabilization policies) and microeconomic efficiency (structural adjustment policies). The former included changes in taxation and government spending, reductions in budget deficits, inflation control, and establishment of competitive currency values. Microeconomic reforms include a large number of targets including regulatory reform, particularly in labor markets, trade openness, privatizations, and a relaxation of rules governing foreign investment. The specifics of the structural adjustment program are meant to be tailored to the unique conditions of the country seeking assistance.

East Asian countries most deeply affected by the crisis did not have histories of macroeconomic imbalances or problems in macroeconomic management. Prior to the crisis, government budgets were in surplus, inflation was a moderate 3–6 percent, and economic growth was better than most places in the world. The crisis was a surprise precisely because they were well managed economies. Consequently, the IMF's decision to impose austerity (budget cuts, interest rate increases) as a condition for receiving aid, has been widely criticized. The IMF's reasoning was that austerity would help defend currencies from further collapse. Higher interest rates would, in theory, make assets in the crisis countries more profitable to investors, attract more capital inflows, and increase demand for the baht, rupiah, won, and ringgit. Higher interest rates also slow the economy and make a recession worse, however, so some or all of the affect in attracting investment may be offset by a decline in economic activity. If the economy is shrinking, higher interest rates do not necessarily compensate for fewer profitable opportunities and may even be indicative of increased risk and a higher probability of default. All other things being equal, higher interest rates attract foreign capital and increase the demand for the domestic currency, but in a financial crisis, all other things are not equal. Specifically, economic activity is collapsing.

The IMF was widely criticized for its contractionary stabilization policies, but its structural adjustments policies may have been even worse. Indonesia was perhaps the most egregious case. It was widely recognized that Indonesia's government routinely favored the interests of President Suharto who, by the time of the crisis, had been in office for more than thirty years. Family and friends that owned enterprises were given state monopolies, subsidized credit, trade protection and other supports that guaranteed their profitability but reduced the overall economic efficiency of the Indonesian economy.

When the IMF set out to reform the Indonesian economy and to eliminate or reduce what many were calling crony capitalism, it inevitably looked like a colonial institution that favored the interests and ideas of Western countries that dominated policymaking at the IMF. In addition, when the IMF tried to reform specific Indonesian industries, it was working outside its areas of core competence. For example, when timber management and production became a target for reform, a lot of observers had to scratch their heads and ask themselves what the IMF's expertise in finance tells it about the lumber industry. In the views of many, both supporters and critics of the IMF, structural adjustment and the push for efficiency had gone too far. And the context compounded the mistakes, given that it was an institution dominated by European and US interests who were telling leaders in developing Asia what they had to do in order to qualify for support. The optics looked horrible.

In the IMF's early years, it limited its crisis intervention to restoring stability and did not engage in wider efforts at structural adjustment. It was criticized for that, however, because many felt it was simply putting bandages on problems with much deeper roots. Consequently, in the 1970s it began to take a more holistic look at the countries it was asked to help and it tried to develop policies that would comprehensively improve the overall functioning of troubled economies. With the Asian Crisis, the pendulum went as far toward intervention and structural adjustment as it could. Since then, and largely due to the pushback against the policies it implemented during the Asian Crisis, structural adjustment and the effort to "fix everything" have been pulled back.

The recoveries came relatively quickly after short but deep recessions. The underlying conditions in each economy that made them successful in the decades before the crisis were still present. Educated populations, deep trade networks, strong manufacturing industries, high savings rates, and stable government finances were not undone even if the crisis and recessions temporarily imbalanced government budgets. The East Asian economies, unlike Latin

America after the onset of its crisis, produced a variety of goods that the world wanted to buy. Trade deficits were quickly converted into trade surpluses that were often quite large relative to the size of the economy. The shift from trade deficits to surpluses was painful since it required less domestic consumption, especially of imports, and more production for export. The key to this shift was that each country produced manufactured goods the rest of the world wanted and were able to arrest the collapse of their currencies with their earnings of dollars and other foreign exchange.

5.6 THE FALLOUT

The IMF played a central role in the crisis response and consequently, its policies and practices were the main focus of the criticisms that arose in the aftermath. There were three main parts to the complaints. First, critics argued that the IMF's push to open capital markets to international flows was one of the main sources of problems in the lead up to the crisis. Open capital markets was a policy of the IMF throughout the 1980s and 1990s, even though the benefits of openness lacked both theoretical and empirical consensus. The free movement of money is not the same as the free movement of goods and services, and the views of economists about the benefits of free trade do not carry over into the field of capital flows. Nevertheless, the IMF, the US Treasury, and other proponents of open capital markets argued that the benefits of increased capital inflows and higher investment levels were sound reasons to support the openness policy. (Chapter 14 explores this idea in more detail.) In the context of East Asia, the main weakness of the argument is that these were all high savings economies and it is not at all certain that they needed external doses of capital in order to fund more investment. In Thailand, for example, the inflows of foreign capital mostly fueled a real estate bubble.

As part of its prescription for responding to the crisis, the IMF encouraged countries to go even further in opening their capital markets. The reasoning was that more open markets would ensure investors that government controls and restrictions on capital movements would not be used and investors did not need to worry about their ability to move assets. Whether this is good advice or not is still debatable but the experiences of Korea and Malaysia serve as two natural experiments. Against IMF advice, Malaysia imposed controls, while Korea followed as directed and opened its capital markets more widely. The outcomes were that recoveries in both countries were not very different. Since this is a one-off case and other factors were different, no generalizations should be drawn other than to think that perhaps this is an area where greater humility and less certainty about the best policy are warranted.

A second criticism of the IMF is that it pushed countries to pursue contractionary monetary and fiscal policies while they were in recession. Higher interest rates and cuts in government spending at the same moment when the private economy is shrinking is the opposite of the ideas taught in Economics 101. By the 1990s, however, a strong set of beliefs in the importance of government budget surpluses as the main determinant of business confidence had grabbed the imaginations of many policymakers. In addition, new theoretical macroeconomic models supported the idea that cuts in government spending and increases in nominal interest rates would not have harmful effects on the level of economic activity. That is, many policy advisors had convinced themselves that contractionary policies are not altogether that contractionary, at least in theory. This notion was part of the rejection of the Keynesian consensus and has not fared well, particularly since the Subprime Crisis.

A third criticism is that the IMF imposed structural adjustment programs that had little or no effect in resolving the crises. In some cases, the structural adjustment reforms may have prolonged the crisis since regulatory and institutional changes create a period of increased uncertainty about new rules and how they will be put into practice. Furthermore, the areas where reforms were required were sometimes far outside the expertise of the IMF and its staff. In pursuing reforms unrelated to the specific problems of a currency crisis, the IMF opened itself up to the charge that it was acting in the interests of firms and industries in the United States, Europe, and Japan that wanted greater access to the resources and markets of East Asia. Whether this was a justified criticism or not, it seemed to confirm the views of those that argued that the IMF had an agenda beyond international financial stability.

These three main criticisms of the IMF have altered how it operates. In the aftermath of the Asian Crisis, it began to reexamine the benefits and costs of open capital markets and has moved away from a blanket policy that favors greater openness. This remains an area of ongoing research and most economists, including those at the IMF, now recognize a wider range of potential policies toward capital flows. The IMF has also backed away from aggressive programs of structural adjustment, although it continues to support them in general.

After the Asian Crisis, the IMF began to look more closely at the effects of government spending on overall economic activity. To its credit, its research department published new research showing that its assumptions about the non-effects or small effects of budget cuts on overall economic activity were flawed, and that the impact was larger than previously thought. There are many caveats to this conclusion, for example whether the economy is in recession or expansion, but in general, the conclusion was that budget cuts can most decidedly make a recession much worse.[11]

Internal changes in IMF policies were not the only lasting effects of the Asian Crisis, nor were they the most important. Two additional responses to the crisis have had profound impacts on the global economy. One was a push by Asian countries to develop alternative institutions for managing crises and for providing infrastructure financing. The second was a push to accumulate large reserves of foreign exchange so that countries could fend off speculation against their currencies. Both these responses have altered international economic relations.

11 Ultimately, when this issue arose again and budget cuts were prescribed for countries in the Eurozone as a response to the budget imbalances created by the Subprime Crisis, the research department and the political leadership of the IMF appeared to be in disagreement. Politics not economics almost always wins those debates.

The push to develop Asian alternatives to the IMF surfaced with the proposal by Eisuke Sakakibara, Japanese Vice Minister of Finance for International Affairs, to create an Asian Monetary Fund (AMF). The proposal was immediately and vigorously rejected by the United States where it was viewed as a breach of protocol for United States–Japan relations and provoked the fear that US influence in Asia might decline under such a proposal. Policymakers in the United States also worried that it would lead to a set of policies that supported greater state intervention in economic decision-making and planning. While the AMF plan was not enacted, it did spur the United States and other countries to increase the quotas they paid into the IMF and to change some of the procedures followed when the IMF provides financial assistance (Blustein, 2001: 151–74).

Some of the ideas behind the AMF proposal were much more widely accepted outside the United States and a number of new initiatives and institutions began to be developed. The ASEAN+3 is an organization of the ten members of the Association of Southeast Asian Nations (ASEAN) plus China, Japan, and South Korea. It serves as a coordinating agency for various policy initiatives and, after the financial crisis, began to take on greater importance in the area of international finance. It has helped countries develop bond markets that allow borrowing in their domestic currencies, rather than having to use the dollar-denominated markets they relied on before the crisis. The Asian Bond Market Initiative (ABMI) has worked to strengthen credit markets, including the creation of credit guarantees for bonds issued in a country's own currency. The Chiang Mai Initiative is another effort by the ASEAN+3 and has led to a program of currency swaps that let countries borrow dollars or other currencies while using their own currency as collateral. These initiatives and programs do not replace the IMF, but they do create an alternative.

Other institutions that were directly or indirectly developed in response to the Asian Crisis include the Asian Infrastructure Investment Bank (AIIB) which provides technical and financial support to promote infrastructure in Asia, and the creation of numerous new trade agreements. According to the Asian Development Bank, the number of free trade agreements in all of Asia stood at five in 1991 but began to grow in that decade. In 1996, the year before the crisis, it reached thirty-three; ten years after that was eighty; and by 2016 it was 147 (Asian Development Bank, 2017). Many factors in addition to the crisis explain the growth of cooperation and trade agreements, but the crisis was nevertheless important. Writing for the Asian Development Bank, two researchers explained that " . . . the 1997–1998 Asian financial crisis made it clear that Asian economies needed to work together in the area of trade and investment in order to sustain growth and stability by addressing common challenges" (Kawai and Wignaraja, 2010). In part, the new elements of cooperation are about growth and stability, but that is not the whole story. Emerging Asian economies, and especially China, want to create new international organizations that are not dominated by Western interests, where they will have greater freedom to support or oppose policies on the basis of their own considerations. At the same time, organizations such as the AIIB are a way for them to influence other countries and to shape how those countries view China and other emerging Asian economies. These developments may have been inevitable as East Asian economies grew in importance and wealth, but the Asian Crisis served as a catalyst.

New institutions and new thinking about international capital markets and crisis resolution were not the only changes that occurred in the wake of the Asian Crisis. Another significant change was a dramatic increase in the current account balances of individual countries, including some that were not caught in the crisis. Current account deficits became surpluses, often large ones, and small surpluses grew much larger. In the crisis countries this was a response to the immediate pressure to earn foreign exchange, and in some non-crisis countries it was an effort to avoid the type of problems that might develop as a result of holding limited reserves of foreign exchange.

The crisis countries were forced to run trade surpluses as a direct result of the crisis, but others observed the benefits of large reserves and

Table 5.2 *Average annual current account balance, percent of GDP*

	1990–97	1998–2007	Difference*
China	1.5	4.0	2.6
Hong Kong	0.5	8.5	7.9
Indonesia	−2.1	2.8	4.9
Korea	−1.5	2.7	4.2
Malaysia	−5.2	11.6	16.9
Singapore	12.3	19.1	6.8
Taiwan	3.8	5.7	1.8
Thailand	−6.2	4.5	10.7

* Numbers are rounded to the nearest one-tenth; differences from the numbers in the table are due to rounding errors.
East Asian economies saw dramatic increases in their current accounts after the crisis.
Source: Author's calculations based on data from World Bank, 2017a; IMF, 2017b.

began to run surpluses in place of deficits, or larger surpluses than previously. Table 5.2 illustrates this point with measures of the average annual current account deficits or surpluses during two periods, expressed as a percentage of each country's GDP. Thailand, for example, had average current account deficits that equaled 6.2 percent of its GDP from 1990 through 1997. From 1998 through 2007, those deficits were converted into surpluses that equaled 4.5 percent of GDP. The last column is the difference in the first two and illustrates the shift in the composition of GDP that is implied by the shift from imports to more exports. For Thailand, this was a very large shift equal to 10.7 percent of its GDP.[12]

12 As noted in previous chapters, large shifts from deficit to surplus in the current account require businesses to invest less, households to consume less, governments to tax more and spend less, or some combination of the three. In all four countries, consumption, investment, and imports fell dramatically in 1998.

An important lesson absorbed by many countries is the need to maintain large reserves of foreign exchange as a tool for dampening speculation against the national currency. Hong Kong, Taiwan, and Singapore all felt the effects of the crisis but none of them were damaged as deeply as Indonesia, Korea, Malaysia, and Thailand. The latter lacked deep foreign exchange reserves, while the former did not. With large reserves, countries were able to prevent speculators from forming expectations that a currency collapse was imminent. The lesson was clear: If a nation wants to avoid the problems caused by speculation against its currency, including potential IMF intervention limiting the autonomy of the nation to make its own policies, it needs large reserves of foreign exchange as a way to fight against speculators. In response, all of the countries in Table 5.2 increased the size of their trade surpluses. When a small city-state such as Singapore runs a large trade surplus, the world barely notices. When China does, it has a major impact. To be sure, the Asian Crisis is not the only factor behind the increase in China's trade surpluses in the 2000s, but it was one significant factor. China's history of foreign intervention has strongly increased its desire to avoid economic problems that might lead to a need for foreign advisors and resources.[13]

The current account surpluses shown in Table 5.2 are part of what Fed Chairman Ben Bernanke referred to in 2005 as a global savings glut (Bernanke, 2005).[14] As noted previously, the current account is a measurement of the difference between domestic income (or production), and domestic expenditure. If the difference is positive, production is greater than expenditure and the difference primarily shows up as exports. In other words, counties that have surpluses with the rest of the world are net savers, and countries with deficits are net borrowers. The global savings glut referred to by Chairman Bernanke

13 China's entrance into the WTO in 2001 was also important in the development of its trade surpluses in the early 2000s. WTO membership gave it much better access to foreign markets and increased its exports. WTO membership, however, could have been done in a more balanced way with more imports as well as exports.

14 Bernanke was on the Board of Governors of the Federal Reserve when he made this speech but was not yet Chairman of the Fed.

was partly a result of the actions by China and other countries to increase their foreign reserves in response to the crisis in East Asia. The increase in Chinese savings and savings by others meant they were accumulating IOUs from the rest of the world, particularly the United States, where federal government deficits and a large and growing financial sector provided a great number of opportunities for foreign investors.[15] This inflow of funds was a major source of financial capital for US firms and consumers and was directed to a wide variety of activities, including in major part, real estate development. China and other East Asian economies were by no means the only countries with large trade surpluses, but they were the ones that were in part motivated by the Asian Crisis.[16] The accumulation of foreign reserves in response to the Asian Crisis is a direct link from it to the Subprime Crisis.

15 China was a major source of funds for the United States, but far from the only one. Oil producers such as Saudi Arabia also accumulated large trade surpluses and invested much of the proceeds in the United States and other overseas markets, and countries with aging populations, Japan for example, accumulated surpluses and the assets they bought in the hope they would be able to support an aging population with many fewer workers.

16 Other deficit countries with large inflows besides the United States included the United Kingdom, Spain, Ireland, and several others that were ground zero in the housing boom that resulted in the Subprime Crisis. Other countries ran surpluses for different reasons. Saudi Arabia and Russia had oil profits they could not absorb, while Japan and to a lesser extent, Germany, have aging populations that are saving for retirement.

6 The Subprime Crisis in the United States

6.1 VULNERABILITIES

The literature on the Subprime Crisis is voluminous and spans a range of different approaches, from popular accounts to technical analysis to memoirs by first responders at the Federal Reserve and in the executive branch of the federal government.[1] This chapter provides an overview and chronology of the main developments and turning points and describes the vulnerabilities present at the onset of the crisis.[2] Chapter 7 examines the contagion effects of the crisis in Europe and how it deepened into a worse slump than the Great Depression of the 1930s.

Before the crisis, many academics, finance experts, and policymakers were captured by "new era thinking" and the "this time is different" syndrome. Financial innovations, preferences for a regulatory light touch, the adoption of new risk models, and a widespread belief that financial globalization had created a new and more stable era in economic relations, all contributed to the belief that financial firms were in control of the risks they faced. Some participants knew they were courting danger and even spoke about it, but many others succumbed to the common problem of

1 Henry Paulson (2010) was Bush's Secretary of the Treasury when the crisis began and Timothy Geithner (2014) was Obama's during his first term in office. Ben Bernanke (2015) was Chairman of the Federal Reserve from February, 2006, to February, 2014, and was the main architect of the central bank's response to the crisis and economic recession. Bernanke (2012) also gave four lectures that were converted into a book on the history of the Federal Reserve and its response to the crisis. The list of outsiders – mostly academics and journalists – that have produced histories of the crisis is extensive. Lo (2012) is a short review of twenty-one books.

2 The Federal Reserve Bank of St. Louis (no date a, b) has a very detailed timeline of the crisis in the United States and the original documents that go with it. See https://fraser.stlouisfed.org/theme/103, and https://fraser.stlouisfed.org/timeline/financial-crisis

overconfidence bias – the belief that one knows enough, has enough control, and enough access to resources to bend conditions to one's advantage.

US home prices increased during the 1990s but around 2000, they hit an inflection point and began to rise at a much more rapid rate. Houses are the most valuable asset consumers own and the increase in prices was unusual, although not unprecedented. In the 1970s house prices also increased dramatically, but that decade's relatively high inflation meant that real price increases were much smaller. In the 2000s, there was a notable regional variation in housing prices, but all markets rose in value. Nationally, the increase from January, 2000, to June, 2006, was approximately 85 percent (Case-Shiller, 2017). A $500,000 California home purchased at the start of 2000, would have been valued at $925,000 by 2006 if it experienced an average price increase but California and several other states were far above average. Home prices in California went up 146 percent, by some estimates (US Federal Housing Finance Agency, 2017). At that rate of increase, a California house that sold for $500,000 in 2000 would sell for $1,230,000 in 2006.

When banks, homeowners, mortgage lenders, realtors, and home builders see such large price increases, it fundamentally alters their incentives and their willingness to take risks. If you do not jump on the bandwagon, you may be sacrificing a once-in-a-lifetime chance to get rich. Such new era thinking begins to have a very powerful pull, and economic life begins to look much easier for a lot of people who begin to see their houses as ATM machines where home equity lines of credit can be used to buy boats, cars, and RVs, to pay for college education, medical bills, vacations, and an infinite variety of other pleasures and necessities. Potential homeowners simply had to find a house for sale, obtain a loan, and then ride the price increases into prosperity.

The asset bubble was supported by the availability of credit for buying houses and by a light regulatory touch over the mortgage industry that became even lighter as the bubble grew. Looking at the credit boom first, there were two main sources of supply, one domestic and one foreign. The conventional image of mortgage finance in the United States is that a home buyer goes to a bank and asks for a loan. The bank examines the borrower's income, assets, and credit worthiness, and then decides whether to make the loan or not. The successful borrower uses the loan to buy the house and begins to make regular monthly mortgage payments to pay back the bank over the maturity of the loan which is commonly thirty years in the United States. This is a simple story of credit intermediation in which a bank pools the savings of depositors in order to provide a loan; it is not how the mortgage market works, however. Banks make loans but the mortgage market is increasingly dominated by specialized mortgage lenders that do not have depositors and technically are not banks. Both institutions make loans that are often resold to either government sponsored enterprises (GSEs) or to private financial institutions such as investment banks or hedge funds. The two main GSEs, Fannie Mae (Federal National Mortgage Association) and Freddie Mac (Federal Home Loan Mortgage Corporation), operate as private firms with stockholders and independent management, but with an ambiguous degree of government protection against failure. They both play a key role in providing liquidity to the housing industry by buying mortgages and packaging them into bond-like instruments that are more liquid than the mortgages and that can be sold in pieces to investors who want a slightly higher return than most alternative investments with the same degree of risk. The mortgage lenders that sell their mortgages to Fannie or Freddie, or to investment banks or other private financial institutions, can use the cash they receive to make additional loans. By turning illiquid mortgage loans into very liquid financial securities, securitizers such as Fannie and Freddie increase the amount of liquidity in the housing market and enable more people to have access to loans. In turn, that increases the effective demand for houses and increases the incentives to build more. Additionally, the GSEs provide guarantees for the mortgages which makes the securities more attractive as investments.

Fannie Mae was created in 1938 as a government agency under the New Deal with the purpose of supporting the mortgage market. It was privatized in 1968 and two years later, Freddie Mac was created as a means to provide competition for Fannie Mae. Ostensibly independent and private, both had ambiguous relations with the federal government. While some believed they were completely independent private entities, many others assumed they each had an implicit federal guarantee against default. That assumption proved correct in September, 2008, when both received bailout funds that ultimately totaled $187 billion and gave the federal government majority ownership in both companies. While the bailout was contentious on many levels, it was not a money loser since the federal government was paid back and had earned nearly $100 billion in profits by mid-2018 (ProPublica, 2018).

Fannie and Freddie supported and expanded the mortgage market not only through their ability to buy up the loans that other institutions made, but also by securitization of the loans they bought. Securitization has been around since the 1970s but began to grow dramatically in the 1990s. Purchasers of MBSs, earn returns that are derived from the payments of the home buyers that obtained the original mortgage. With the added feature of a mortgage guarantee provided by Fannie or Freddie, the return on the security is often higher than alternative investments with the same or similar risks, particularly when overall interest rates are low. In addition to the potential returns, the financial entities that create MBS earn fees and commissions. Fannie and Freddie were the main actors in the mortgage securitization movement but private investment firms increasingly challenged the two GSEs for market share over the early years of the new century. Mortgage securitization is an attractive market to financial firms because they can earn significant fees and they create new assets that often earn better returns than many alternatives, particularly in low interest rate environments. Furthermore, before the crisis, ratings agencies were willing to rate most mortgage securities as nearly risk free. This significantly increased the size of the market for mortgage securities by making them available to pension funds, insurance companies, and other investors restricted to low risk investments.[3] In 2003, Fannie and Freddie held approximately half of all mortgages, but by 2006, on the eve of the crisis, their share had fallen to approximately 32 percent of the mortgage market (Urban Institute, 2017).[4] Not content to lose market share, in 2004 Fannie and Freddie began to relax their lending standards to try to win back a larger slice of the mortgage market. They also began to move into market segments that they had previously shunned, such as the so-called Subprime and Alt-A mortgage markets, where Alt-A is a mortgage industry short-hand for "alternative to A-rated credit" and is intermediate between the subprime and prime credit markets.

Reasonable observers disagree about the importance of Fannie and Freddie in causing the Subprime Crisis. At one end of the spectrum is the argument that they were the primary cause of the crisis, while at the other end is the view that they were one element of a complex set of causes. Observers that blame the GSEs argue that their aggressive use of mortgage securities to extend credit to borrowers with low credit ratings, coupled with a number of poor management decisions, led to the collapse in the mortgage security market. This view also stresses that GSEs responded to political pressures under both Republican and Democratic presidential administrations to expand lending and home ownership (Wallison, 2015).[5]

3 Ratings agencies fell down on the job, but counter to conventional wisdom and normal intuition, creating a security comprised of thousands of different mortgages can reduce some of the risk. The key is that the new security is sold in slices, or tranches, each with a different level of risk. It is possible to load most of the risk into only one or a few parts of the security so that the remaining tranches have much lower risks, mathematically speaking. This requires the tranches to have independently determined default probabilities, which is not a bad assumption if you believe that regional mortgage markets do not move together. If, however, house prices fall everywhere, as happened in the 1930s and again during the Subprime Crisis, it is a deadly assumption.

4 There is a third and much smaller GSE in the mortgage market, called Ginnie Mae, that handles Veterans Administration and Federal Housing Authority loans. If included in the GSE total, the share in 2006 is approximately 35 percent of all mortgages.

5 Similarly, Rajan (2011) while not blaming the GSEs for the crisis, argues that the failure of the United States to address problems of inequality led to the political expediency of expanding mortgage credit so that even households with stagnant incomes could buy a house.

There are two main criticisms of the idea that government housing policies in general and Fannie and Freddie specifically were to blame for the crisis. One stresses the fact that the GSEs share of the mortgage market was at its lowest ever historical point when the crisis began. That does not prove they were not responsible, but it is difficult to reconcile with the idea that they caused the crisis. A second counter-argument is that complex phenomenon, such as financial crises, rarely have a single cause and many different factors have to be present simultaneously. In the case of the Subprime Crisis, other factors included large capital inflows from abroad, the lack of adequate regulation in financial markets in general, financial incentives for executives in financial services firms to take on too much risk, the sudden loss of confidence in short-term lending markets, failures in rating agencies, mistaken beliefs about housing markets, and a number of other factors. In a poll of 100 European and US economists, government housing policies were considered an important cause of the crisis, but ranked number nine out of twelve main factors (IGM Forum, 2017).

In sum, it is impossible to state definitively the importance or irrelevancy of the GSEs in causing the financial crisis. In all likelihood, the decisions made by the managers of the GSE's contributed to the crisis, but were not the sole cause or even necessarily a prime cause. Many vulnerabilities were present at the time the crisis began, and removing the GSEs from the equation would probably not have avoided a crisis given the erosion in lending standards, the growth of securitization, and the failures of regulatory oversight. Furthermore, several European countries suffered similar crises even though they had nothing equivalent to Fannie and Freddie.

If the GSEs had not existed there would have been less liquidity in the mortgage market and perhaps that would have calmed the price bubble, but it would not have stopped the credit boom which was not dependent solely on domestic forces. Securitization, both by the GSEs and by private investors, increased market liquidity but the United States probably could not have had a housing bubble without access to foreign credit given the low US savings rates. As noted in Chapter 5, foreign capital inflows were partly driven by policies outside the United States where there was a push to accumulate foreign reserves. Foreigners were willing to accumulate dollar reserves in the United States (and elsewhere) because dollars are used in international transactions, the United States is a secure place to put savings, and there were attractive investments, such as MBS and other forms of securitized debt that paid higher returns than were available elsewhere.[6] In a speech given a year before he became Chairman of the Federal Reserve, Ben Bernanke described these flows as a global savings glut (Bernanke, 2005). Whether that was an apt expression or not, the savings of China, Germany, Japan, and oil producers such as Saudi Arabia and Russia, found their way into the United States, Ireland, Spain, the United Kingdom and other countries, where they helped drive up construction spending and housing prices.

Cumulatively, from 2000 to 2007, the United States pulled in 4.7 trillion dollars in foreign funds (IMF, 2017b).[7] The money came from countries with large saving surpluses, where total expenditures on goods and services were less than total income. As noted in Chapter 5, the global savings glut and the availability of funds for investment in housing markets were two of the indirect consequences of the Asian Crisis as countries like China sought to accumulate large foreign reserves in order to maintain their autonomy and to avoid reliance on the IMF or other outsiders. Japan and Germany's motives for running large surpluses were partly demographic, given their aging populations and the need to save for a growing wave of retirements, but also partly the result of economic policies that encouraged trade surpluses. Other large pools of savings were the result of oil exports that generated more income than could be immediately consumed or put to work through productive investments in the markets of the oil producers.

6 MBS are a form of a general class of securities called collateralized debt obligations (CDOs). A CDO can be composed of mortgages, like a MBS, or any other form of debt that has a regular payment, such as student loans, credit card debt, auto loans, or some combination of any of them. These assets have collateral that the creditor can seize in case of default, such as a car, a house, or a lien against wages.

7 Technically, this is the cumulative value of US current account deficits, which are trade deficits plus net income payments abroad. In effect, it is a measure of the difference between the United States' absorption of goods and services and its income.

Two additional vulnerabilities were exposed by the large capital inflows to the United States and other countries. One, the availability of credit supported a huge buildup of private debt by both households and businesses, and particularly by financial enterprises. And two, regulatory oversight of the financial system was weak in places and had large gaps in others. Increasing debt and inadequate regulatory oversight interacted in disastrous ways. Home buyers were given mortgages they could not afford, with the expectation they would refinance after home prices rose and their equity increased. Financial institutions then borrowed heavily to buy the mortgages so they could turn them into more liquid securities.[8] Once accomplished, the securities would be sold to other investors or held on the books of the firm that created them or a combination of both. This process required large amounts financing, most of it short-term debt which could be used to fund daily operations. Plentiful credit made it relatively easy to obtain ever larger amounts of debt, even for non-traditional housing finance firms. Given that many of the financial institutions involved were not banks, many types of financial transactions were either lightly regulated or fell through gaps in the regulatory system. For example, much of the short-term borrowing preferred by many investment banks and hedge funds avoids oversight by the US Securities and Exchange Commission.[9] And when regulation was present, there were a variety of ways that financial institutions could switch between the

8 "From 2001 to 2007, the average mortgage debt per household increased sixty-three percent, while wages remained flat. After approximately 2004, the financial system provided this credit with enthusiasm, even to individuals with low or undisclosed income, then packaged the loans into securities that were also bought on credit. The financial sector now held $36 trillion worth of debt, a twelvefold increase over three decades" (Geithner, 2014: 106–107).

9 Repurchase agreements, or repo, is one way. Repo is a very short-term loan that has a maturity of overnight or only a few days. The borrower provides some collateral, usually in the form of a financial instrument it is holding, such as a CDO. The lender provides the loan and receives the collateral. Repo enables pension funds, money market funds, insurance companies and other financial services firms to earn interest on the cash they have to keep for precautionary reasons such as a potential payout on an insurance policy, withdrawals by money market depositors, and so forth. Repo lets large financial firms, investment banks for example, use short-term financing to fund their operations.

different regulators in order to take advantage of the one with the lowest standards. Regulatory arbitrage, the practice of switching from a more rigorous to a less rigorous regulator, became a common practice and was often allowed under the rules of US financial regulation (Financial Crisis Inquiry Commission, 2011: 40).

Even when regulators were present, they were too frequently ineffective. Credit rating agencies gave triple-A ratings to many MBS and collateralized debt obligations (CDOs) that ultimately defaulted, and regulators stood on the sidelines and watched as the standards for giving home loans eroded severely.[10] Rating agencies justified their lack of oversight with the claim that securities were low risk if they were comprised of mortgages from a geographically diversified cross section of communities spread throughout the United States. The argument of low risk could only be justified if there was no memory of the nationwide collapse in home prices during the Great Depression, or if there was a belief that another depression with home prices falling simultaneously across the country could never happen again. Even if MBSs and CDOs were relatively safe, regulators made little effort to understand what assets they contained and, as a result, they granted far too many AAA ratings.[11] In this case, financial innovation outstripped everyone's ability to keep up. It was not uncommon that even the firms that created mortgage securities were not aware of the specific contents of the MBS and CDOs they designed. Everyone understood that they contained mortgages, but the regions that originated the mortgage and the risk profiles of the borrowers were buried in a mass of data that were not closely examined.

Looking again at the list of risk factors, the only one not present was an overvalued currency. All the others, including an asset bubble,

10 There are ten nationally recognized rating agencies, but over 95 percent of all ratings are performed by three companies. These are Moody's, Standard and Poor's, and Fitch (Securities and Exchange Commission, 2015: 10–11).

11 This is one of the more amusing and surprising points made by Michael Lewis' (2010) entertaining description of the Subprime Crisis, *The Big Short*. The protagonists who profited from the crisis took advantage of the fact that almost no one knew what was contained in the mortgage backed securities they sold to investors. That included the banks that sold the securities.

a credit boom, weak supervision, open capital markets, large trade deficits, and a huge debt buildup, were present. If only one or two factors had occurred at the same time, things might have turned out differently, but the interactions of so many risk factors overwhelmed the financial system and ultimately created one of the worst recessions since the Great Depression.

6.2 CHRONOLOGY

The Subprime Crisis began in 2007, reached its most intense stage during the late summer and fall of 2008, and then began to subside around the middle of 2009. While the trigger for the crisis seems to have been the decline in home prices, the actual date at which that occurred depends on the index consulted. The Federal Housing Finance Agency (FHFA), an independent federal regulatory agency, estimates that home prices peaked in April, 2007, while the S&P Case-Shiller index estimates that the peak was reached nearly a year earlier, in July of 2006 (FHFA, 2017; Case-Shiller, 2017; Blinder, 2013: 17–18). The beginning of the decline in home prices did not occur at the same time everywhere, nor was the decline the same across the United States. Nevertheless, once average house prices turned down, the entire edifice of residential construction, mortgage loans, securitized loans, and other related financial instruments began to break down. Many homeowners borrowed in anticipation of a rise in home prices that would let them refinance their loans, but as house prices fell, that possibility disappeared. As defaults in the mortgage market grew, it affected the underlying value of the MBSs and made it harder to use them as collateral for loans in the short-term funding markets. In turn, a lack of access to short-term loans hurt the financial viability of some participants in the securities markets.

In June of 2007, two hedge funds owned by Bear Stearns, the smallest of the five largest US investment banks, went broke. These were perhaps the first negative signs of the crisis (Paulson, 2010, 70; Bernanke, 2015: 140). In August of the same year, the French bank, BNP Paribas stopped payouts from three mutual funds that were exposed to the US housing market, and in September, the Bank of England was forced to provide support to Northern Rock, a mortgage lender. By the end of 2007, the banking system in the United States was under a great deal of stress due to the growing losses in housing markets. Defaults on home loans were spreading into financial markets more broadly, and from there into the real economy. In December, 2007, the United States entered a recession.

The Federal Reserve's response was to implement a standard anti-recession monetary policy. They supported the economy though interest rate cuts and a variety of programs to ensure that credit continued to be available to solvent but illiquid financial firms. In March, 2008, Bear Stearns, was on the verge of collapse before the Fed helped arrange a takeover by JP Morgan, another, larger, investment bank. Bear's stock was valued at $172 per share in January, 2007, but sold to JP Morgan in mid-March, 2008, for $10 per share. Uncertainty about the value of mortgage related assets continued to grow throughout the summer of 2008, causing credit markets to shrink and forcing up the cost of insuring assets against defaults.

By September, financial markets were in terrible shape and the real economy was feeling it. The number of officially unemployed workers rose from 6.8 million in May, 2007, to over 10 million in October, 2008, and was continuing to rise quickly. A year later, in October 2009, it would hit over 15.3 million people unemployed, which translated into an unemployment rate over 10 percent (BLS, 2017). The banking crisis in the United States and abroad continued to worsen as weak banks were merged into stronger ones, governments took over some banks, and provided funding to others. Governments in the United Kingdom, Belgium, Iceland, Switzerland, Portugal, Spain, the Netherlands, and Denmark, were particularly challenged to find solutions to escalating problems in the banking sector. The Bagehot Rule that central banks should provide liquidity at penalty interest rates to solvent banks ran up against the fact that many of the insolvent banks were essential to the entire financial system. Insolvent banks, according to Bagehot, should be allowed to fail, and that may have been good advice to follow in the nineteenth century when banks were smaller, but in 2008, when some of the failing banks threatened to bring down the entire financial system and a big part of the real economy with it, Bagehot's Rule seemed too risky. No one was certain what would happen if the largest elements of the financial system went under, but no one wanted to find out either.

6.2.1 Too Big to Fail

The problem of failing banks was complicated by the fact that a number of financial services institutions that were too big to fail were not banks. Failures of systemically important institutions led to several bailouts in September, 2008, and threw the US economy into its worst period since the Great Depression. On September 7, the US Treasury Department took control of Fannie Mae and Freddie Mac. Their takeover of the two GSEs had been planned in July when the Treasury, anticipating what was to come, asked for and was granted Congressional approval to take control. The September 7 takeover of Fannie and Freddie was followed on September 15 by Fed support for Bank of America's acquisition of the failing brokerage firm Merrill Lynch, and the bankruptcy of the fourth largest investment bank, Lehman Brothers. The next day, September 16, insurance giant AIG received a bailout of $85 billion from the Federal Reserve. None of these failing institutions – Merrill Lynch, Lehman, AIG – were legally considered banks. Merrill was primarily a stock brokerage firm, AIG was a diversified financial services firm, but primarily an insurance company with a financial products division that managed to lose billions, and Lehman was an investment bank without a retail side that took deposits or made ordinary business loans.

The Federal Reserve was relatively unrestricted in its abilities to make loans to firms in an emergency. These powers have been limited by financial reforms passed after the Subprime Crisis, but prior to then it was empowered to make loans to banks it regulated without having to justify its decision, while Section 13 of the Federal Reserve's charter gave it the power to lend to "individuals, partnerships, and corporations" under "unusual and exigent circumstances." When it used Section 13 to make loans to non-banking firms, the Fed was required to justify its support and explain to the House of Representatives and the Senate the terms and conditions imposed. One of the requirements was that the Fed was confident that the recipient was solvent and could pay back the loan. When it bailed out AIG, it gambled that market uncertainty caused the company's assets to be temporarily undervalued, but that they would eventually pay off. Ultimately, the Fed and the Treasury Department provided over $180 billion in support, all of which was paid back by early 2011, with a profit of $9.4 billion (FRB New York, no date).

In the case of Lehman, the Fed decided that the investment bank's insolvency prohibited it from lending money under the terms of Section 13. The Treasury Department could have lent Lehman money, but was most likely worried that doing so would create a moral hazard for other institutions. This is perhaps the most significant and controversial case because Lehman's failure triggered a frightening intensification of the financial crisis and has become the main exhibit in discussions of government bailouts and their consequences. Some observers believe bailouts are a mistake because they only encourage others to take on too much risk and heavy debt loads. The counterargument is that when the financial sector is collapsing and threatening to take down the economy with it, the responsible thing to do is to stop the damage as quickly as possible and worry later about the lessons for the future. Moral hazard, in this view, is an issue to be addressed during periods of relative normalcy and not during a crisis. To use a metaphor, when a house is burning down, it isn't the right moment to teach about fire safety. Ball (2018) goes so far as to argue that if the Fed or Treasury had saved Lehman from failure, the Great Recession would not have happened and many subsequent failures in the financial system would have been avoided.

6.2.2 *Maintaining Credit Availability*

Throughout 2008 and 2009, the Fed continued to expand its programs supporting credit availability. It introduced a highly expansionary monetary policy in late 2008, called quantitative easing (QE), which was designed to support the flow of credit in the system. QE is unconventional and no one was certain it would have a positive effect, but given that interest rates were near zero, the Fed's traditional policy of interest rate decreases was exhausted. Therefore, instead of normal open market operations with short-term government bills, the Fed bought all kinds of assets from a wide range of enterprises, including firms that are not banks. The impact on the banking system was dramatic as excess reserves, which are normally close to zero, began rising and were over $767 billion by the end of the year. A year later, at the end of 2009, they were over $1 trillion. Eventually, excess reserves grew to more than $2.5 trillion (FRB St. Louis, 2017a).[12]

Some observers feared the inflationary consequences of a policy that increased reserves so dramatically. There is a difference, however, between excess reserves and the actual money supply. As long as the bank reserves were held by banks, they did not enter circulation and did not become part of the money supply. And as long as interest rates were low, markets were indicating that there was little demand for borrowed money. More astute observers correctly predicted no inflation. Worries also arose about the value of the dollar, and many of the same individuals who expressed very public opinions about a coming dollar debasement were surprised to see the dollar rise in value. Markets again were telling a different story, proclaiming that there was little demand for loans but a huge demand for secure, liquid assets, such as US Treasury bills. Insecurity in the global economy

12 The increase in excess reserves has had a profound and unexpected effect on monetary policy. The Fed pays interest on reserves in order to manage the quantity held by banks. Consequently, monetary policy which used to be described as buying and selling short term government securities (open market operations) is now more focused on managing the level of excess reserves. Changes in the interest rate paid on reserves affects the quantity of excess reserves and spending.

caused by the spread of the financial crisis led to a rise in the demand for the dollar and any asset perceived to be less risky.[13]

By the middle of 2009, the recession was over although it was impossible to know that at the time and it did not feel like the end of the recession to most people. The recession's end did not mean that recovery had taken place, only that the decline had been arrested. Unemployment was still high and GDP was below the peak it reached in 2007, but economic growth was slightly positive in the second half of 2009. The end of the recession was helped along by nearly $800 billion in fiscal stimulus that was passed in February, 2009, one month into President Obama's administration. Many economists argued that the stimulus was too small, but the stimulus opposition among the ranks of politicians and observers professing concerns about large deficits probably made a larger stimulus politically impossible. In any event, most economists agreed in retrospect, that the stimulus had a significantly positive effect on the economy (IGM Forum, 2012 and 2014a).

On the monetary and financial front, the Federal Reserve continued to protect credit markets as best it could, while continuing its large unconventional monetary stimulus. In 2009 it added a diagnostic tool in the form of stress tests for individual banks. Stress tests were a gamble since any bank that failed to pass would undermine the tentative and fragile return of confidence in the financial system. Banks were required to show that they could withstand the types of negative shocks that might challenge their ability to maintain their solvency. If they had not been able to weather these shocks and pass the tests, it undoubtedly would have heightened fears about the banking system and the weak recovery that was underway in mid-2009.

13 In November, 2010, more than twenty prominent academics and investment advisors sent Fed Chairman Ben Bernanke a letter predicting that QE would cause high inflation and depreciation of the dollar. Although many economists disagreed and subsequent events showed the letter signers to be wrong, many continued to insist that inflation and depreciation were coming. The text of the letter and the names if its signatories are available at: https://blogs.wsj.com/economics/2010/11/15/open-letter-to-ben-bernanke/.

The upside was that if they passed the tests, and if the tests were accepted as credible, then it could further the perception that the worst was over and recovery was underway. Fortunately, US banks passed and appeared to be capable of handling likely shocks. The tests were not without their critics, particularly among those who thought they were not rigorous enough and doubted whether they were real tests. Nevertheless, the bulk of public sentiment seemed to favor the idea that the worst of the financial crisis was over.

The end of the financial crisis is a somewhat arbitrary date. By May of 2009, after the positive results on the stress tests, the worst was over. By October, 2009, the St. Louis Federal Reserve's financial stress index showed that financial stress levels in markets had returned to normal. Economically, the 2007–2009 recession officially ended in June of 2009. Growth was anemic, however, and rates of unemployment remained high in the slow recovery (FRB St. Louis, 2017b; NBER, 2016e). Politically, the 2010 midterm elections represented a legislative shift away from crisis management and back toward more traditional legislative issues. The federal budget deficit had ballooned in size, as deficits always do during a financial crisis, and many opponents of additional stimulus focused on potential future deficit problems. The 2010 midterm elections returned the House of Representatives to Republican control and shrank the Democratic majority in the Senate. As opponents of activist government policies gained power, further stimulus became impossible, and a turn toward austerity probable. After 2010, any additional fiscal policy stimulus was not possible and unconventional monetary policies were the only tools left to fight slow growth and high unemployment.

6.3 FINANCIAL REFORMS

As it became clear that the crisis was ending and that the emergency was receding, policymakers began to ask questions about the causes of the crisis. Politicians on both the left and the right shared a sense that there was something terribly wrong with a financial system that could collapse suddenly and seemingly without warning. The legislative response was the Dodd–Frank Wall Street Reform and Consumer Protection Act which was signed into law on July 21, 2010. It is the primary response to the Subprime Crisis and remains largely intact several years later (2018) despite amendments and legislative and executive attempts to eliminate some of its provisions. The bill reflects widespread agreement about the problem areas of finance, even though there are deep disagreements about specific reforms and the best way to address recognized problems.[14] Dodd–Frank does not attempt to eliminate the risk factors described in Chapter 1 except in the case of strengthening regulatory institutions that provide oversight and enforce rules.[15] With respect to the other vulnerabilities described in the beginning of this book, complete elimination would be impossible and even if it could be done, would impose such severe restrictions on finance and the economy that the cure would be worse than the disease. Nevertheless, Dodd–Frank has two major goals consistent with harm reduction. These are crisis prevention and crisis mitigation.

6.3.1 Crisis Prevention

On the crisis prevention side, the goal is to prevent the intensification of vulnerabilities that might grow into a crisis. Dodd–Frank makes several important changes in the rules for banking, derivatives, and mortgages, and perhaps most importantly, it attempts to incorporate a supervisorial and regulatory perspective that is not limited to one institution or even one market, but takes into account the entire

[14] Oppenheimer, Kessler, and Liner (2014) have a succinct and balanced statement of the main elements of Dodd–Frank. See also the overview given by Bernanke (2012). The reforms required by Dodd–Frank overlap significantly with several of the key ideas contained in the influential *Squam Lake Report: Fixing the Financial System*, a 2010 collection of essays by fifteen distinguished financial economists that began meeting in 2008 to develop a set of policy proposals that would "offer guidance on the reform of financial regulation" (French, et. al., 2010, vii.) Hoshi (2011) compares two central ideas of the Dodd–Frank bill – orderly liquidation and too big to fail – to the recommendations given in the *Squam Lake Report*.

[15] This is not surprising given that there is a strong consensus among both European and US economists that flawed financial sector regulation and supervision was the most important factor contributing to the crisis (IGM Forum, 2017).

financial system as a way to address the problem of too big to fail. This is done through the implementation of new regulatory oversight and with more careful monitoring of overall conditions in the financial system. In perhaps the most meaningful reform contained in the legislation, the US Treasury Department is required to form a Financial Stability Oversight Council (FSOC), comprised of twelve federal regulators, with the purpose of providing oversight for the entire financial system.[16] The FSOC is aided by a newly created Office of Financial Research which is directed by the FSOC and is designed to provide research and information about emerging threats to financial stability.

The FSOC is the most direct attempt to address criticisms that arose during the Subprime Crisis and its aftermath that no regulator was concerned about the stability of the financial system as a whole, that each agency or office was focused on a limited set of financial institutions that interacted in complex ways with institutions outside the purview of any single regulatory body. Those criticisms gave rise to a call for more attention to be paid to the new idea of macroprudential regulation. The goal of macroprudential regulation is to close gaps in financial regulation that left some important firms essentially unregulated and, perhaps most critically, to require regulatory bodies to consider a bigger picture than only the set of institutions they are required to regulate or monitor. Given that no single regulatory body has the expertise or the legal authority to cover the entire system, and rather than creating an entirely new centralized agency with macroprudential responsibilities, Dodd–Frank creates a consortium of existing agencies, housed in the Treasury Department, and charged with the responsibility of monitoring for new financial threats to stability.

16 The twelve members are the Board of Governors of the Federal Reserve, the Commodity Futures Trading Commission, the FDIC, the FHFA, the National Credit Union Administration, the Office of the Comptroller of the Currency, the SEC, the Treasury Department, and the Consumer Financial Protection Bureau. In addition, non-voting members include representatives of state insurance commissioners, state banking supervisors, and state securities commissioners. There is also a representative from the newly created Office of Financial Research.

The FSOC has also been given authority to designate firms as SIFI which are required to undergo additional supervision. A SIFI designated institution need not be a bank but can be any large institution that plays an important financial role as part of an interlinked financial network. These firms are considered systemically important to overall stability, regardless of their definition as a bank or other type of enterprise.

In addition to the introduction of macroprudential regulation as a goal of the regulatory system, the Dodd–Frank bill implements a number of specific rules and regulations that increase bank capital and liquidity requirements, try to limit excessive speculation by federally insured banks (the Volcker Rule), impose regular stress tests for large banks, create greater transparency in derivatives markets, establish new standards in mortgage markets, and protect whistleblowers. The rules are not unimportant, but as rules, they are naturally more contentious and are perhaps less certain as best practices. For example, as discussed in Chapter 10, there is widespread but not unanimous agreement that bank capital levels should be higher than the approximately 3–5 percent level from before the recent crisis. But should they be 5–6 percent as is now the case for most large institutions under Dodd–Frank, or 20–30 percent as some financial experts have advocated? There are similar uncertainties about the specifics for rules concerning liquidity requirements, excessive speculation, and the others. The definition of a particular standard is often somewhat subjective and is the result of strong lobbying efforts by interested parties rather than the careful consideration of research and analysis.

6.3.2 *Crisis Mitigation*

Beyond crisis prevention through macroprudential regulation and numerous changes in specific rules, Dodd–Frank also seeks to mitigate crises once they occur. The most notable effort in this direction is with new authority given to the FDIC to require large financial institutions to develop a procedure for their own orderly liquidation if that should become necessary. This is the main way that the new legislation addresses the problem of too big to fail. Future bailouts of banks and other large financial institutions became politically impossible almost as soon as they occurred in 2008 and 2009. The bailouts caused a high level of moral outrage and repugnance as wealthy executives landed softly in spite of the fact that their management led to the hard crashes of the financial system and the global economy. Moral judgments aside, however, US and European policymakers decided in the moment of the crisis that the failure of systemically important institutions would be more damaging than bailouts.

Bailouts raise the issue of moral hazards and create fears that the natural discipline of the marketplace is removed. Yet allowing the financial system to collapse in order to avoid making life easier for wealthy executives or to possibly make future executives more careful does not seem like a good tradeoff. The orderly liquidation components of Dodd–Frank require large financial firms to develop a plan for bankruptcy that minimizes the damage they might cause the financial system in the event of a future crisis. It is uncertain if these plans will accomplish the intended goal, and without doubt, the answer will depend on the specific characteristics of a future crisis that causes one or more firms to fail.

A separate but important element of the Dodd–Frank bill is the creation of a Consumer Financial Protection Bureau (CFPB). The CFPB's mission is to assist consumers in nearly all financial matters that intersect with consumers and households. This includes mortgage lending, student loans, credit cards, pay-day loans, auto loans, retirement plans, financial planning, and many others. Its mission is to provide information and educational resources and it has the authority to implement new rules in areas of consumer finance. The CFPB plays an important role in protecting the fairness of the financial system, and as such, it helps to legitimate finance in the eyes of citizens. In this respect, its role is more fundamental to the health of the financial system than simple rulemaking, since the system is extremely vulnerable if it is thought to be unfair or a tool used by the wealthy and powerful to exploit the rest of society. The CFPB is perhaps the part of the Dodd–Frank that has had the strongest opposition from financial services interests.

6.3.3 Prognosis

Criticism of Dodd–Frank comes in two predictable flavors: one that it does not do enough and the other that it does too much. The fact that the legislation is criticized by both those favoring more and fewer restrictions does not mean it has hit the Goldilocks "just right" spot since the new rules are untested. To date, efforts targeted on changes to the bill are mostly attempts to weaken some of its restrictions and to fix problems where there is a significant amount of agreement.[17] The general direction of changes, toward weaker rules and standards, is not a reflection of any consensus, but rather reflects the current composition of Congress and the White House. Financial regulation in practice is at least as much or probably more about interest groups and politics as it is about best practices and economics.

The Dodd–Frank Wall Street Reform and Consumer Protection Act is a set of rules and procedures embedded in a US institutional framework. While it encourages consultation and coordination with foreign institutions such as the European Central Bank and other regulators, its rules apply primarily to financial services offered in the United States. That is one limit to its effectiveness, particularly as finance becomes ever more integrated across national boundaries that are nearly always the boundaries for rules and regulations. Tomorrow's financial system will almost certainly operate on a greater international scale than today's, yet the institutions

17 Partisan changes to date (June, 2018) include an interpretation of rules implemented by the CFPB that weaken consumer protections, and an increase in the minimum value of assets a firm must have to be subject to tougher capital and liquidity standards. Another change is a weakening of the Volcker Rule. That rule tries to partially separate investment banking and commercial banking by limiting the trades banks can make if they are a federally insured depository institution. The consequences of this and the other rule changes are too uncertain at this point to know if they are harmful or beneficial, but in either case, they are a move towards laxer regulations. On a bipartisan basis, there is agreement that the original law imposed too many new rules on lending by small banks and that too has been relaxed.

available across national boundaries are rudimentary for the purposes of coordination and cooperation, and nearly nonexistent for rulemaking and enforcement.

Legislation is an essential part of the effort to protect the integrity of financial services and to guard against activities that threaten the entire financial system, but rules and regulations are only part of the story of financial crises. There are also risks associated with the use of government budgets, interest rates, and exchange rates, for explicitly political purposes without regard for economic constraints. And there are risks stemming from the movement of large capital flows from one place to another, from the use of complex financial instruments, from financial innovation, and from the development of interconnected businesses in a global economy. Dodd–Frank is a reaction by US legislators to the perceived lessons of the Subprime Crisis. It does not, cannot, embody all that was learned, but instead it is what was politically possible at the time legislation was proposed.

7 The Financial Crisis in Europe

7.1 THE SINGLE CURRENCY PROJECT

The institutional origins of the European Union began with the signing of several treaty agreements by a handful of European countries in the 1950s. These were important but not comprehensive, covering coal and steel trade, peaceful development of atomic power, and a six-nation free trade agreement.[1] The original goals of the founders were motivated by a desire for deeper political integration as a means to end the "frequent and bloody wars between neighbors" (European Union, 2018). The movement toward political integration required countries to cede some sovereignty to a federal European authority but that proved to be beyond the reach of political leaders. It was possible to reduce economic barriers, however, and movement toward economic integration encouraged the belief that trade agreements could serve as a platform for approaching deeper political ties. Today, the original six countries have expanded into twenty-eight and the free trade area is an economic union of more than 500 million people and nearly $20 trillion in GDP. Perhaps more importantly, it has helped to bring peace and prosperity to a region with a long history of war and deep cultural and linguistic divisions. The EU is one of the world's great institutional achievements of the second half of the twentieth century.

Its achievements have not been easy and the possibility remains that some elements of the union could be reversed. The Subprime

1 It included the large nations of France, Germany, and Italy, and the smaller countries of Belgium, Netherlands, and Luxembourg. The United Kingdom opted not to join at the start but became a member in 1973. It is currently negotiating the terms of its withdrawal.

Crisis exposed deep flaws in the design of the single currency and pushed several countries into a far more virulent crisis than the one that hit the United States. In several countries, the 2007–2009 financial crisis was deeper and the recovery slower than in the United States or the strongest EU economies, largely due to a series of counterproductive economic policies that were promoted by national governments and EU institutions and rules.[2] The most severely affected countries were the so-called GIIPS: Greece, Ireland, Italy, Portugal, and Spain. The crisis exposed their loss of competitiveness and with the exception of Ireland, they all suffered longer and deeper recessions than the rest of the Eurozone. Greece ultimately defaulted on its sovereign debt and all have struggled with debt sustainability. Chapter 13 examines the issue of the single currency more directly, while in the remainder of this chapter, the chronology of the crisis in Europe and the responses of policy makers are described.

The founding treaty of the European Union, the Treaty of Rome, was signed in 1957 and implemented on January 1, 1958. Over the decades, the treaty has been amended to increase its scope while the addition of new members has widened the agreement from the original six to its current twenty-eight. The EU today is an economic union with a set of governance institutions, a small budget, free trade in goods and services, free movement of capital and labor, and some coordination of fiscal policies. Since, 1999, a subset of its members have shared a common currency and a common monetary policy. Currently (2018), nineteen of twenty-eight countries use the euro. Countries must qualify for the euro by achieving specific macroeconomic targets in the areas of budget deficits, inflation, debt levels, and exchange rates, but in practice, no countries have been kept out.

Economic theory tells us that a geographical region should adopt a single currency only if the different parts of the region have synchronized business cycles. This is a necessary requirement since

2 Frieden (2018) asserts that the fundamental mistakes in economic policy were due to decisions made by national governments and not EU institutions. This is a matter of interpretation since EU institutions reflect the preferences of national governments.

a common currency means that individual countries give up their ability to conduct their own monetary policies. Only one policy is possible for the entire area sharing the currency, regardless whether all regions need the same monetary policy or not. For example, the states of the United States share the dollar and New York cannot have a different monetary policy than New Jersey. Historically, the United States has relied on the fact that if business cycles vary across states, with one region expanding and another contracting, then the free movement of capital and workers will smooth out the differences between regions by causing unemployed people and capital to move from the slow growth region to places that are expanding and need workers and capital for investment. Since 1992, the EU allows free movement of labor and capital and, in theory at least, it is possible for unemployed workers in one country to move to a different country in search of work. In practice, high skilled workers and professionals are able to migrate but less skilled workers less so, mostly due to financial costs and language barriers.

The experience of the EU tells us that monetary unions also require a system of transfers to smooth out differences in business cycles. This point is not recognized or accepted by all of the Eurozone's politicians and policymakers, but it is understood by most economists. In the United States' system, transfers from one region or state to another occur through federal taxation and expenditure programs that automatically adjust when states enter a recession. Federal income and social security taxes are reduced automatically when incomes decline, and expenditures such as social security pensions, federal highway funds, income maintenance expenditures, either increase or at least remain the same. In effect, states with good economic conditions automatically increase the share of federal taxes they pay, while states in recession automatically see a decline in their share of taxes and an increase in federal expenditures received. By contrast, the European Union and the Eurozone have no equivalent institutional structures for burden sharing during a downturn that occurs in only in one part of the region. When Greece or Spain enter a recession, there are no significant payments from the parts of the European Union not in recession.

In the 1990s, several institutional limits on macroeconomic policies were adopted by the European Union as a part of the 1992 announcement of negotiations for the establishment of a single currency. It seemed that the member countries were about to become far more integrated economically, and that their individual differences were going to diminish as a new level of prosperity spread throughout the region. Or such was the prediction of many of the proponents of the euro.[3] One of the greatest political obstacles to a single currency was the fear that countries with stronger economies would be forced to support the weaker ones with subsidies and other expenditures. In order to convince the electorate that they would not be responsible for weaker or badly managed economies, member countries agreed that there would be no fiscal transfers and that each nation was responsible for its own fiscal order. The newly created European Central Bank was required to manage the currency and was also prohibited from directly lending to national governments, even if they were facing a financial crisis. In effect that meant that there would be no lender of last resort function in the central bank and consequently, no bailouts of individual member countries. In effect, membership in the Eurozone requires countries to give up the use of monetary policy and exchange rate policy, and it puts severe limits on the use of fiscal policy since the size of budget deficits is constrained.

Citizens in the European Union were far less enthusiastic than their leaders about the benefits of surrendering their currencies, and they conveyed their reservations to national politicians. Investors, however, were more enthusiastic about the disappearance of exchange rate risk between Eurozone countries and began to reduce the interest

3 Important politicians such as Germany's Chancellor Helmut Kohl recognized the problems of combining weaker and stronger economies into a single currency but sold the idea politically by repeating that German and other taxpayers would never be responsible for the mistakes of policymakers in other countries and that the single currency would create a new higher level of prosperity across the European Union (Mody, 2018: 65–123).

differentials they charged Greece and other borrowers with traditionally higher rates. Interest rates paid by Greek, Italian, and other governments converged toward the lowest rates in the European Union. In the case of Greece, interest rates on ten-year government bonds fell from a differential of approximately sixteen percentage points above German rates in 1992, to less than two percentage points in 1999. Given that it is difficult to justify the interest rate convergence on the basis of the elimination of exchange rate risk alone, it must be the case that purchasers of Greek bonds were perhaps assuming that the euro would discipline Greece and other countries with historically higher borrowing costs and force them to reduce their borrowing needs. Rules limiting deficits and debt levels in the Eurozone might lower the risk of default and enforce greater fiscal discipline, if the rules are credible. Another possible explanation for the disappearance of interest rate differentials is that purchasers of government bonds might have expected the single currency to introduce smaller inflation differentials. Or perhaps, purchasers assumed there would be bailouts if a Eurozone country needed them, even though policy explicitly said otherwise. Regardless of the assumptions, interest rate differentials disappeared over the 1990s and into the 2000s so that by 2005 investors demanded the same or nearly the same interest rate on bonds sold by Germany, Greece, and other Eurozone countries.

7.2 AN UNEVEN CRISIS

With the elimination of exchange rate risk and the assumed disappearance of country and inflation risks, capital flowed from countries with lower interest rates to those with higher rates. Specifically, capital moved from the center of the European Union toward the periphery, from Germany and the Netherlands and France into Greece, Spain, Portugal, and Ireland. Capital flows encouraged and reinforced housing and construction booms in the latter, and enabled governments to borrow more easily at lower interest rates. As housing and construction took off in the early 2000s, prices and wages rose in the capital receiving countries. By 2008, as the crisis was in full bloom, prices in Portugal had climbed 9 percent higher than German prices, relative to what they were in 2000. The pattern was even more notable in other countries where the crisis was more severe. By 2008, prices in Ireland were 11 percent higher than in Germany, in Spain they were 12 percent higher, and in Greece,13 percent higher. The direct effect of price level increases was to reduce competitiveness and increase trade deficits.

If the Eurozone countries had retained their own currencies, a depreciation would have played a key role in restoring their competitiveness. In fact, this was the methods that several Eurozone countries, including Italy, France, and others, had used throughout the previous decades. Depreciation would have enabled Greece, Spain, and the others to reduce the prices of their goods and services relative to Germany and restore their competitiveness. With the common currency, however, the elimination of the price differentials that had crept in during the boom in construction can only be accomplished by achieving a lower rate of inflation than their trading partners. To restore competitiveness, Greece, Spain, and the others would have to reduce their inflation rates to a level below that of Germany and the other leading economies, which would achieve the same outcome as a devaluation. Price cuts and disinflation are the solution in theory, but in practice it was extremely difficult to achieve. Germany's inflation rate was consistently below the EU average before and after the crisis began in 2007, so countries would have to achieve a much lower rate of inflation. Given that monetary policy is not controlled by individual nations, the primary means to reduce inflation was through a reduction in the level of economic activity and, consequently, steep recessions became the main mechanism for trying to restore competitiveness. This strategy only works slowly and at the cost of enormous output losses, high unemployment, bankruptcies and the human tragedy those economic conditions imply.

The loss of competitiveness was but one of the problems in the countries that received large capital inflows during the first years of the euro. A second and more immediate problem was that the decline in asset values brought on by the collapse of housing prices in the United States and the resulting pressures on EU banks. Banks and other financial institutions, including pension funds, insurance companies, and investment banks in the European Union participated fully in financial globalization, including buying CDOs from US investment firms and banks, investing in US banks and financial firms, and borrowing heavily in short term credit markets in order to fund construction projects that matured over the longer run. When falling house prices in the United States created uncertainty about the value of mortgage based assets and CDOs, the entire web of interconnected global finance began to unravel. EU banks suddenly found themselves without access to short term loans and the dollars they had come to depend on while simultaneously their assets were falling in value. By design, the problem of insolvent banks in the European Union is a national problem and not directly a EU problem. Individual nations must decide how they will treat a failing bank, whether depositors will be protected, and how much of a loss, if any, bank owners and creditors will be required to take. While bank failures or banking problems are a national responsibility, all nations in the European Union are impacted and key EU decision makers have a significant stake and are deeply involved.[4]

7.3 BANK DEBT BECOMES NATIONAL DEBT

The stronger preference was to use the borrowing capacity of national governments to guarantee the debts of the banks. This avoided a wave of bank failures but only by turning banking losses into government debt and dramatically increasing government borrowing needs. The preference for this strategy, rather than one that allowed banks

4 "Key decision makers" is intentionally ambiguous because there were no formal lines of authority for many of the decisions that were taken. However, the important figures included the Chair of the European Central Bank (ECB) (Jean-Claude Trichet), the leaders of the largest economies in 2010 when key decisions were made (Angela Merkel, Chancellor of Germany; Nicolas Sarkozy, President of France), their finance ministers, and the President of the European Commission (the executive body of the European Union). This is not a definitive or exhaustive list but conveys the idea that policy became ad hoc and that countries with larger economies had stronger voices.

to fail and bank depositors and creditors to lose some or all of their assets, stemmed from the fear that a wave of bank failures would be highly contagious, even if in the beginning it affected only one country. There is strong disagreement about whether contagion from wiping out the creditors of failing banks and letting them absorb the losses on the loans they made would spread through the European Union and even, perhaps, challenge the euro's existence. The president of the ECB, Jean-Claude Trichet, and the German minister of finance, Wolfgang Schauble, were both proponents of the view that contagion from letting bank creditors go under would have disastrous effects on the European Union. Notably, neither of them are economists by training. According to Mody (2018: 250–254), there was little empirical evidence for the idea that contagion posed a threat. Nevertheless, the fear of contagion spread, and countries with struggling banking sectors were encouraged to use the power and authority of their national governments to protect bank creditors who were at risk of losing their investments. The European Union had agreed that there would be no bailouts, but that meant that it would not provide bailouts. National governments, on the other hand, were encouraged to bail out bank creditors and to ensure they were paid back.

In the years leading up to the crisis, government finances in the Eurozone were varied. This was the case in spite of an agreement, called the Stability and Growth Pact, that countries would limit budget deficits to less than 3 percent of their GDP. There is no consistent pattern before the crisis to the countries that exceeded the deficit limit for three or more years (France Germany, Greece, Portugal), or those that ran surpluses in three or more years (Ireland, Netherlands, Spain). As part of the euro negotiations, German leader Helmut Kohl had proposed the 3 percent ceiling with financial penalties for exceeding it, yet Germany exceeded it every year from 2001–2005. By contrast, Spain and Ireland consistently had budget surpluses or very small deficits before intensification of the crisis in 2008 even though the lead-up to the introduction of the euro dramatically reduced their borrowing costs. Greece and Portugal were yet another case, as their borrowing costs also fell dramatically when the euro was introduced and both used the cheaper access to funding to increase spending which caused them to have larger deficits. By 2009, as the crisis reached it most intense period, every country had a deficit and only three small countries (Estonia, Finland, and Luxembourg) were below the 3 percent deficit ceiling (IMF, 2017b).

7.4 THE DOOM LOOP

From the inception of the crisis in 2007 until a few years after the worst had passed, the Eurozone's path through crisis and recession was similar to the United States, both in terms of its depth and its timing. In the third quarter of 2009, GDP growth became positive in most Eurozone countries, in the European Union as a whole, and in the United States. EU and US policies were similar to that point as both the Federal Reserve and the ECB provided monetary support and, depending on the EU country, national governments applied fiscal stimulus. In 2010, however, the president of the ECB, Jean-Claude Trichet, interpreted early signs of growth and the beginning of an expansion as a reason for concern and prematurely raised interest rates. Monetary tightening at such an early stage of recovery was a major mistake but it was not solely due to a misreading of the economic recovery. The ECB has a single mandate to maintain price stability alone and, unlike the Fed which has a dual mandate to provide price stability and support economic growth, the ECB focuses exclusively on preventing inflation. In 1998, as the euro was about to start life, a group of economists that included two Nobel Laureates in the field of macroeconomics, Franco Modigliani and Robert Solow, predicted that the single mandate would lead to policy mistakes. They wrote that high unemployment rates in Europe were likely to continue if, among other things, the ECB did not adopt a dual mandate to support growth and to maintain price stability. The single mandate, they argued, would cause the bank to err on the side of too much anti-inflation policy and too little support for aggregate demand (Modigliani, et al., 1998). Their warning was focused on long run rates of unemployment and not policies during a recession caused by a financial crisis, but it was prescient. The recovery in the Eurozone economies, like the United States, had not yet been consolidated when the interest rate hikes hit the markets in 2010 and 2011. In the second quarter of 2011, GDP growth in the Eurozone hit zero and then turned negative in the fourth quarter and remained negative through 2012 and the first quarter of 2013 (OECD, 2018). With a return to recession and the resulting loss of tax revenues, budget problems worsened in the hardest hit countries. By contrast, in Germany which had one of the least severely affected economies, the double-dip recession was relatively mild. This was partly due to Germany's export competitiveness but also to the good fortune of a very strong stimulus package passed by China where the demand for German auto and machinery exports was strong. But in countries without competitive manufacturing sectors, the recession intensified problems. In addition to deficit problems and growing debt levels, solvency questions began to arise in countries with banking sector problems. Macroeconomic questions about borrowing limits, insolvencies, and spillovers to other countries raised the level of uncertainty and institutional questions about bailouts, the costs of leaving the euro, the role of the ECB, and ultimately, the viability of the euro were under discussion.

As noted, governments were encouraged to support their banking systems as a measure to minimize potential problems of contagion. In countries with banking crises, support meant government support for the banks and the avoidance of losses by creditors. Support for the banking sector put additional pressures on governments that were already struggling with rising debt levels and the associated increase in interest payments which were intensified by the ECB misstep on interest rates. As the recession caused governments to struggle to reduce expenditures, and as growing debt problems increased the risks for lenders, interest rates began to rise on the debt sold by weaker governments. This was an unsustainable cycle of debt and bailouts in which governments borrowed to supports banks that, in turn, held government bonds of deteriorating quality. Bank balance sheets also included bad real estate loans and financial assets tied to the Subprime Crisis in the United States. If government debt was not sustainable and seemed likely to provoke defaults, then creditors were more likely to try to take money out of the banking sector since banks were dependent on government support. Fears of bank failures weakened the overall economy through effects on credit markets and intensified fears of a government default since a weak economy hurts tax revenues and increases expenditures on social welfare at precisely the moment government support for banks becomes more urgent. This was labeled the doom loop of the Eurozone crisis: Fears of a government default lead to fears of bank failures, both worsen economic performance and lead to more fears of a government default (Baldwin and Giavazzi, 2015).

By 2012, most of the countries that had received large capital inflows during the first years of the 2000s were stuck in this scenario. Matters were worse than a normal recession because most of the traditional avenues of escape were not available. A currency devaluation would have helped restore competitiveness and confidence in the economy, but membership in the Eurozone made that impossible. A central bank that could perform the function of lender of last resort and directly lend to governments was another theoretical possibility, but that was not allowed under the terms of the ECB's charter. In a normal recession, expansionary monetary policy can help return an economy to positive growth, but interest rates were still relatively low and yet there was no stimulatory effect from monetary policy.[5] And fiscal policy such as increased spending and cuts in taxes were off

5 The conditions of the Subprime Crisis in both United States and the European Union created a "zero lower bound" or liquidity trap. In this situation, high levels of uncertainty cause investors to prefer liquidity (cash and cash-like assets) to other types of assets. Increasing the money supply does not lead to lower interest rates since they are at zero or close to it. Furthermore, investors prefer liquidity–cash–to illiquid investments, so expansion of the money supply does not generate spending or investment. The theory of the zero lower bound was first sketched by Keynes in the 1930s, but was considered an oddity until the 1990s when Japan's long period of expansionary monetary policy, low interest rates, and deflation, caused economists to reexamine the phenomenon (Krugman, 1998).

the table due to worries over national debt levels and the fear that more spending would worsen the situation.

7.5 EMERGENCY ACTIONS

In retrospect, it is clear that the European Union did not have a credible strategy for addressing the crisis once the recession returned in late 2011. Its policy choices were severely limited by a number of factors, some of which were built into the design of the euro, such as the institutional restrictions limiting support for national governments. But other limiting factors were operational as well, such as the absence of a Eurozone monetary policy focused on growth as well as inflation, and the contradictory goals that required national governments to support their banking systems while they simultaneously reduced their borrowing and shrank their debt levels. Support for employment and households were secondary, at best, while maintenance of financial obligations was primary. For example, after the Irish government assumed the debt of its banks, its debt-to-GDP ratio rose from 24 percent in 2007 to 116 percent in 2013. Similarly, Spain's debt rose from 36 percent of GDP to 94 percent.

The proponents of the euro had argued that there would be no bailouts of national governments by the ECB. The prohibition on bailouts served the political purpose of assuring a skeptical EU citizenry that they would not be forced to pay for the mistakes of policymakers in other countries. Without that guarantee, it is unlikely that resistance to giving up national currencies would have been overcome and the euro probably would not have been established. Such assurances are always uncertain, however, because in a time of deep crisis, the tradeoffs look different than they do when they are abstract and hypothetical. As the Greek economy faced the real likelihood of a default on its bonds, some of which were held by banks in France, Germany, and other EU countries, the existential threat of a national default, an intensification of the banking crisis across the European Union, and the possible breakup of the euro, changed the cost-benefit ratio of bailouts.

The first bailout was a $146 (€110) billion loan to Greece granted by the European Union and the IMF in May, 2010. Disbursement of the loan was over three years and in return, Greece promised an austerity program of spending cuts and tax increases. The purpose of the loan was to support banks inside and outside Greece by supporting the ability of the Greek government to make its scheduled payments (BBC News, 2010, 2 May; Bilefsky and Thomas, 2010 2 May). The second bailout was provided to Ireland, in November, 2010, and a third was given to Portugal in May, 2011. Between the Ireland and Portugal bailouts, Greece received a second, larger loan in February, 2011. The second loan required private bondholders to accept a haircut of 53.5 percent, and Greece agreed to make spending cuts and tax increases to reduce its debt-to-GDP ratio from 160 to 120 percent by 2020 (Council on Foreign Relations, 2017). As was true in Latin America during its debt crisis, austerity programs have a poor record of debt reduction. Spending cuts and tax increases slow the economy and reduce the ability of governments to pay down debt. Over the next few years Greece was granted a slightly relaxed debt target and lower interest rates (2012), accepted new austerity programs (2013) and, in 2015, defaulted on its debt when it missed a payment to the IMF. The government agreed to even more cuts in spending, and received a third bailout in August, 2015, although this time the IMF refused to participate because it viewed Greece's debt as unsustainable. Finally, in 2018, EU Economic Affairs Commissioner, Pierre Moscovici, declared the debt crisis over when a new deal was agreed giving Greece a relatively small loan, reduction in interest payments, and a longer repayment period on previous loans (BBC, 2018 22 June). Between the first bailout in 2010 and the declaration that the debt crisis was over in 2018, Greece's debt-to-GDP ratio rose from 146 percent to an estimated 191 percent despite the fact that government expenditures fell by 25 percent, from €118 billion to €89 billion (IMF, 2018). If the strategy was to reduce Greek debt, it failed. If the strategy was to cut government spending, it succeeded, but at the cost of a prolonged recession. And, if the strategy was to reform the Greek economy with the goal of eliminating inefficiencies and corruption, the jury is out. Growth finally turned positive in 2017, after ten years of a recession that shrank the economy by one-fourth.

Bailouts were not the only emergency actions. In May of 2010, shortly after the first bailout for Greece, the ECB announced a program of secondary market purchases of Eurozone government bonds. Because direct purchases by the ECB of newly issued government bonds is not permitted, the work-around involved banks buying the initial offerings, and then selling them to the ECB. This program, called the Securities Markets Program (SMP), was incorporated into a similar program begun in 2012, called Outright Monetary Transactions (OMT). The purpose of both SMP and OMT was to support the Eurozone member governments through the creation of increased demand for their short term debt and to gradually shift holdings of risky government bonds away from banks and other private lenders and toward the ECB and other governmental institutions. In the wake of the OMT, interest rate differentials shrank and countries that had been forced to pay higher rates received some relief.

In July 2012, one month before the launch of the OMT program and at a low point in international confidence in the euro, ECB President Mario Draghi sought to assure the public that the euro would not disappear. While speaking to a Global Investment Conference in London, he asserted that "Within our mandate, the ECB is ready to do whatever it takes to preserve the euro. And believe me, it will be enough" (Draghi, 2012). No one knew what that meant exactly, nor was it clear that the ECB could save the euro if pressures grew too great, but his comment helped change public expectations and solidified confidence in the ECB's commitment to saving the currency. His comment, together with the announcement of the OMT program a month later, shifted expectations and supported the belief that no country was going to leave the euro and that the currency was safe. Interest rates fell, countries that needed to borrow were more easily able to obtain funds, and the most intense period of the crisis passed. But the recession did not.

7.6 RECESSIONS PROLONGED

Draghi's comment played an important role in ending the crisis in confidence in the euro, but his actions could not address the second round of recessions that began in 2011 and 2012. The timing of recessions varied by country, but by 2012, the economies of most of the Eurozone countries were shrinking. EU leaders, afraid of more debt and worried that some countries were acting irresponsibly in managing their government accounts, settled on the idea that the core problem was a loss of business confidence in Eurozone countries with budget deficits. This view was pushed hard by Germany and its closest followers such as the Netherlands, Austria, and Finland. Germany's role as a supplier of capital prior to the crisis and its slow growth in the years leading up to it, meant that it did not enter the crisis with rising prices and wages and that it did not have a credit boom. Consequently, it performed relatively better during the crisis, and together with its absolute size as the largest EU economy, it has a disproportionately large voice in EU affairs. When its leaders called for austerity as a way to boost economic growth, they found support among other Eurozone members.[6]

European Union and German policy makers based their call for austerity on the belief that contractionary fiscal policy would be expansionary since it would restore confidence in governments that practiced fiscal austerity. The idea that fiscal austerity might be expansionary – called "expansionary austerity" – became a common policy response to the European Union's growing crisis. The concept of expansionary austerity directly contradicts fundamental principles of economics taught in most introductory classes and has never achieved widespread support in the economics profession since there

6 Germany had been the source of much of the capital invested in the peripheral countries in the early 2000s as its own economy was not growing fast enough to absorb all its savings. By the start of the crisis in 2007, its economy was healthy again. As the crisis developed, Germany's ability to rely on foreigners as a major source of demand for its manufactured goods, caused its crisis to be shorter and kept economic growth slightly positive in 2012 and 2013 when many other Eurozone countries fell back into recession.

is little or no empirical evidence for it. Chapter 12 discusses this fallacious idea in more detail, but it is worth considering why it became the favored policy response in the European Union and particularly in the Eurozone.

Several factors led to the adoption of contractionary fiscal policies, but their justification as expansionary was a result of motivated reasoning. Cynics would argue that EU politicians knew better but pushed fiscal contraction anyway. A more charitable view is that they were ignorant but wanted to believe that fiscal austerity was a solution. A third possibility, and the one that is perhaps most likely, is that political leaders in Germany and other relatively strong economies mistakenly assumed that Greece's fiscal mismanagement was representative of all struggling countries. Hence, they assumed that discipline and rules and austerity were needed to restore balance. This assumption was partly financial and partly a moral belief that the crisis countries were not misfortunate as much as they were profligate, careless, and even corrupt in the management of their public finances. The primary evidence for this view was the fact that for several years before the beginning of the crisis and up to 2009, the Greek government published falsified statistics about the size of its deficits. When large intentional errors in the deficit estimates were exposed in October, 2009, the Greek government lost the confidence of the EU's leadership.[7] There was irony in this since a newly elected government exposed the errors of its predecessor, but the messenger became the target of the criticism and hostility directed toward Greece. It was not the only country with budget deficits before the crisis, but its circumstances and behavior reinforced the idea that a significant part of the problem was widespread economic mismanagement and corruption.

7 In the lead up to joining the Eurozone in 2002, Greece had repeatedly underreported its deficits. Membership requires deficits below 3 percent of GDP, which was too difficult a target. In order to stay on track for membership, and once it joined, to avoid penalties for not meeting the deficit target, it cooked the numbers. By 2009, the gap between the actual and the reported deficits was so large it could not be ignored. It created a firestorm of anger towards Greek politicians.

The problem with this view is that it ignores the differences across the Eurozone and the fact that Spain and Ireland ran fiscal surpluses before the crisis. Even Italy's finances were stable in spite of the legacy of debt it had accumulated in decades past. Furthermore, austerity usually increases debt through its negative effects on economic activity. And perhaps most importantly, perpetual austerity, which seems to be the policy in Greece and elsewhere, is politically dangerous as it undermines the democratic legitimacy of the European Union and the governments that impose it. The viability of the European Union depends on a widespread sense of solidarity among different political classes and across average citizens in different countries. The Subprime Crisis and its aftermath undermined that sense of solidarity and the policies that perpetuate negative growth or that prolong a steep recession must, in the long run, undermine support for the institutions that implement them.

To be sure, non-crisis countries fear that crisis resolution might require large transfers which will be defined geographically as transfers from the core to the periphery, or from Northern Europe to Southern Europe. Functional economic unions such as the United States have fiscal systems that automatically create transfers when there are regional differences in economic conditions but it is another matter altogether to create those transfers explicitly when they have not existed previously. In the European Union today, it is highly unlikely that a system of transfers will be developed but at the same time, the results of expansionary austerity are not positive. On average, it took Eurozone countries 6.6 years to return to their pre-crisis levels of GDP, not counting the three countries, Cyprus, Greece, and Italy, that as of 2017 had not reached their previous peaks. In the six hardest hit countries with debt problems and strong austerity programs, except for Ireland, average annual growth has been near zero, 2009–2017. And growth in the rest of the Eurozone has been anemic in the majority of countries.

Problems in the Eurozone have mostly dissipated after the long period of slow or no recovery. Nevertheless, they are likely to reappear in the future unless there are institutional changes that address the tendency for recessions to cause divergence between weaker and stronger economies. One side of the debate, represented most notably by France and Italy, proposes institutional changes that would allow more transfers and greater risk sharing during recessions. The other side, most notably Germany, proposes more rules to limit problems caused by mismanagement of the macroeconomy, and more market discipline. There is a lack of consensus in the European Union and the Eurozone, and neither side is likely to realize its program without causing injury to the institutions. Nevertheless, the fundamental need to move beyond a stalemate has prompted researchers to look for a compromise set of policies that mediate between more rules and more transfers, or more market discipline and more risk sharing, in order to find a path toward greater macroeconomic, fiscal and financial stability (Bénassy-Quéré, et al., 2018). These issues are discussed in more detail in Chapters 12 and 13.

PART III Lessons

Eight lessons are explored in the following chapters. These lessons are drawn from all of the crises but weighted more heavily toward the Subprime Crisis and the Eurozone Crisis since they have not been as thoroughly considered. Several of the lessons have been incorporated into the economics mainstream and a few others remain contentious, largely for political reasons, as discussed in the conclusion.

8 Markets Do Not Self-Regulate

8.1 OVERCONFIDENCE IN THE MARKET

The idea that markets self-regulate, or come close to self-regulation, is a surprisingly robust proposition. Practical experience and simple reflection would seem to run contrary to this notion, but for a period of time from the 1980s forward, the idea that markets worked best if left to their own regulatory efforts seemed to gain support, particularly in the financial services industry. The key to making it sound reasonable is to not carry it too far and to support it with the right kind of story. It also helps if the story is buttressed with a large dose of cynicism regarding the ability of governments to get things right.

The story goes like this: Financial markets are places where firms and individuals can gain or lose enormous sums of money; reasonable people will not venture into those markets without doing all the necessary background checks and research; and financial firms that do business with one another will not establish relationships if their potential partner's corruption or incompetence will hurt their own reputation and profitability. In sum, individual firms have a lot to gain or lose in their dealings with each other, they have strong incentives to avoid shady deals that would harm their profitability or their reputation, and they are the most reliable source of oversight. Unfortunately, this view of finance is similar to thinking that the ocean has no sharks.

The idea that markets self-regulate, particularly financial markets, was often expressed by no less a credible source than Alan Greenspan, former Chairman of the Federal Reserve. One example will illustrate his view. In his speech to the Annual Conference of the Association of Private Enterprise Education, Greenspan reviewed the history of banking in the United States, focusing on the ability of banks to self-regulate and their successes at doing so except during times when government regulation interfered. He begins his presentation with the following:

> It is most important to recognize that no market is ever truly unregulated in that the self-interest of participants generates private market regulation. Counterparties thoroughly scrutinize each other, often requiring collateral and special legal protections . . .

Greenspan's view is reasonable – firms will not contract with each other without first doing due diligence. That makes sense, but if their scrutiny of potential counterparties is effective, how can he explain the many episodes in US history where bank crises occurred? Did banks stop exercising their normal levels of scrutiny? Why would they do that? He has a clear answer to these questions: government interference. He goes on in the same speech to argue:

> At worst, the introduction of government rules may actually weaken the effectiveness of regulation if government regulation is itself ineffective or, more importantly, undermines incentives for private market regulation . . . If private market participants believe that government is protecting their interests, their own efforts to do so will diminish (Greenspan, 1997, April 12).

This was a perspective that Greenspan frequently voiced and was instrumental in promoting, both as an idea and as actual legislation. He was not a voice in the wilderness, however, and many interests and influential individuals took a similar perspective. The notion of market self-regulation was "in the air" and had become a significant element of official opinion that contributed to the deregulation of many parts of the US financial services industry through the 1980s and 1990s.

There was also some hubris and historical ignorance mixed in with ideas about regulation. After the Asian Crisis (Chapter 5), most analysts recognized the need to improve the regulation of financial markets in developing countries where it was presumed that institutions were weaker, supervision less rigorous, regulatory experiences fewer, and markets more volatile. Developed countries such as the United States, however, were presumed to have the ability to allow financial markets freer reign since institutional protections were stronger in the areas of property rights, investor protections, and the rule of law. Institutional considerations aside, it is a misreading of the historical record to assume that richer countries have fewer crises. As noted in Chapter 2, over the long term, countries in Europe and North America have had many more banking crises than those in Asia, Latin America, or Africa, and countries with financial centers tend to have even more frequent banking crises. There are exceptions, but the general historical pattern makes clear that banking crises at least are "An Equal-Opportunity Menace" and not something countries grow out of as income per capita rises (Reinhart and Rogoff, 2009a: 150–55; 2013).

There are many possible reasons for the higher incidence of banking crises in high income countries. For one, their financial sectors are more extensive, with greater linkages to the outside world and deeper financial relations inside the home country. In that sense, more frequent banking crises may simply reflect a larger financial sector and a kind of pathology of wealth, like heart disease. This cannot be the whole story, however, and a substantial amount of research prior to the Great Recession (and more research since) shows that deregulation of financial markets was risky business. There are well-known theoretical reasons for this, as well as a number of practical concerns.

The idea that financial markets are self-regulating if freed from government restrictions was a radical departure from traditional thinking. As far back as Adam Smith, economists recognized regulation was prudent and in the public interest. When discussing banking regulation specifically, Adam Smith wrote:

> Such regulations may, no doubt, be considered as in some respect a violation of natural liberty. But those exertions of the natural liberty of a few individuals, which might endanger the security of the whole society, are, and ought to be, restrained by the laws of all governments; of the most free, as well as or the most despotical (Smith, 1776 [1937]: 308).

While Smith understood the need for regulations in industries such as banking, where failure of the industry threatened everyone's security, the pendulum in the United States and elsewhere began to swing toward less regulation in the 1970s and 1980s. This was a worldwide trend, not limited to the United States, as many countries and regions adopted more market oriented policies around this time. Examples include the United States under Presidents Carter and Reagan, the United Kingdom under Prime Minister Thatcher, China under Deng Xiao Ping, India under Manmohan Singh, across Latin America, and even the Soviet Union.[1] Markets around the globe were ascendant and governments were in retreat as a negative view of regulation and government became embedded not just in individual perspectives, but in the policies of more and more countries.

Nobel laureates Akerlof and Shiller (2015: 150) describe an overconfident belief in the optimality of market outcomes as "... an unsophisticated interpretation of standard economics" which holds that free markets, subject to a couple of caveats, lead to the "... best of all possible worlds." Hence, an unsophisticated understanding of standard economics supposes that the freer we make our markets, and the more we are "free to choose," the greater our material well-being.[2] In reality, the relationship between markets and economic prosperity is complicated and nuanced. Markets are necessary to prosperity, as attested by the failed attempts in the former Soviet Union

1 Yergin and Stanislaw (1998) describe the worldwide shift towards more market oriented policies though an examination of specific regions, countries, and personalities.

2 *Free to Choose* is the title of a bestselling book and TV series by Milton and Rose Friedman advocating minimal government regulation.

and China to build prosperous societies without markets. Nevertheless, there is a difference between extolling the virtues of markets on the one hand and arguing that they are optimized if there are no restrictions on the other. A sophisticated understanding of standard economics recognizes that markets need regulations in order to function properly because without them, they will generate a variety of pathologies, inefficiencies, and generally undesirable outcomes.

8.2 MARKET REALITY

Economists have studied and catalogued many of the reasons why markets fail to achieve optimal outcomes when they are unregulated. In what follows, the focus is on a general issue that is particularly germane to financial markets and has a large number of specific instances and subcategories. This is the problems of asymmetric information. In 2001, the Nobel Memorial Prize in Economic Science was awarded to three economists, George Akerlof, Michael Spence, and Joseph Stiglitz, for their fundamental research into the problems of markets under conditions of asymmetric information. The next year, 2002, it was shared by Daniel Kahneman (with Vernon Smith) for his research into the role of our cognitive biases and flawed decision-making when information is difficult to obtain and circumstances pose a high level of uncertainty. Kahneman's work in particular has given rise to the field of behavioral economics which gave rise to behavioral finance and led to Shiller's work.[3] More recently, Shiller and Akerlof have examined a particularly antisocial consequence of asymmetric information, which they have labeled "phishing for phools" (Akerlof and Shiller, 2015). The purpose of their work is to remind us of something that is often ignored by market fundamentalists, namely that in addition to the wealth and prosperity created by markets, profit making can also contain a fair amount of trickery and deceit.

3 Kahneman's work also led to another Nobel for a behavioral economist in 2017, this time for Richard Thaler.

Asymmetric information is the idea that the two sides of the market, the buyer and seller, have different information sets. Consequently, the buyer may be purchasing a good or a service with unknown characteristics, as when someone buys a car without knowing it has a bad transmission, or invests in a complicated financial asset without understanding that it has a high probability of default. Market trading cannot be said to be optimal in either case because buyers are purchasing goods that are significantly different from what they think they are paying for and if they knew the real characteristics of the car or security, they would pay less or not buy at all. The idea of asymmetric information has withstood both theoretical and empirical attempts to dismiss its importance. As described in Chapter 5, asymmetric information was a central issue in the Asian Crisis, when lenders to Thai banks became uncertain about bank solvency and decided to cut their lending. It was also present in the loans the Indonesian and other governments made to preferred borrowers who were well connected to political leaders. And it also played a key role in the recent financial crisis of 2007–2009 when buyers and sellers of mortgages, MBSs, and insurance policies on those securities, operated with different information about the risks involved.

In finance and insurance markets, asymmetric information leads to the problem of adverse selection. Borrowers know more than lenders about their credit worthiness and ability to repay, and purchasers of insurance know more about their risky behaviors or illnesses than do sellers of insurance. Normally, in most markets, it is desirable to sell to the highest bidder, but in these cases, a borrower willing to pay a higher interest rate or someone buying insurance who is willing to pay a higher premium may actually be less desirable customers. A borrower willing to pay more may be desperate to obtain funding, while an insured person or company willing to pay a higher premium is more likely to need the insurance for what they know to be a high risk situation.

Asymmetric information played a large role in the recent global financial crisis and in previous banking crises in the United States.

There are many examples. Originators of mortgages sometimes pushed homebuyers into more expensive mortgages because they earned higher fees for the loan originator. Firms that securitized mortgages custom-made and sold to clients securities that were stuffed with a large number of subprime mortgages. Given that the MBSs mortgage backed securities often carried AAA ratings, the probability of default appeared very low even though the reality was different.[4] Prior to the collapse of the US savings and loan industry in the late 1980s, some land developers obtained large real estate loans that were ostensibly for development projects but were used to support lavish lifestyles. Ultimately, when the developer defaulted, they walked away from the project in what has been described as "bankruptcy for profit" (Akerlof and Romer, 1993). In both the Savings and Loan Crisis of the late 1980s and the Subprime Crisis, information available on one side of the market was not readily available to the other side. It is conceivable that home buyers could have shopped for better loans, purchasers of MBSs could have looked more closely at the thousands of individual mortgages in the security they were buying, and savings and loan companies could have examined more closely the reputations and financial histories of their borrowers, but the costs and effort to do so were often prohibitive.

The problem of asymmetric information can be compounded by "phishing for phools" (Akerlof and Shiller, 2015). Anyone with an email account knows the term phishing as an attempt by the sender of an email to use trickery or deceit to get others to do something not in their own interest. It does not necessarily involve illegal activities and is often simply an attempt to get consumers or businesses to make bad choices that benefit the originator of the phishing. Sometimes illegality is involved, however, as Akerlof and Shiller (2015) concede. There are other obvious phishes, such as tobacco companies that persuade us to

4 This is more complicated than it seems at first glance. A firm that securitizes a large number of mortgages with different risk levels and then sells slices or tranches of the security can load the risk into selected tranches in a way that (mathematically speaking, under some assumptions of independence) turns the rest of the security into a low risk asset even though it contains higher risk components.

smoke even though we all know the potential consequences or soft drink makers that encourage us to consume too much sugar. But there are less obvious phishes, such as the idea that one can buy a more expensive home than is actually affordable, or that a particular financial advisor can provide investment expertise that is not available at a lower price, or that a financial product is worthwhile because a respected name and reputation are attached to it. As Akerlof and Shiller point out, competitive market equilibriums will exhaust all profit making opportunities, even ones that make the other side of the market worse off through the use of trickery, deceit, and manipulation.

A prominent example of phishing is through reputation mining. If consumers associate a high quality with a particular brand, then there is an opportunity for the brand owner to lower their costs and quality in order to exploit the premium consumers are willing to pay. There is a nearly inexhaustible supply of examples of this type of behavior, from mislabeling by Whole Foods, to exhaust emissions cheating at Volkswagen, to fraudulent education at Trump University, to carelessness on the part of ratings agencies, to risky financial assets sold by credible Wall Street firms, and many others. Some of the actions are illegal, as in the VW case, but others are not. It is not clear that Moody's, Standard and Poor's, or Fitch, for example, broke any laws when they gave AAA ratings to financial instruments that did not deserve them.

Asymmetric information and its malevolent cousin, phishing, are two key reasons why unregulated financial markets fail to achieve the efficient market equilibrium that opponents of government regulations hypothesize. There are a number of subcategories of asymmetric information that pose problems for unregulated markets, many of which are common sense and do not require advanced training in economics in order to see the dangers. For example, economists use the term "principal–agent problem" to describe a case where the interests of a firm or individual acting as an agent for a client may not be aligned with the interests of the client (the principal). This is not uncommon in finance and is the reason the Consumer Finance Protection Bureau implemented a rule requiring investment advisors to give their clients information in the clients interest. Another case is the common problem in financial markets of moral hazards. Moral hazard occurs when there is a financial incentive to incur risks that will fall on someone else if things go badly, as when a mortgage loan originator collects higher fees by persuading a home buyer to purchase a more expensive house than they can afford and ultimately the bank making the loan or the purchaser of a mortgage security containing the loan are injured. Moral hazard is a form of asymmetric information since different actors have different knowledge of their motivations and the risks posed by a particular situation.

8.3 EMPIRICALLY SPEAKING

The Federal Reserve is one of the most important financial regulatory bodies in the United States yet it partially lost sight of that role under its former chairman, Alan Greenspan. As one of the top financial regulators, Greenspan's Fed should have been more attuned to the substantial body of empirical work showing the relationship between financial deregulation and financial crises.[5] Numerous empirical studies, done before the Subprime Crisis, show a correlation between financial crises and banking supervision and regulation, and financial crisis and financial liberalization. Studies done since the crisis have continued in this vein with similar results.[6] Empirical research into

5 Caprio (1998) summarizes the research into the leading causes of financial crises and notes that multiple causes are usually at work, but bank supervision is key. Guttentag (1994), Bartholomew, Mote and Whalen (1995), also point towards regulation and management issues, as well as the problems associated with rapid financial liberalization (deregulation). Caprio and Klingebiel (1997) note that banks need better regulatory systems in order to absorb shocks more effectively, while Demirgüç-Kunt and Detragiache (1999) find that financial liberalization increases the probability of a crisis.

6 Tallman and Wicker (2010) find that banking crises in US history are correlated with financial liberalization, and Dell'Ariccia, Igan, Laeven and Tong (2014) conclude that several types of regulation are useful and necessary for limiting risks of a banking crisis. The latter study looks at 170 countries over the fifty years from 1960 to 2010. Freixas and Laux (2012) explore how information deficiencies in financial markets make self-regulation ineffective. In his recent study of the role of the IMF during a number of different crises, Joyce (2013) views the key lesson of the recent global financial crisis (2007–2009) to be the need for regulation of the financial sector. And a poll of European and US economists found that weak supervision, regulatory laxity, and similar issues were the number one cause of the financial crisis (IGM Forum, 2017, 17 October).

cases of financial crises has been clear and consistent: Financial liberalization (deregulation) increases the probability of a financial crisis. There are nuances to this outcome, but it is robust over time and across countries.

These studies offer a variety of suggestions for limiting the risk of a banking crisis, although none claim that crises can be completely eliminated. Since the global financial crisis, much research and thought has gone into the topic of financial system regulation. Policy makers have traditionally focused on measures to limit risks to individual firms or types of firms, such as commercial banks. More recently, they have developed interest in macroprudential regulation which seeks to limit overall risk to the entire financial system rather than focusing on one institution or one type of institution at a time. For example, the post-crisis Dodd–Frank legislation passed by the United States includes provisions for a new Financial Stability Oversight Council that brings together financial regulators for regular consultations on the overall stability of the financial system (US Department of the Treasury, no date). Dodd–Frank also created the CFPB with the goal to increase the fairness of financial institutions and to limit their ability to "phish for phools" in consumer finance (CFPB, 2018).

Dodd--Frank has a large number of additional regulatory changes, some of which are likely to endure and others that may prove to be counterproductive, or of limited use, or that are captured by the interests they seek to regulate. For example the naming of SIFIs is meant to identify the individual firms that are so large and/or so interconnected that their failure would cause substantial damage to the entire financial system. The goal is to impose a stricter set of rules regarding capital requirements, lending and borrowing, and provisions for dissolving the firm in the event of a bankruptcy. No one knows how this will work in an actual crisis and financial institutions have begun to push back against being so identified. (See Chapter 6, on the Subprime Crisis in the United States.)

Another completely different approach that is not contemplated in Dodd–Frank, is to limit competition among financial firms. The core idea is that firms take on too much risk when they are competing too fiercely against one another. Normally, increased competition is viewed as positive, but in cases where it pushes firms to engage is riskier and riskier strategies in order to win customers or gain market share, competition can lead to a higher probability of a crisis. This approach to regulation protects the franchise value or charter value of banks and other financial services providers by limiting the amount of competition and making it easier for them to earn respectable profits without resorting to higher risk, higher reward strategies. In effect, it is a call to return to an earlier era of banking and financial services, when bankers could be on the golf course by three in the afternoon and banks were treated similar to public utilities.[7]

This strategy is unlikely to be adopted since it would require putting the genie back in the bottle through much stricter limits on the range of activities individual institutions can pursue. It is worth noting, however, that Canada completely avoided the financial crisis, in part because its banking sector is dominated by five large firms that engage in very limited competition against each other. Each firm has its profits assured, there is no reason to try to take market share away from each other, resulting in relatively greater stability in the banking sector. Reducing competitive pressures in finance may sound like a radical idea, but it is one with a prestigious pedigree. Nobel laureate James Tobin hypothesized that financial systems work best when there is some "sand in the gears." His specific policy proposal was to impose a financial transactions tax, first proposed for the buying and selling of foreign currencies (Tobin, 1978). (When he was writing in the 1970s, foreign currency fluctuations were a major issue.) Protecting the charter value of a bank or other institution requires some similar reduction in competition so that "grasping for yield" has smaller rewards and larger penalties.

7 Hellman, Murdock, and Stiglitz (1997) argue that a moderate amount of excess profits for banks is useful since they will monitor their borrowers more closely and expand efforts to mobilize deposits. In their view, both the quality and quantity of financial intermediation can be higher than under greater financial liberalization.

In sum, there is little doubt that the failure of regulation played a significant role in the financial crisis of 2007–2009. A poll of European and North American economists cited regulatory problems as the number one cause of the Subprime Crisis (IGM Forum, 2017, 17 October), and the US's FCIC which investigated the crisis stated:

> We conclude widespread failures in financial regulation and supervision proved devastating to the stability of the nation's financial markets. The sentries were not at their posts, in no small part due to the widely accepted faith in the self correcting nature of the markets and the ability of financial institutions to effectively police themselves (FCIC, 2011: xviii).

Economies need finance, but they also need stability. That requires regulation of the financial sector since, as Smith noted, a collapse of the financial sector "endangers the security of the whole society" (Smith, 1776 [1937]: 308). It is a balancing act – too much regulation suppresses finance to the detriment of economic growth, while too little creates a higher probability of crisis and economic instability. The optimal amount and type of regulation in financial markets is a technical question, but it is clear that it is not zero.

9 Shadow Banks are Banks

9.1 NO BAILOUT?

The financial crisis of 2007–2009 worsened dramatically on September 15, 2008, when Lehman Brothers, the fourth largest investment bank in the United States, collapsed into bankruptcy and triggered the most intense period of financial chaos. The next day, the Federal Reserve provided an $85 billion loan to the insurance giant and financial conglomerate, American International Group (AIG). The Bush Administration immediately went to Congress and asked for $700 billion to buy up bad debt held by banks and other financial institutions. By March of 2009, the stock market had fallen 38 percent, GDP was still shrinking, and people around the world watched in shock as the United States and Western Europe spiraled down into financial chaos.

The debate over letting Lehman Brothers collapse without federal intervention of some sort has not gone away. Six months earlier, in March, 2008, the Treasury Department and the Federal Reserve had engineered a merger in which JP Morgan acquired Bear Stearns, the fifth largest US investment bank, to avoid Bear's complete collapse, and when Lehman began to wobble, its CEO felt entitled to support. The Fed argued it had no authority in Lehman's case, the details differing just enough from Bear Stearns to raise legal issues. Others thought the Fed and the Treasury were sick of bailouts and hoped that the six months after the collapse of Bear Stearns, investors were sufficiently prepared and had protected themselves against the worst that could happen with a Lehman bankruptcy. The debate might never be resolved over whether there should have been a bailout, whether the Fed had legal authority or not, and what the Fed's actual intentions were when it helped with a merger at Bear Stearns but allowed Lehman to collapse (Blinder, 2013: 124–7; Cline and Gagnon, 2013). In defense of the Federal Reserve's decision not to bail out Lehman, Chairman Bernanke (2015: 250–69) described the thinking at the Federal Reserve in light of the rapidly changing circumstances of a financial crisis that was growing worse by the hour. Lacking the legal authority to act directly given Lehman's insolvency, the Federal Reserve tried two strategies. One was to find a buyer, the other was to build a consortium to take over the bank's assets and liabilities. But the bank's rapid deterioration, its slowness in responding, and the lack of legal authority, ultimately left it no choice but to allow the bank to fail. The Federal Reserve and Bernanke have been heavily criticized for their failure to prevent Lehman's disorderly collapse. Some critics have argued that the central bank could have acted sooner, before Lehman's finances deteriorated as far as they did. Others argue that it could have taken over some of Lehman's problem assets, or supported a third party willing to take them (DeLong, 2013). Nearly everyone agrees that if the Fed had acted, the Subprime Crisis might have been milder. Ball (2016, 2018) argues that there would not have been a Subprime Crisis or a Great Recession, only perhaps a mild recession.

None of those questions, however, were the strangest part of the collapse and subsequent fallout from Lehman. Rather, the biggest puzzle was how a bank that was not regulated like a bank could become so central to the financial system of the world economy. Further, Lehman was only the fourth largest institution of its type in the United States; three other firms in the United States and several outside were even larger. Could they fail too? And if they did, what would happen? Queen Elizabeth is famously purported to have questioned why no one saw the financial crisis coming; similarly, we might ask why economists and policymakers did not see shadow banks and the existential threats they posed to the economy.

9.2 SHADOW BANKS

Shadow banks have become central to the financial systems of high income countries and some developing countries, including China. Although the name implies something quasi-legal because it is in the shadows, shadow banks are completely legal. The term refers to their characteristics as businesses that are not quite banks in the way we traditionally think of them, but perform many of the functions of banks. Shadow banks do not take deposits and they do not engage in the type of retail banking functions that are a central part of the business of commercial banks, for example offering checking accounts. Their operations parallel those of ordinary commercial banks, however, in that they borrow short term to invest in a variety of assets, from stocks and bonds, to real estate loans, commodities, currencies, derivatives, and others, that are difficult to imagine, such as helping rock star David Bowie sell securities that give the buyer a piece of his future royalties, or providing insurance policies on assets that the buyer of insurance does not own. Investment banks in the United States are part of the shadow banking system, but so are money-market funds, insurance companies, hedge funds, and a number of other entities. What they all have in common is that they borrow money short term and they lend it long term – which is what a bank does – but they do not take deposits like a bank so they were outside the main regulatory framework of banking before the Dodd–Frank financial reforms were passed in 2010.

Some examples will clarify the differences between commercial banks and shadow banks. Shadow banks and large successful corporations can borrow in the commercial paper and repo markets. These are similar to bond markets, except that they are very short-term lending markets and, consequently, have less oversight and regulation than bond markets. Commercial paper is a short-term debt instrument that provides no collateral and is not guaranteed. The lack of a guarantee limits its use to the largest, highest rated, firms, but as with all things financial, there are variations. For example, asset backed commercial paper (ABCP) is a form of commercial paper – a short-term loan – that is backed by collateral owned by the borrowing firm. There are many other variations, as well. Repo, formally called a repurchase agreement, is another form of short-term borrowing but with collateral. When a company sells a repurchase agreement, it technically sells an asset which it promises to repurchase as soon as the following day or soon thereafter. The seller of repo gets a short-term loan and the purchaser has the asset as collateral. If for some reason the shadow bank cannot come up with the funds to repurchase its asset, the lender can sell it and recoup the money it lent. Repo and commercial paper both provide liquidity to the borrowing firms by converting an asset with a longer maturity into one that is very liquid and has a short maturity.

Large firms use commercial paper and repo to manage their cash flow and current expenses, and together they are a key element of the day-to-day financing of industrial and financial enterprises. Since they are short term, interest rates tend to be lower. The downside for companies using these instruments to raise funding is that they must continually refinance the debt by extending the loan for another short period or by paying off one lender with funds borrowed from another. Before its bankruptcy, Lehman followed the common practice of financing a portion of its investment operations with short-term debt. This continues to be a common practice by shadow banks today. As is often true in the financial world, it works well until, suddenly, it doesn't. Several factors were at play in the Lehman case specifically and the overall financial crisis in general, but one of the keys was that the collateral Lehman provided became uncertain. When Lehman sold repo, it was selling assets that it promised to buy back the next day or in a few days or weeks. When the value of the assets it used as collateral became questionable, Lehman's creditors became more cautious and unwilling to value the assets and they stopped buying the offered repo, which is to say they stopped lending to Lehman. Lehman had no other way to raise funds and was left holding a large portfolio of questionable value.

9.3 SECURITIZATION

A second part of the story of Lehman and shadow banks is the story of securitization. Securitization is a useful financial technique that can turn illiquid debt like mortgages into a more liquid bond that can be bought and sold. Securitization is the process of combining many people's debt, such as home loans, credit card debt, student loans, car loans, or other debt that has a stream of payments. Every month, households pay their mortgage, their student loans, car loans, and so on. Shadow banks buy these mortgages, student loans, and other debts, then use the securitization process to combine them into one large asset which can, in turn, be cut up into of pieces and sold. For example, MBSs are like bonds that pay their holders out of the stream of mortgage payments made by households. The purchaser of a piece of the MBS receives an income that is not dependent on one person's mortgage or even several people's, but rather a share of the payments made by thousands of homeowners who, theoretically, can be distributed across the country. Regional diversification of the mortgages included in the MBS means that home prices and default rates in one place have little or no effect on the overall value of the security. The return an investor receives should, in theory, match the return on a bond of similar maturity and risk, but in the lead-up to the financial crisis, these assets paid a slightly higher rate of return and were highly favored by financial institutions looking to increase their profitability.

A MBS as described can also be considered a type of derivative, or more specifically, a collateralized debt obligation (CDO). Part of the mystery of finance is the use of specialized jargon which obscures the meaning of transactions and financial instruments. The word derivative is a generic term for a large class of securities, like a MBS, whose value is derived from another asset, such as the value of a mortgage payment. There are many, many, different types of derivatives, all with valuations that are tied to something else, such as interest rates, currencies, debt payments, and so forth. A CDO is a type of derivative, but one that has collateral. For example, a MBS has collateral in the form of the houses on which payments are being made. Securities formed out of student debt have the wages of the ex-student as collateral, and those formed out of auto loans have the cars the loans were used to purchase. All of these debt forms – mortgages, student loans, car loans, credit card debt – can and are securitized into CDOs. The innovators of CDOs in the 1980s argued that they increased liquidity in financial markets by turning fixed debt and debt payments into a tradable financial instrument. A bank can sell their mortgage loans to another firm, for example Lehman or another investment bank, who then creates a CDO, turning the mortgage into a more liquid security. The CDO, in turn, can be cut into slices, called tranches, which are grouped by risk characteristics.

CDOs, repurchase agreements, MBS, commercial paper, and their variants are an important part of the story of shadow banking because these financial instruments played prominent roles in the financial crisis. They also illustrate some of the vulnerabilities of our complex financial system. No one was certain, for example, what the CDOs with mortgage debt contained. Michael Lewis' very entertaining story of three small firms that saw the crisis coming and took advantage of it, recounts how hard it was for them to find out what mortgages were in a CDO (Lewis, 2010). Often, even the firms selling CDOs did not know the profiles of the thousands of mortgages contained in a bundle they engineered. Key pieces of information were unknown: What was the regional composition of the CDO, how many loans for homes in Nevada, how many in Florida, New York, and so on? What were the income levels of the homeowners and what percent of the mortgages were made to households with bad credit or incomes insufficient to service their home loan?

9.4 REGULATORS AND INCENTIVES

Answers to the questions just posed are things that a normal investor might want to know before buying a CDO, or a slice of a CDO. The fact that almost no one had that information illustrates another failure of the system: most of the CDOs were given the highest ratings possible by the ratings agencies. The high ratings opened the door to investment by pension funds and other regulated entities that are limited in the amount of risk they can take on. The highest rating possible is the debt of the US Treasury, which is as close to zero risk as possible. Obviously, the rating agencies failed to do their job of providing a correct gauge of the risks posed by the CDOs and in this way they were also responsible for the crisis. Portraying an investment as risk-free or nearly risk-free encourages their purchase and makes it less likely that the purchaser will adequately protect itself.[1]

Problems in the ratings agencies were a key system weakness. Ratings agencies had strong incentives to issue favorable ratings regardless of the characteristics of the asset. Rating agencies are paid to rate assets by the firms selling assets. Naturally enough, the firms want the best possible ratings since it will determine the interest they have to pay. Rating agencies want repeat business and therefore have an incentive to be lenient in their evaluations. A second problem, then and now, is that many rating agency employees eventually seek much more lucrative work with the financial firms whose assets they evaluate. A third problem stemmed from the complexity of the instruments they were asked to rate. The description given here of the MBS and CDOs is simplified and partial, and does not convey the complexity of those instruments or the others derived from them. For example, firms also sold CDO-squared, which were securities whose value depended on CDOs, and CDOs-cubed, which depended on CDO-squared and so on. The lead-up to the financial crisis was a period in which financial firms were hiring PhDs in mathematics, physics, and

1 Without going too far into the weeds, note that it is possible to design a CDO or other securitized instrument that loads most of the risk into one tranche. This means that the least risky tranches have very low probabilities of default and, in that case, may deserve a triple-A rating. In order to do this, however, one has to assume that the risks for each of the tranches are independent of each other so that whatever causes the riskiest tranche to fail will not change the probability of failure for the less risky ones. As long as housing markets were not synchronized across the country, and as long as the securities included a regional diversity of mortgages, the assumption that the risks were independent was not far off. However, when housing markets across the country started to collapse, both the high risk and low risk parts of the collateralized mortgage securities started to fail.

computer science, and tasking them with designing newer and ever more complex financial instruments. No one, including the CEOs of the top firms, fully understood the complexity of the instruments they were creating. Nor did they think that was their job since they had models of risk that told them the probabilities for how much money they would gain or lose in different scenarios. As long as the models worked, that was sufficient for keeping the firm out of danger.

Shadow banks were one of the primary creators of CDOs and other asset-backed securities. The money they used to buy up the mortgages and assets they compressed into the new securities came from the repo market and the commercial paper market. The collateral used in the repo market could be a CDO, or piece of a CDO that they created previously. Shadow banks not only sold CDOs but also kept them on their books since they often paid a slightly higher rate of return than alternative investments and made managers look smart by returning more money to their shareholders.

9.5 SHADOW BANK DEPOSITORS

The depositors in this shadow banking system are the firms that buy repo and commercial paper issued by the investment banks, hedge funds, insurance companies, and other firms that borrowed short term. Lenders are mostly enterprises with significant cash flow such as pension funds, mutual funds, insurance companies, hedge funds, and other banks. It also included foreign governments with large holdings of dollars and other currencies that they kept in reserve for meeting unexpected contingencies.[2] Lenders to shadow banks typically have large amounts of cash on hand – workers pay into their pension funds every month, households and businesses pay their insurance premiums, foreign governments accumulate dollars through their trade surpluses. Lenders to shadow banks can partly

2 According to Federal Reserve Bank Governor Tarullo, foreign governmental entities invested about $1.6 trillion in highly liquid assets in the US in the four years prior to the crisis (Tarullo, 2012).

invest longer term, but must also keep some liquidity available for meeting their obligations to new retirees, insurance claimants, mutual fund withdrawals, and so on. The system works the same as the commercial banking system except that a variety of entities are lending money to the shadow banks via the commercial paper and repo markets instead of individuals lending money to banks via their deposits into their accounts. All of these sellers and purchasers of asset-backed securities share the common need for something equivalent to a checking account: a safe, liquid, short-term asset that lets them store their cash and earn a small return.

In the shadow banking sector we can think of the lenders to shadow banks as depositors. In a simple banking system, banks take their depositor's money and use it to make real estate and other loans. Shadow banks behave similarly but instead of supporting the purchase of a new home or the expansion of a business, they put their borrowed funds into a variety of investments such as CDOs and other, sometimes extremely complex, financial instruments. These pay a return to the shadow bank which is greater than the cost of the borrowed money and can also be used as collateral to borrow more money so they can make more investments. In other words, shadow banks, like regular commercial banks, borrow short term so they can invest in long term assets that are less liquid than their borrowed money, or liabilities.

Financial economist and economic historian Gary Gorton (2010, 2012) asserts that nearly all financial crises are banking panics, and the crisis of 2007–2009 was no exception. It looked different at first, however, because it happened in shadow banking rather than in commercial banking. A traditional bank panic in commercial banking occurs when depositors begin to worry that their banks will not be able to provide them with their money if they request a withdrawal. Commercial banks operate with a fractional reserve system and maintain only a fraction of their deposits on reserve. Consequently, banks do not have sufficient funds on hand if everyone decides to withdraw their deposits at once. A bank panic begins when rumors of a bank failure spread, depositors rush to withdraw their money, and even solvent banks fail because they do not have sufficient liquidity to meet the withdrawals.

One simple way to avoid the calamity of a traditional bank panic is to implement a system of deposit insurance. This is exactly what the United States did after the collapse of thousands of banks and the loss of savings by millions of households and businesses during the Great Depression. Deposit insurance is a double edged sword, however. During normal times, there is evidence that it increases risk taking and decreases banking stability even if during a crisis period, it reduces instability (Anginer, Demirgüç-Kunt, and Zhu, 2014). The key, as usual, turns out to be the system of bank supervision and oversight. An adequately regulated banking sector will mitigate the moral hazard of deposit insurance during normal times and calm the fears of depositors that their money is at risk during a crisis.

9.6 BANK PANICS WITH SHADOW BANKS

The shadow bank equivalent of a banking panic occurs when lenders to shadow banks become uncertain about the value of the assets used for collateral by shadow banks. If asset values fall significantly or, as happened in 2007 and 2008, it becomes difficult to evaluate their worth, then the pension funds and money-market funds that buy repo and commercial paper from shadow banks will pull back. In 2007 and 2008, as housing prices began to fall, the value of the CDOs held by Lehman and Bear Stearns and others became difficult to price. What is the value of a security composed of thousands of mortgages if default rates on mortgages are suddenly rising? Rather than risk losing their loan and ending up stuck with collateral of reduced value, the lenders pulled back, setting in motion the shadow bank equivalent of an old fashioned bank panic.

Once the shadow banks were cut off from short-term borrowing, they were in serious trouble. They needed to borrow today in order to pay off the very short-term loans they obtained yesterday or in the previous week. When they could not sell repo or commercial paper, they were in a bind. The only way out was to sell off whatever assets they had available but this created the further problem of a fall in asset prices. The American economist Irving Fischer called attention to this problem during the Great Depression when he described how the scramble by debtors to sell assets would push down asset prices and increase the probability of bankruptcy (Fisher, 1933). As Lehman and others began to liquidate their CDOs, prices for the assets fell, and as their value came into question, firms stopped buying them.

Recall from earlier chapters the rule proposed by the nineteenth century British financial journalist, Walter Bagehot. Bagehot's rule says that to manage a bank panic, the central bank must lend freely during the panic, but only to solvent banks, against good collateral, and at penalty interest rates. Insolvent banks should be resolved quickly and completely. This rule was often cited during the financial crisis, as it is during nearly every crisis since Bagehot first formulated it. It has lasted for more than a century because it works: It avoids inaction which allows the crisis to deepen, and it avoids over-reaction which costs governments large sums and does not solve the problem of insolvency. It is a less clear guide to action, however, when the insolvent institutions threaten to wreck the entire financial system.

There were two major interrelated problems confronting the Federal Reserve and other central banks. First, a number of shadow banks were so large and so intertwined with national and global finance that their failure threatened to collapse the entire financial system. Bagehot's rule presupposes that banks are not systemically important and can, if insolvent, be allowed to fail without dire effects on the rest of the financial system. Smaller banks in the US were allowed to fail, but the growth of finance since the 1970s has produced a number of banking and financial behemoths whose failure would create enormous costs to the economy. Secondly, if the banks are insolvent, but they are systemically important, how should central banks resolve them? In the United States, some observers argue that the Federal Reserve and the Treasury Department did not have legal authority to guide or manage the process of resolving failing shadow banks (Wallach, 2015). The Fed argued that Section 13(3) gives it legal authority to intervene, but regardless whether the Fed's actions were legal or not, resolution of the financial crisis with extensive interventions by the Federal Reserve and federal government raised questions about the rule of law and generated widespread repugnance by both sides of the debate. As a result, post-crisis legislation has focused on avoiding systemic failures, creating an orderly resolution process, and limiting direct intervention by the Federal Reserve and federal government.

9.7 THE RISE OF FINANCE

Economists were aware of shadow banks before the crisis but did not pay them much attention for the simple reason that finance did not seem particularly important to the macroeconomy. To be sure, this view was changing by 2000, but in the view of many economists, finance is about transacting, exchanging one type of asset for another, and it was hard to see in 2000 or 2006 how that could have much impact on the overall economy. Business cycles, monetary and fiscal policies, unemployment, investment, consumption, and the other topics of macroeconomics did not seem to depend in any important way on the manner in which transactions occurred. So the financial system, while important for a healthy economy, was a seen as a kind of accounting system that kept track of credits and debits, but did not seem to have characteristics that required it to be explicitly taken into account when thinking about or modeling the macroeconomy.

There were exceptions to this myopic view. Federal Reserve Chairman Ben Bernanke, for example, had published a paper in 1983 in the *American Economic Review* pointing out that the collapse of the financial system in the United States during the 1930s had significantly deepened and prolonged the Great Depression (Bernanke, 1983). He had followed that work up with research showing that the extent of a country's banking crisis was one of the two key factors explaining the depth of the 1930s depression (Bernanke, 1995). Economists knew banking crises were harmful, but there was not an agreed idea about the role of the financial system beyond its function as a kind of utility that enables households and businesses to transact with one another. Consequently, not many economists were paying attention to the shadow banking system until the crisis occurred.

This gap in thinking about finance was also fed by the general expectation that large sophisticated shadow banks like Lehman knew what they were doing. They are not in business to go bankrupt and prudent firms do not foolishly engage in extremely risky activities. Furthermore, the rapid evolution of the financial system, including innovations in financial instruments such as the many forms of securitization, new technologies, and new financial organizations, outpaced awareness of the changes. In the United States, there had always been investment banks that traded in various markets but the extent to which their technologies, incentives, and organizational forms had changed ran ahead of the analysis of the possibilities.

Until the 1990s, the United States had a clear separation between retail banks and investment banks. Retail banks were the kind of business that most of us think of when we think of a bank. They take in deposits and make loans to households and small businesses. They tend to be small operations, at least in comparison to the financial behemoths that are common today. Investment banks on the other hand did not engage in commercial banking in the sense of taking deposits and making loans. Instead, they assisted firms with acquisitions and mergers, with initial public stock offerings, in placing bonds and commercial paper, and they traded in financial markets for themselves and for their clients.

Investment banks were partnerships until the 1980s when many of them went public. Many observers argue that once the management of investment banks began to invest with other people's money rather than their own, as they had when they were partnerships, they made much riskier investments (Lewis, 1989; Shiller, 2012; and Kay, 2015). If that is true, then the shadow banks of 2007 would have behaved differently if the managers were gambling with their own capital instead of their shareholders' and lenders'. And once deregulation of finance ended the legal separation between investment banks and commercial (retail) banks, all forms of financial services could be bundled together, from insurance to specialized mortgage lending to investment services. The risk that a crisis would spread through the entire financial system expanded correspondingly.[3]

The growth of the shadow banking sector tells us that there is a demonstrable need for the services they render. Specifically, many types of firms inside and outside the financial sector, as well as foreign governments and their agencies, have a need for liquid, short-term assets that are safe (Gorton, 2009). This is parallel to the need that households have for checking accounts. Bank checking and savings accounts are guaranteed and do not change in value depending on the latest economic data. They are, in Gorton's words, "information insensitive." Similarly, many firms that deposited funds with the shadow banking sector believed that they had a safe, liquid place to put their money.

The challenge for the Federal Reserve and other bank regulators is to bring these enterprises into a regulatory system that minimizes the risks to society. The fragmentation of US financial regulation, the implicit and sometimes explicit assumption that financial markets are best left to self-regulate, and the incentives for shadow banks to rely on short-term debt funding, was a toxic mix when many of the firms involved turned out to be systemically important. When small banks fail, it has little impact outside the immediate effect on its employees, stockholders, and the local community, but when behemoth shadow banks become insolvent, it threatens the entire financial system and the global economy.

It is clear that the Great Recession is not leading to a wholesale redesign of the financial system as occurred during the Great

3 The Banking Act of 1933 and its most popularly known provision, the Glass–Stegall Act, created a legal separation of commercial and investment banking. Regulatory interpretations of the act in the 1970s and 1980s gradually eroded the distinction between investment and commercial banks, until it was repealed completely in 1999 by the passage and signing of the Financial Services Modernization Act, also known as the Gramm–Leach–Bliley Act.

Depression. Hence, most steps taken to make shadow banking safer do not call for a complete change in the structure of the industry, but look to implement changes at the margin that are believed to add stability. These include changes designed to decrease the vulnerabilities of money-market funds to sudden withdrawals, the addition of liquidity and capital requirements, greater transparency in the repo market along with measures to more forcefully convey its associated risks, and greater oversight based on the type of transaction rather than the type of financial firm (Tarullo, 2013; Carney, 2014; Yellen, 2013). In sum, the goals are to reduce the threat of a systemic failure by increasing the transparency of shadow banks and by imposing a set of requirements and rules that prevent excessive risk taking. These are changes at the margin; there are no plans for a systemic redesign of the financial system.

10 Banks Need More Capital, Less Debt

10.1 OTHER PEOPLE'S MONEY

> The financial crisis revealed that banking firms around the world did not have enough high-quality capital to absorb losses during periods of severe stress
>
> Janet Yellen, 2013.

Banks take deposits – other people's money – which they use to fund their own activities. Bank deposits are loans by depositors and a form of bank debt, even if most people with checking accounts probably do not think about the fact that they are loaning money to a bank. Deposits are the primary source of funding for most retail banks, which also have other sources of funding, including capital invested by the bank owners or shareholders, and loans from sources other than depositors. Taken together, deposits, other borrowed money, and capital, make up the liabilities side of the bank balance sheet.

Banks increase their resources by borrowing more from depositors and other sources, and by increasing their capital, which they do by selling more shares or by withholding profits. Debt and capital are the two sources of funding, but there is an important distinction between the two. Bank capital, unlike debt, is not a bank liability since it is not a legal contract requiring repayment. In effect, it is a buffer against defaults by borrowers from the bank. When a default on a bank loan happens, the bank loses an asset while its liabilities to depositors and lenders do not change. In that case, the bank's capital helps ensure that bank resources are adequate for meeting the withdrawal and repayment demands of its depositors and lenders.

Over the course of the nineteenth and twentieth centuries, banks gradually increased their reliance on borrowed funds, mostly deposits, and decreased their holdings of capital. Estimates of the share of bank funding derived from capital vary but it was probably around 30–40 percent of the value of bank assets in the mid 1800s, when banks were sole proprietorships or partnerships, and declined gradually to the range of 5–10 percent by 2000.[1] According to the Government Accountability Office, in the years before the onset of the Subprime Crisis, the largest US investment banks had capital ratios between 3–4 percent of the value of their assets, while the Congressional Financial Crisis Inquiry Commission reported them to be around 2.5 percent by some measures (US Government Accountability Office, 2009: 18; FCIC, 2011: 19). European banks used even less capital in funding themselves and had ratios in the 2–4 percent range before the crisis. A capital ratio of 2.5 percent implies that there is only $1 of capital to support each $40 of assets, and that a 2.5 percent decline in asset values wipes out all the capital. By contrast, US firms outside of finance rarely have less than 30 percent equity, or capital, and average values are much higher. In terms of funding, the reliance of banks on debt is very different from other sectors of the economy. If banks hold the equivalent of 3–4 percent of their assets in the form of capital, then 96–97 percent of their operating funds come from borrowed money, mostly from depositors but also other lenders.

In the aftermath of the Subprime Crisis, researchers, policy makers, and others, including the Federal Reserve Bank of Minneapolis, called for banks to use more capital and less debt.[2]

1 Jordà, et al. (2017) estimate an average capital ratio (capital/assets) of 30 percent around 1850 for a group of high income countries; Admati and Hellwig (2013: 178) claim it was somewhat higher, perhaps 40–50 percent. Both agree that the use of capital fell over the subsequent 150 years, although Jordà and his colleagues argue that it stopped declining and perhaps rose gradually after 1975. They estimate capital ratios at the time of the Subprime Crisis as 5–10 percent while Admati and Hellwig assert it was less than 5 percent, particularly in Europe.

2 Admati and Hellwig (2013) and Admati (2014) set forth the clearest arguments. Cline (2017) offers a critique. The latest update to the Minneapolis Plan to End Too Big to Fail (FRB Minneapolis, 2018) is available online.

This continued the trend begun in 1988 when the G-10 industrialized countries signed the Basel I agreement raising minimum capital standards. In 2010, the Basel III agreement responded to the crisis with additional rules and slightly higher capital standards. Basel I was more concerned with creating a level playing field for banks operating across international boundaries, but Basel III was directly in response to the crisis and was based on the assumption that very low capital ratios increased the probability of bank failures and worsened the financial crisis. In the United States, the 2010 Dodd–Frank financial reform legislation raised the minimum for bank capital.

Common sense seems to tell us that less capital makes banks more vulnerable to crises because it means that banks hold smaller buffers against asset losses caused by borrower defaults. In addition, there is an argument that more debt creates a moral hazard for bank executives and encourages them to take more risk. This was a second reason why there were calls to increase capital requirements for banks. So, not only does less capital and more debt increase vulnerability to a crisis directly through less protection against losses, but it also does so indirectly through an incentive for bank managers to take more risks which inevitably increases the probability of a crisis. Both the issue of debt versus capital to fund banks and the incentives for bankers created by more debt are worth elucidating because they are at the core of the reasons why there has been a push to increase capital ratios. There is a need for additional research on these issues, however, and the answers are perhaps less clear than desired.

10.2 LEVERAGE

Leverage is a measure of the value of an asset relative to the equity share, or capital, of the asset owner. Algebraically, it is (asset value)/(capital). Higher leverage means the asset owners have invested less capital. For example, if the buyer of a house makes a 10 percent down payment, leverage is ten since the down payment is their equity, or capital. With a 20 percent down payment leverage is five, and so forth. Leverage increases the return on investment, but it also increases risk. Consider a bank that funds itself mostly by taking deposits which it combines with its own capital. If the bank makes loans with these funds, then most of the interest they receive is earned through the deployment of the depositor's money, not the bank's own capital. This increases the return on the bank owner's capital relative to what it would have been if they used more capital and fewer deposits (debt) to fund their business. Consider the purchaser of a house again. With a 10 percent down payment, all of the increase in the value of the house is a return on their 10 percent down payment since the buyer of the house gets to keep all the increase in price, if any. A 20 percent down payment may have the benefit of reducing the probability that they might someday owe more than the value of the house if prices fall, but if instead, the house value rises, the gain is spread over a larger investment and earns a smaller rate of return for any given increase in the price.

Leverage is the same principal that helped homebuyers become temporarily rich during the housing boom before the Subprime Crisis, and that stock market speculators used before the Crash of 1929. Before the Subprime Crisis, zero down payment was not uncommon in the United States, and extremely low amounts were the norm. If a homebuyer puts 2 percent down on their new home so that their leverage ratio is fifty, and then the house price rises by 5 percent, the return on investment is 250 percent (five times fifty). Leverage also works in reverse, however, as many subprime borrowers and 1929 stock speculators discovered. A relatively small decline – 2 percent – in house prices will completely wipe out the homeowner's equity. If it is a bank that is using large amounts of leverage, then a small increase in the rate of default on its loans will wipe out the bank's capital and make it insolvent. The lesson is that the higher the leverage ratio, the more fragile the bank, since smaller capital buffers and more debt imply that a smaller downturn in the economy and a smaller increase in loan defaults wipe out the bank's capital and turn a solvent bank into an insolvent one.

The issue of incentives and compensation schemes for bank executives is another reason behind the support for an increase in bank capital requirements. Existing compensation schemes are viewed partly as a system weakness that increases risk and partly as an explanation for the resistance by banks to using more capital and less debt. The argument is that debt provides greater leverage and higher rates of return, while the argument about risky behavior is that bank executives, like everyone else, are less prudent when playing with other people's money. The use of debt causes them to take greater risks to earn higher returns, and since their compensation is often related to the return on bank equity, using debt ultimately causes higher salaries and bonuses for executives.

Whether or not compensation schemes contributed to the crisis is debated. Many economists think it did, including the bipartisan group of fifteen that issued the influential *Squam Lake Report* analyzing the causes of the crisis (French, et al., 2010: 75–85). Several other economists that have written extensively about finance and the crisis agree with this perspective (Blinder, 2013: 81–84; Stiglitz, 2010: 151–153; Shiller, 2012: 23–24). Lo (2012), on the other hand, cites research showing that executive compensation was so heavily weighted toward bonuses and stock options that any rational executive would not have taken excessive risks since they would have put their own income and wealth in jeopardy. Lo's point is that executives were not gambling with other people's money only, but were also gambling with their own, and many of them lost large fortunes when the crisis began. As examples, he cites the cases of Ken Lewis at Bank of America and Jimmy Cayne at Bear Stearns. Lewis' $190 million in stocks and options at the end of 2006 were worth $48 million by the end of 2008, while Cayne managed to sell his interest in Bear Stearns for $61 million in 2008, after it was valued at over $1 billion in 2007. Those are both big losses, but even so, it is hard to see Lewis or Cayne as victims and it is easy to believe that executives at large financial firms might often believe that they are somehow different, that they are capable of managing risk in ways that others cannot. This would mean that they are just normal human beings who suffer from the all too common malady of overconfidence bias. Overconfidence and the illusion of control explain the finding that executives take more risks, not fewer, when they have their own money at stake (Malmendier and Tate, 2008; Kahneman, 2011: 258).

10.3 LIMITS TO RISK MODELS

Bank executives argue that their high leverage ratios are not as risky as they seem, primarily because they are experts at managing risk and their assets are diversified over a wide range of asset types, including loans to other banks, securities, derivatives, currencies, real estate, and so forth. Diversification and other risk management techniques, they claim, enable them to avoid a concentration of assets that will simultaneously fall in value. When there is turmoil, some asset may lose value but others will gain. Hence, the probability of a significant decline in the overall value of their portfolio is extremely unlikely, so unlikely as to be negligible.

In a famous quote during the financial crisis, the *Financial Times* cites David Viniar, Chief Financial Officer of Goldman Sachs, one of the largest US investment banks before the crisis, as claiming: "We were seeing things that were 25-standard deviation moves, several days in a row" (Dowd et al, 2008, 13 August). Probabilities in finance and other fields are measured statistically, often with the concept of "sigma" which is one standard deviation. A two-sigma event has a 2.275 percent probability; three-sigma is well below 1 percent probability (0.135 percent) and so on, with the probabilities for higher sigma falling nonlinearly. A six-sigma event is so unlikely that it would only occur once every 4,039,906 years. A twenty-five-sigma event is hard to measure given the nonlinearities but according to one estimate, a twenty-sigma event "corresponds to an expected occurrence period measured in years that is ten times larger than the higher of the estimates of the number of particles in the Universe." And that is a twenty-sigma event, not twenty-five-sigma (Dowd, et al., 2008).

As the Chief Financial Officer for Goldman Sachs, Mr. Viniar undoubtedly knows something about probability. His exclamation has to be seen as an exaggeration made to emphasize his view that events in the market were highly unusual. Outsiders not familiar with Goldman Sachs's risk models or its trading strategies in 2007 have two choices. We can agree that the events were completely unusual, albeit not twenty-five-sigma, or we can believe that the risk models used by Mr. Viniar were not appropriately calibrated to measure the real probabilities. That is, either we observed something extremely unlikely or our idea of unlikely is incorrect. When confronted with two explanations, Occam's razor tells us that the one that relies on more likely events is almost always the better choice.

Mutual fund companies are obligated to provide a prospectus to individuals thinking about investing with them, and the disclaimer that past performance is no guarantee of future performance. Risk models should come with a similar disclaimer, but unfortunately they do not. Models of risk are incredibly complex but are inevitably based on historical relationships. The reason history plays a role is because risk models have to analyze how one variable, say interest rates, influences another variable, say exchange rates. We can theorize a relationship such that, all else being equal, a rise in interest rates will cause a rise in the value of currency used to buy those assets, but we don't know the strength of that relationship or what other variables might be changing simultaneously. Is the interest rate–currency relationship constant or does it change over time; is it strong or weak, and how important are other variables? Builders of economic models calibrate them with actual measurements of the strength of these relationships under different scenarios by looking at data from a range of times and places. But once they step into the real world of actual measurements, they are relying on current and historical patterns that only go back as far as their datasets. A lot of economic data loses its granularity after thirty to forty years into the past, and although datasets are improving as economic historians put together more complete time series for more countries, there are still very great limits. Most financial data are hardly long enough or complete enough for econometricians to have observed all possible relationships or to have reliable measures for the probabilities of all possible scenarios.

These models have increased dramatically in mathematical sophistication in recent decades, but that simply means they contain a more sophisticated and complex understanding of the underlying connectedness between different variables. The probabilities of different scenarios remain as uncertain as ever. That is, we can say that given the way economic variables behaved from, say, 1980 to 2015, we know what the probabilities of different scenarios are as long as those variables continue to behave as they did in the past and as long as nothing fundamentally new enters the picture. This is not a reason for confidence in our knowledge of possible outcomes, a point that is reenforced by the fact that risk models frequently perform very well right up to the point when they stop performing well. The most dramatic breakdown in models happens when unusual patterns such as those during the Great Depression occur. For example, housing prices rarely fall simultaneously in all fifty states of the United States, but occasionally they do, and the probability of an infrequent event such as that can hardly be captured by thirty or forty years of measurement with only one or possibly two examples. Inherently, there is no way to accurately estimate the probability of a simultaneous decline in house prices throughout the entire country. Risk models are incredibly sophisticated and necessary and can perform very well over periods of time, but there is a fundamental level of uncertainty about the future that they cannot address.

10.4 RESISTANCE TO INCREASING CAPITAL

In addition to the bank executive's confidence in their ability to manage risk, another reason given for rejecting the greater use of equity to fund bank operations is that the claim that it increases banking costs. This point is debated with good arguments on both sides. A famous theorem in financial economics, called the Modigliani–Miller Theorem, states that under a number of assumptions, there is no difference in costs to firms if they are financed with debt or equity (Modigliani and Miller, 1958). Referring back to the discussion of leverage or debt financing, it was argued that leverage increases returns to the invested capital. However, what was not mentioned is that if a firm has higher risks associated with higher debt financing, then its lenders will charge higher interest rates and capital investors will demand higher returns as compensation for the greater risk. All else being equal, greater debt financing increases unit borrowing costs and reduces the share price. Leverage increases with more debt, but according to the Modigliani–Miller Theorem, the advantages are offset by higher costs, and in the end, it does not matter for their overall costs if banks and other firms use debt or equity to finance themselves. One of the assumptions of the theorem, however, is that there are no taxes or subsidies. This assumption is not met, in part because the largest banks, especially those that have been identified as systemically important banks (SIBs), receive significant subsidies which reduce the costs of using debt financing. The subsidies exist because large and SIBs are likely to be bailed out.[3] The IMF describes the consequences as follows:

> Because the creditors of SIBs do not bear the full cost of failure, they are willing to provide funding at a lower cost than warranted by the institutions risk profiles. They also have little incentive to monitor and punish excessive risk taking. SIBs then may take advantage of the lower funding cost to increase their leverage and engage in riskier activities (IMF, 2014b: 102).

How large are the subsidies? This point is difficult to answer with any certainty but the IMF's research shows that subsidies are worth twenty to sixty billion dollars a year in the United States and ninety to three hundred billion dollars in the euro area, where less has been

3 Note that the Dodd–Frank legislation passed after the financial crisis requires regulators to specify banks and other financial institutions that are considered SIFIs. Dodd–Frank limits the ability of the Fed or the Treasury Department to bailout banks. In effect, this subsidy described has been removed, although in the event of a crisis that threatens the system, it is uncertain what will happen. The Fed or the Treasury could do nothing, or they could go to Congress to seek permission to act.

done to eliminate the subsidies and too big to fail is a more serious problem. Others have argued that in the United States at least, the subsidies have become small and are disappearing as a result of the financial reforms put into place after the crisis (Konczal, 2015). The IMF estimates of twenty to sixty billion dollars is consistent with this point given that the estimate is for the entire financial sector and represents only a tiny fraction of the assets available.

Does the Modigliani–Miller Theorem apply, or are the deviations from the key assumptions so large that it is not relevant or only partially relevant as Cline (2017) asserts? At this point there is not a strong consensus in any direction, but the debate about the costs of equity versus debt financing is somewhat of a sideshow. The most important question is about the very large economic and social costs of banking crises. The costs of a banking crisis, particularly if it is contagious and spreads through the system, impact many businesses and individuals beyond the banking system. Therefore, a slightly higher cost of doing banking business, if it exists, may be well worth the price from a societal standpoint if increased capital ratios reduce the probability of a crisis. Banking interests have lobbied hard against being forced to rely on more equity and less debt financing, as is only normal for an industry that believes its costs will be pushed up by those changes. But if regulations can be implemented to reduce the probability of a systemic banking crisis, the benefits to society almost surely outweigh the costs.

10.5 CAPITAL AND RISK REDUCTION

Capital requirements specify the minimum amount of capital as a share of assets that banks must use to finance their operations. Capital can be acquired in two main ways. Either a firm sells shares or, more commonly, it retains some of its profits. The questions for reformers are whether increased capital requirements will reduce the probability of banking crises and what effects they will have on recovery from a crisis. It has been a common assumption that increased capital requirements will reduce the probability of financial crises, but not all analysts agree. Jordà, et al., (2017) compile historical data for bank assets and liabilities in seventeen advanced economies between 1870 and 2013, and find no reduction in crisis probabilities with an increase in bank capital ratios.[4] Their sample is limited to a subset of advanced economies, but it is one of the few papers that does not rely on case studies or a theoretical model. In a similar vein, other analysts argue that increased capital levels would not have prevented the Subprime Crisis, since it started in the relatively unregulated shadow banking sector, and financial innovation, credit booms, and other factors are more important (Gorton, 2010).

If a decline in the probability of crises is uncertain with an increase in capital ratios, it does not mean that increases are unnecessary or unwarranted. This is because low capital ratios cause the costs of financial crises to be greater, with longer recovery periods. When capital ratios are lower, the breakdown in the financial system is more severe and takes longer to repair, delaying recovery throughout the economy. Empirical research on the relationship between capital ratios and the probability of financial crises is still developing but regardless of the outcome, there is robust evidence that the severity of the crisis is greater when capital ratios are lower and bank debt is higher.

A final question is the optimal level of capital. There is not an agreed answer and estimates by academic researchers vary widely, from around 5 percent to the 20–30 percent range. Furthermore, there are questions surrounding the risk characteristics of different types of assets, and general agreement that capital requirements can be less when assets are less risky. Capital too is not homogenous and certain types of capital are considered less adequate than other types. Under the Dodd–Frank financial reforms, capital requirements for many larger US banks are in the 8–10 percent range and 4–5 percent

4 In fact, they find the opposite: crises were more frequent when capital ratios were higher. They argue that this is likely due to reverse causation as financial crises cause banks to add to their capital. Crises, in their view, are much more likely to be triggered by credit booms.

of assets for smaller, regional banks. Two of the leading experts on this issue, Anat Admati and Martin Hellwig (2013) argue that capital ratios should be much higher, more like 20–30 percent, while Cline (2017) estimates an "optimum" at 7–8 percent of total assets, which is 12–14 percent once the risk characteristics are taken into account. This puts the Dodd–Frank standard slightly below his estimated optimum, and well below the standard proposed by Admati and Hellwig (2013) or by the Federal Reserve Bank of Minneapolis (FRB Minneapolis, 2018).

Increases in bank capital may or may not raise the cost of banking, and may or may not reduce the probability of crises. These are issues that require more research in order to have a clearer picture of the situation. More capital will not prevent all future crises and, as noted, probably would not have prevented the last one (Gorton, 2010). As long as shadow banks or some new version of financial intermediation are outside the system of bank regulation, increased capital requirements for regular banks has no effect. What increased capital requirements are likely to accomplish, however, is a reduction in the severity of financial crises and faster recoveries from their worst effects.

11 Monetary Policy Does Not Always Work

11.1 OVERCONFIDENCE

In the 1980s and 1990s, Americans began to believe that a well-run Federal Reserve could use the tools of monetary policy to keep the economy on a steady growth path with low rates of inflation. The Fed could not eliminate all recessions, but as long as it did its job correctly it could limit their length and depth to the point that a long, protracted economic decline was no longer probable. This point of view developed out of the hard won victory of monetary policy against inflation in the early 1980s, and out of a grand theoretical argument that fiscal policy, the primary tool for countering recession in the 1960s and 1970s, was flawed and ineffective.

Confidence in monetary policy's ability to keep the economy out of serious trouble meant that most observers and policy makers were quickly overwhelmed by the magnitude of the Subprime Crisis and were without a clear action plan once interest rates began to approach zero. If a zero rate of interest does not stimulate recovery, then what? Conventional monetary policy ceases to have much of a role once interest rates are at their lower bound.[1] The Chairman of the Federal Reserve, Ben Bernanke, was a student of both the 1930s and Japan's long economic stagnation of the 1990s and 2000s. Consequently, the Federal Reserve in collaboration with the Treasury Department and the FDIC developed a variety of strategies, including the unconventional monetary policy known as quantitative

1 Economists also believed that a zero interest rate was a natural lower bound. We have learned that it is not, and central banks have paid negative interest. Interest rates have not yet gone much below zero, however, so this chapter continues to talk about a zero lower bound while recognizing that it is not an absolute limit.

easing (QE) (Bernanke, 2015: 337–46, 418–421). As interest rates approached 0 percent, the Fed moved to a more aggressive set policies. Those included lending and asset purchases which were intended to restore liquidity, to make a market for assets with uncertain values, and to rescue systemically important financial institutions, including nonbanks. A majority of economists agree that the monetary measures were helpful in avoiding another Great Depression but even so, the recession lasted longer than any since the 1930s, and was followed by a period of such weak growth that many Americans continued to believe the country was still in recession long after it was technically over (IGM Forum, 2014b). The length of time before the economy returned to its pre-recession level of output was nearly twice as long as any since the 1930s, and was more than three times longer than the average of the ten other post-World War II recessions (NBER, 2010). While recessions accompanied by a financial crisis tend to be deeper and to last longer than recessions without a crisis, the lesson from this experience was that monetary policy helped avoid another Great Depression, but it clearly was not able to stop a very serious recession.

11.2 THE RISE OF MONETARY POLICY

How did policy makers come to believe that monetary policy could be effective in the face a Great Depression-scale event? The answer has several strands, including Friedman and Schwartz's research on the Great Depression, the taming of inflation in the 1980s by the Fed under the leadership of Paul Volcker, the rejection of Keynesianism by macroeconomists in the 1980s, and an unusual period of low volatility in the US economy from the mid-1980s until the Great Recession. Each of these elements played a role in shaping a belief that the normal pattern of expansion and recession had been tamed by the judicious application of monetary policy. Not everyone shared this belief, but there developed a general sense among mainstream economists that history was over. Never again would an advanced industrial economy have to experience something like the Great Depression, and even the much smaller swings of the business cycle during normal times would be better controlled. The story begins with the work of Friedman and Schwartz on the problem of the Great Depression.

Milton Friedman's campaign to restore the quantity theory of money was mostly ignored in the 1950s and 1960s, and monetary policy as a tool to regulate economic fluctuations was mostly dismissed. When he and Anna Schwartz published their monumental *The Monetary History of the United States* with the long chapter devoted to the failings of the Federal Reserve in the 1930s, their arguments began to gain traction. The consistent logic of monetary theory, Friedman and Schwartz's use of supporting data to show the role of monetary policy in the Great Depression, and the growing problem of inflation in the United States, were all strong arguments in favor of monetarism. Monetarism is the proposition that the level of prices is determined by the quantity of money in circulation and that inflation is everywhere and at all times a monetary phenomenon. Further, there was an added belief that monetary policy could be a powerful and useful tool for managing short-run swings in economic activity.

In August, 1979, Paul Volcker became the Chairman of the Federal Reserve Bank. Inflation was 11.8 percent that month. It began a long gradual increase in the mid-1960s that culminated in a relatively sudden jump to higher levels beginning in 1976. Volcker turned Fed policy toward an exclusive focus on combatting rising prices, and in the process he temporarily sacrificed the Fed's other mandate to ensure adequate economic growth. The result was a brief recession in 1980, followed by a more prolonged one in 1981 and 1982, but a rapid decline in the inflation rate after it peaked at 14.6 percent in March, 1980. Volcker's restriction on money supply growth successfully tamed inflation and also seemed to confirm the teachings of Friedman and Schwartz that inflation is a monetary phenomenon.

Volcker's success was widely admired and appreciated as rising inflation was a plague on American households and businesses. Before monetary policy brought it under control, inflation caused thirty-year fixed mortgages to climb above 18 percent in 1981, shrank the real value of most bank savings accounts, and reduced the purchasing power of Americans living on fixed incomes. The recessions induced by Volcker's contractionary monetary policy were painful, but they stopped inflation and eliminated the uncertainty caused by high and rising prices. The success of Volcker's experiment raised the credibility of monetary policy as an effective, flexible tool, for managing the macroeconomy, in part by showing that it could be deployed far more rapidly than fiscal policy and, most importantly, more effectively. Monetary policy was ascendant.

At more or less the same time as Volcker's monetary approach to controlling inflation, developments in the field of macroeconomics pointed toward a theory of the business cycle that left no room for managing the economy through fiscal policy. This was a direct assault on Keynes' theory that a slump caused by a lack of demand in the economy could be shortened and made less severe through increased government spending. A fundamental tenet of orthodox Keynesianism as it was developed by his followers in the 1950s and 1960s was that an economic slowdown caused by a decline in demand can be counteracted by an increase in spending, as for example, when wartime spending definitely ended the Great Depression of the 1930s. The focus of Keynes's theory was a Great Depression-type event in which an economic slump is caused by a lack of demand, but the supply shocks of the 1970s were entirely different. A shortage of demand was not the problem, instead it was supply constraints on output that were caused mainly by oil shortages. Under those circumstances, more government spending worsened inflation and made fiscal policy appear as an ineffective tool for managing the economy. The failure of Keynesian policies of the 1950s and 1960s to resolve macroeconomic problems caused by supply bottlenecks in the 1970s had an explanation in the new macroeconomic theories emerging around the same time. These new theories showed that instead of government spending increasing output, it simply crowded out private spending and had no real effect on the economy whatsoever. It did cause inflation, though, as the increase in demand pushed up prices.

This anti-Keynesian counterrevolution was led by a group of mathematically sophisticated economists, including Robert Lucas, Thomas Sargent, and Edward Prescott, who were each eventually awarded Nobel Prizes.

11.3 NEW CLASSICAL ECONOMICS

The new ideas came to be known as the New Classical synthesis. It hypothesized that recessions were caused by changes in output such as sudden temporary declines in productivity that raised production costs and led to layoffs. In the models proposed by Lucas, Prescott, and Sargent, wages and prices would adjust quickly, so that unemployment would correct itself through wage declines. These ideas were consistent with Friedman's work which assumed that market economies were quickly self-adjusting if left alone by governments, and that output would naturally tend toward its long run level with an adequate number of jobs for those that wanted to work. If workers remained unemployed, it is because they choose not to accept the new lower wage rate, or because unions prevented them from going back to work, or because government interfered with work incentives in the form of unemployment insurance, food stamps and other income supports. If left to itself, the market would quickly reestablish full employment, albeit at lower wages and prices. In the end, no one would be worse off since the real level of output would be the same as it was before the temporary productivity shift.

This model of the economy is called New Classical economics because it represents a return to pre-Keynesian ideas of self-correcting markets that never deviate far from a full employment equilibrium, except when governments, unions, trade associations, or other organizations intervene. These models were supported by a higher degree of mathematical consistency and elegance than the typical Keynesian model in which wages and prices do not move up and down symmetrically. In the typical Keynesian model, wages and prices are sticky downwards and are much less likely to fall during a recession than they are to rise during a boom. Exactly why wages do not easily fall is difficult to incorporate into a mathematical model that assumes profit maximization by firms and utility maximization by workers. New Classical economists, by contrast, get around this difficulty by assuming that prices and wages are symmetrical in their ability to move up and down. Furthermore, their models of the macroeconomy usually assumed that price and wage adjustments result from the individual microlevel maximization decisions of workers and firms, so the models were preferred because they built up a macroeconomy out of the micro-units that comprise it. If a worker is unemployed, he or she can find work by lowering their wage demands; if they refuse to do so, then they are being unreasonable (irrational) and apparently, do not want work at the (new) prevailing wage and cannot be considered unemployed.

By the late 1970s, New Classical economics was gaining strength and by the late 1980s it had captured most graduate programs, economic journals, and the research agenda of macroeconomists. Keynesian models did not disappear altogether, but they were no longer at the frontier of the field and were seen as less rigorous and out-of-date. They did have a couple of strengths, however. Keynesian models could be used to forecast the economy, unlike New Classical models which assumed that the economy was at full employment except when it was feeling the effects of a random, unpredictable, shift in productivity. Consequently, Wall Street firms, large corporations, and the Federal Reserve continued to use Keynesian models in their planning and forecasting units. A second advantage is that Keynesian models offer policy choices when there is a recession. New Classical models can only tell policy makers to hold on, wait for the crisis to end; it will be over soon if you do nothing. The New Classical story does not sell well to many businesses and government agencies, and some economists have noted that we are all Keynesians in a recession.

While the causes of the business cycle hypothesized by New Classical economists held that fiscal policy was ineffective, support was growing for the use of monetary policy. In part, this was a result of the work of Friedman and his colleagues, in part it was due to the experiment with monetary policy carried out by Federal Reserve Chairman Paul Volcker, and in part it was the result of the Fed's management of inflation and economic growth through monetary policy after Volcker. As the 1980s unfolded, economic fluctuations seemed to lessen. Changes to the money supply helped to smooth adjustments in the economy by providing a temporary monetary stimulus to counter a slowdown or a temporary monetary contraction to counter an unsustainable expansion. Eventually, the period from the mid-1980s until the Great Recession of 2007–2009 came to be called the Great Moderation and was noted for the mildness of both the downturns and the expansions and for the decline in inflation volatility.[2]

11.4 THE GREAT MODERATION

It is only a step or two from observing a reduction in economic fluctuations to believing that the business cycle has been tamed. Many economists, perhaps most, began to believe that with the right application of monetary policy, the United States could avoid both serious inflation and serious recession. Nobel Prize Winner and macroeconomic theorist Robert Lucas was prominent in this group, proclaiming in his 2003 Presidential Address to the American Economic Association that the "central problem of depression prevention has been solved, for all practical purposes, and has in fact been solved for many decades" (Lucas, 2003). Lucas reflected the mainstream of US economic thought and many other economists adopted similar views, including those less inclined to see the economy as always tending to be at or near full employment (DeLong and Tyson, 2013).

After the Great Recession and the slow recovery, it is much harder to justify this view. It even seems a bit odd that anyone would have taken this position, although it continues to be revived

2 Some economists have argued that it is not over; see Gadea, Gomez-Loscos, and Pérez-Quirós (2015).

(Quiggin, 2010). In fact, there are several reasons why economists began to believe they had conquered the business cycle. First, until the Great Recession, data indicated that economic fluctuations were significantly reduced and, importantly, there was a credible story about the role of central banks together with a more advanced understanding of monetary policy. The story was key since it explained the data and lent force to the claim that radical swings in the business cycle were a thing of the past. Furthermore, it was a happy story about advances in economic management, and it fed the prejudices of those who wanted to reduce the importance of presidents and congresses in economic management – relatively simple monetary policy was all that was needed to keep the economy on track. Politics were taken out of economic management since elected officials did not have a role to play in avoiding economic fluctuations.

The fact that there was not a long enough data series to be certain that economic fluctuations had been reduced permanently should have been cautionary since it opened the door to a variety of cognitive biases. Perhaps most importantly, the narrative bias lets people see patterns in past outcomes that tell the story we want to tell (Kahneman, 2011). Claims of so momentous an achievement as conquering the business cycle should have produced a great deal of skepticism, particularly when it was based on fifteen or twenty years of data. But it was a story of great achievement in economic science and was too good to question, particularly since it supported a more hands-off approach to managing the economy. In addition to the narrative bias, research economists probably suffered from confirmation bias the bane of every scientist, particularly social scientists, that caused them to accept confirmatory interpretations of their results and reject unsupportive ones.

Economists should also have been more skeptical of their own interpretations of the Great Moderation because most of them above the age of fifty in 2000, were taught about the liquidity trap and a period in the 1930s when monetary policy was ineffective. Once interest rates hit zero, there is very little monetary stimulus left to be provided by a central bank unless it turns to highly unconventional and uncertain policies. Older economists were taught this, but the lesson seemed irrelevant by 2000. This may have been due to a view of 0 percent interest rates as a form of out-of-date, old-school Keynesianism, or because it was believed that monetary policy had improved dramatically and would never allow zero interest rates. Japan's economy in the 1990s was a counter-example to the idea that zero interest rates are unlikely if not impossible, and that monetary policy might be ineffective at some point. But perhaps the Japanese case was considered exotic and not particularly relevant to Western economies by all but a handful of Western economists (Krugman, 1998; Bernanke, 2000a). The failure to consider the possibility of a return to 1930s-type problems may also have reflected a general lack of historical imagination by economists, most of whom trained in programs that have eliminated economic history requirements over the last decades. Perhaps it was some of all of these reasons, in varying proportions with different economists. What is certain, however, is that the profession was not sufficiently skeptical of grandiose claims of having tamed the business cycle.

11.5 ZERO LOWER BOUND

To be certain, not all economists were on the bandwagon. Paul Krugman, for example, wrote a well-known paper in 1998 that developed a more up-to-date model of monetary policy ineffectiveness and used it to argue that Japanese economic stagnation in the 1990s reflected a liquidity trap, defined as a condition in which monetary policy is ineffective (Krugman, 1998). And Richard Koo, a business economist and somewhat of an outsider since he does not work in academia, also explored the Japanese case of stagnation in the 1990s, and the failure of monetary policy to end the malaise (Koo, 2008).

Japan was the canary in the mine for monetary policy. In the 1980s it was one of the fastest growing economies in the world with its GDP per capita on a trajectory to pass the United States in a few years. The bursting of bubbles in real estate and stock prices in 1989 brought an end to its high growth and turned the 1990s and 2000s into years of on-again, off-again, recession, frequently falling prices, and 0 percent interest rates on Japanese treasury bills. The economy of Japan has been a real-time lesson for analysts of stagnation and ineffective monetary policy.

There is no shortage of explanations and policy proposals: The aging of Japan's population and its demographic decline has reduced the demand for goods and services and contributes to slower growth and low inflation; monetary stimulus, when it was tried, was too timid and was not left in place long enough; fiscal stimulus also has not been consistent; and the government and private firms both have too much debt on their books. All of these arguments have been put forward but perhaps the most interesting was made by Ben Bernanke in 1999 while still teaching at Princeton and before he became a member of the Federal Reserve Board (Bernanke, 2000a). In a paper written for the American Economic Association annual conference and later published in a small volume devoted to Japan's crisis, Bernanke argued that Japan could escape its period of slow growth and monetary ineffectiveness with unconventional, extremely expansive, monetary policies. His argument foreshadowed the actions he would take nearly a decade later in 2008 when, as Chairman of the Federal Reserve, he would begin a series of unconventional monetary policy actions known as quantitative easing.

Normal monetary policy is conducted primarily through buying and selling short term government treasury bills. In order to stimulate the economy, the Fed buys T-Bills from banks and others. The seller gets cash or more precisely, an increase in the reserves it holds with the Fed. The increase in reserves causes interest rates to fall and, under normal conditions, business investment and consumer purchases of big-ticket items like appliances, cars, and houses, will increase. In theory, the Fed can only influence short term rates. Long term rates are determined in the private economy, and are understood to be a reflection of private sector expectations for future short term rates. By comparison, the goal of QE is to influence long term interest rates. With QE, the central bank buys very large amounts of longer term government bonds and private-sector bonds in an attempt to bring down long term interest rates. It is about the only option for monetary policy once short term rates hit zero and the central bank can no longer use them to stimulate the economy.

QE was the policy Bernanke advised for the Bank of Japan in 1999, it is the policy the Federal Reserve implemented beginning in 2008, and it was adopted by the European Central Bank some years after the Fed. At the beginning of the financial crisis in August, 2007, the Fed's balance sheet had just over $870 billion in assets. By the end of December, 2008, its assets had grown to $2.2 trillion (157 percent increase) and by the end of 2014 it reached $4.5 trillion, more than a five-fold increase since 2007 (Board of Governors, 2015). The Fed clearly was not making the same mistake it made in the 1930s when it failed to support the financial system with increased liquidity. The Fed's expansion of its balance sheet through asset purchases created a market for stressed securities and provided liquidity to financial institutions. It was exactly the kind of policy action that Bernanke, Friedman, and other students of the Great Depression, criticized the Fed for failing to do in the 1930s. It was expansionary monetary policy on steroids, and it was extreme because conditions were extreme.

If a five-fold increase in the monetary base cannot pull the economy out of a liquidity trap, then perhaps it is time to rethink the theory. In truth, however, the theory of liquidity traps and what to do about them has not reached a consensus and economists continue to debate the issues. Bernanke's position when writing about Japan, and in light of his studies of the 1930s, was that the liquidity had to be added to the economy in great quantity (Bernanke, 2000a). Once businesses and households see that this will add to inflation, it will encourage them to make purchases before prices rise. Consequently, the Fed under his leadership adopted the unconventional and very extensive programs of QE1, QE2, and QE3. While each of these were somewhat different in the assets they bought and how they put liquidity into the market, together they led to the noted five-fold increase in the monetary base and the expectation among some observers that inflation was about to take off. A decade after the start of QE1, inflation remained low and some might argue that the Fed should have doubled the money supply again if it wanted to end the recession and slow growth period sooner. While there may be economic justification, there was no political space for the Fed to undertake such an experiment. Consequently, Bernanke's idea, drawn from the work of Friedman and Schwartz on the monetary history of the Great Depression, that monetary expansion of sufficient size can solve the problem of economic stagnation, will probably never be put to its ultimate test. But the existing expansion, as extensive as it was, seems to have settled the issue as to whether a monetary expansion can always pull an economy out of stagnation – it can help, but it cannot do the job alone.

This has led some to argue that a fiscal expansion is the only way out of slow growth and the stagnation of prices and wages. Since his 1998 paper, Krugman has consistently argued that the monetary authority should convince businesses and households that it will act irresponsibly – that inflation is coming because the increases in the money supply are permanent, not temporary (Krugman, 1998). But the threat to act irresponsibly and to let inflation take off has to be accompanied by a fiscal expansion or else the threat may not appear credible. In other words, monetary expansion by itself is insufficient.

As always, there were observers who thought the Fed did act irresponsibly and that its policies would undoubtedly cause high inflation and rising interest rates. This view, which was a mix of different arguments, has gone into hiding after a decade of no inflationary pressures. Some anti-QE views were outright conspiracy theories about government underreporting inflation, while others used theoretical models in which a five-fold increase in the monetary base must cause a significant jump in inflation, and still others simply wanted interest rates to rise. None of these positions grappled directly with the problems caused by the ineffectiveness of monetary policy in a liquidity trap.

If anything, the Great Recession has left macroeconomists with a giant question: in a financial meltdown such as the Great Depression or the Great Recession, after monetary policy has failed to restore growth and interest rates are at zero, what else can be done? A growing consensus of economists holds that fiscal policy consisting of increased government expenditures and selected tax cuts are the only way to shorten the crisis. This has highly charged political implications, however, and is unacceptable to some on the grounds that it requires active government policy, regardless of its efficacy in restoring the economy. Monetary policy does work in many recessions and economic slowdowns, and the cases when it does not have been relatively rare, to date. That could change, however, like everything else, but the assumed infrequency of zero lower bound cases reduces the sense of urgency to prepare an economic strategy for those cases. The fact remains, however: The Great Recession taught those who were paying attention that monetary policy alone cannot prevent all recessions, and it is unwise to think that we have tamed the business cycle.

12 Fiscal Multipliers Are Larger Than Expected

12.1 ACTS OF NATURE

As the United States descended into the Great Depression of the 1930s, economic advice was contradictory and confused. The business community, politicians, and academics called for a variety of different policies: Some wanted government to do nothing, believing that there was not much that government could do, that recessions had to work their way through the economic system, like a poison that has no antidote; others thought government should encourage firms to invest, that they should be allowed to form cartels to control prices and wages and output; and still others favored public works that would put the unemployed back to work. To a large degree, Roosevelt was more successful than Hoover because he kept trying one thing after another. He did not have a comprehensive economic model, or even much of any kind of model, but focused on humanitarian relief as something government could do even if it did not understand how to systematically counter the recession. At least government could aid those who lost their jobs, their homes, and their farms. Roosevelt did not end the Great Depression and we now know that many of his policies and those of his contemporaries were counterproductive and prolonged the recession.

In the 1920s and 1930s, contemporaries of President Hoover and President Roosevelt viewed recessions and depressions as acts of nature that could not be resisted. A depression was seen as an economic equivalent of a hurricane, and if one was coming, it was unavoidable. All you could do was to find shelter and then pick up the pieces after it was over. Recession avoidance and recession cure were not in the tool boxes of economists, and were far outside the considerations of politicians and the general public. Written in the

1930s, John Maynard Keynes's work eventually changed this idea of recessions as unavoidable natural disasters. His simple yet fundamental insight persuasively showed that in a recession caused by a low level of demand for goods and services, there are tools available to policymakers for increasing demand and putting the economy back onto a track toward full employment. If businesses do not invest and households will not or cannot purchase consumer goods, then government can increase aggregate demand in the economy by buying goods and services. This was a new insight largely because Keynes was able to explain that the increase in government spending did not crowd out private spending. Most of his predecessors and most of his contemporaries in business and politics believed that any increase in government purchases would cause a crowding out and lead to a decline in purchases by businesses and households, with zero net increase in the demand for goods and services. Keynes explained how an economy with idle capacity in the form of unemployed labor, shuttered factories, and fallow farmland, can increase aggregate demand and total output: When there is idle capacity, new spending does not crowd out existing spending but can lead to the re-employment of idle labor, capital, and land.

Keynes and nearly all economists then and today believe that depressed economies will return to full employment and normal growth even if there is no intervention. Keynes and most economists today agree that market-based economies tend toward an equilibrium that is at or near full employment, that market economies have powers of self-correction, and that a spell of unemployment and idle resources will pass after a time, even with no actions to counter the slowdown. The main question is how much time has to pass before an economy restores itself to full employment? On this point, the length of the economic slump of the 1930s indicated that the return to normal could be lengthy. Better then, to speed up the process if there are adequate techniques for doing so.

12.2 THE KEYNESIAN CONSENSUS

The remarkable fact about Keynesian economics is that it went from standard theory taught in all textbooks and recommended by all economic advisors in the 1950s and 1960s, to completely ignored by the 1990s and sometimes disparaged as wrong-headed, irrelevant, and even dangerous. How Keynes's insights went from consensus to abandonment is not the story of scientific progress. Not all of its practitioners dropped it since elements of the theories that developed around Keynes's ideas remained practical and useful to business and government, as described in the Chapter 11. Keynesian-type models remained relatively widely used on Wall Street, the Federal Reserve, and other venues where analysts had to evaluate their predictions by holding them up to actual market outcomes. As the Great Recession developed, the "master returned," to paraphrase the title of a book by the economic historian Robert Skidelsky (2009). Keynesian models performed far better than the alternative anti-Keynesian ones, and were much clearer and more accurate in their predictions about the effects of the economic stimulus, austerity, and the unconventional monetary policies adopted first by the Federal Reserve in 2009 and then, later, by the European Central Bank. The story of the rejection of Keynesian modes of analysis is more about politics than it is about economic analysis. It is about the limits to what we know and the overconfidence of academics and policymakers when we reached that point.

The Keynesian Consensus was standard macroeconomic policy after World War II. In particular, the US presidential administrations of Kennedy, Johnson, and Nixon embraced the idea that the federal budget could be used to do even more than Keynes claimed. Not only could government spending and taxing be used to avoid or shorten recessions, but they could be used to "fine-tune" the economy so it did not deviate far from full employment. If a recession threatened, the federal government only needed to increase spending a little, or cut taxes so consumers and businesses might spend more. By the 1960s,

Keynes's great insight into how to counteract a long run decline in output had developed a short run counterpart with his name attached to it. As with many ideas, simplification and blind application were not equivalent to the original idea, nor did they lead to happy outcomes.

In 1964, President Johnson reached an agreement with Congress on a set of tax cuts previously proposed by President Kennedy. The tax cuts affected both individual and corporate taxes in an attempt to provide some stimulus to the economy. Generally, they are regarded as successful and are often considered the high-water mark of the application of Keynes's ideas to fiscal policy. In addition to the tax cuts, however, there was new spending on public programs like food stamps and health care for the elderly (Medicare), as well as new military spending to pursue the Vietnam War. Between 1964 and 1968, the civilian unemployment rate fell by nearly 2.5 percentage points to 3.4 percent in September, 1968, where it stayed until May of 1969. Not surprisingly, inflation which was below 2 percent in the early 1960s began to ratchet upwards. Increases came in waves, with each successive wave reaching higher than the last. The first wave pushed inflation above 6 percent in 1970, then the second peaked above 12 percent in 1974, and the third was more than 14 percent in 1980. Between those peaks, the rate fell, but not as far as the pre-peak average, and each subsequent decline in inflation did not bring it down to earlier levels. The twenty years from approximately 1965 to 1984 would become known as the "Great Inflation."

The respective roles of policy misunderstanding (bad ideas) and politics in the creation of the Great Inflation are still disputed (Meltzer, 2005; Romer, 2005). There is no doubt that the oil shocks of 1973 and 1979 contributed to the inflation, with oil price increases at a time when there were few alternatives to fossil fuels and conservation efforts were just beginning, but Federal Reserve policy accommodated the price increases with relatively easy money. Their behavior led to retrospective questions as to whether Fed officials understood that they could counteract the price effects of a supply-side shock with a demand-side monetary contraction, or whether the Fed was simply trying to support incumbent presidents with accommodative monetary policy. In either case, the Great Inflation was the turning point in support for Keynesian ideas.

There is a complex interaction between economic ideas and political trends. Economists and other social scientists are rooted in a time and place to the extent that it is impossible to completely disentangle the effects of political ideology on academic theorizing. The Great Inflation of the 1970s led directly into a rejection of Keynesian modes of analysis by academic economists at nearly the same time as political thinking began to favor more free-market policies. Ronald Reagan's election in 1980 followed on the heels of Margaret Thatcher's election in the United Kingdom, and both were accompanied by radical shifts in the political landscape around the globe. Throughout the 1980s, state led development was rejected outright or its importance played down in places as disparate as Latin America, China, and even the USSR by the end of the decade (Yergin and Stanislaw, 1998).

12.3 THE MULTIPLIER

Political trends were moving against the idea that states must play an active role in economic management and were reinforced by internal problems of Keynesian analysis. Throughout the 1960s and 1970s, proponents of Keynesian policies had not been able to precisely calibrate Keynes's central insight so that it could be turned into a ready-to-use policy. Keynes had argued that during a recession caused by a lack of demand, increases in government spending or cuts in taxes would stimulate the economy and push it in the direction of full employment. But how much spending or tax cutting was necessary? That was impossible to answer with any certainty. If a government increased spending by $100 billion, for example, what would the effect be on GDP? $100 billion? Or would the additional spending cause other changes, such as encouraging businesses to make new investments, so that the ultimate effect was more than that? Or, if the spending and consequent increase in economic activity caused prices and interest rates to rise, could the effect be less than the original $100 million? The effect, whatever it was, came to be called the multiplier. For example, if an intentional increase in government spending of $100 causes a net change in GDP of $100, the multiplier is one. If the net change is $200, the multiplier is two, and if it is only $50, then the multiplier is one-half.

It is difficult to state precisely what the multiplier is because it changes, depending on a variety of other, often unpredictable, factors. If monetary policy is restrictive, it will offset some of the expansion set in motion by the fiscal policy. If the economy has bottlenecks or is near full employment, then the multiplier cannot be as large since there is not enough slack in the economy to produce significantly greater output and the result of increased government spending will be mostly in the form of higher prices. Other relevant factors include changes in interest rates, currency values, and debt levels in both the private and the public sectors. Economists of the 1960s and 1970s were aware of some of these issues but did not have the data or computing power to investigate them in the way that is possible today.

Confusion about the precise impact of a change in government spending was a weakness in the analysis and added to the criticisms of Keynesianism that it was inflationary and increased the size of the deficit. Nor were these the only problems. In addition, it was cumbersome since changes in spending and taxation had to pass through Congress first, which delayed their implementation and made them less useful for managing short-run changes in the business cycle. The economy is in constant motion and by the time a president and Congress could agree on a course of action, appropriate necessary funding, and begin to implement a policy, economic conditions would almost certainly be different. The lag in policymaking and its implementation meant that Keynesian fiscal policy was often responding to conditions from last year or the year before.

The lack of precision and the cumbersomeness involved in using Keynesian fiscal policies were practical problems but there were also theoretical problems that developed at more or less the same time as the Great Inflation. Policy makers during the Kennedy and Johnson administrations of the 1960s believed that there was a permanent tradeoff between inflation and unemployment. In effect, they held that there was a menu of inflation–unemployment pairs and policy makers could choose whichever felt most comfortable. If they wanted relatively low unemployment, then inflation would be relatively higher, and vice versa. The hypothesized relationship between unemployment and inflation is called the Phillips Curve and seemed to be a stable tradeoff until the Great Inflation (Phillips, 1958).[1] Most economists now agree that it is stable as long as expectations of future inflation do not change. In the 1950s and early 1960s, when everyone expected inflation to be near zero, the tradeoff seemed to hold. In the late 1960s, as the Great Inflation began to takeoff, expectations about future inflation began to change, and along with it, there were changes in the tradeoffs between inflation and unemployment. During the Great Inflation, a 4 percent unemployment rate that was previously associated with a 2 percent rate of inflation became associated with a 4 percent rate of inflation, then a 6 percent rate, and so on, as everyone began to revise their expectations based on their experiences of rising inflation.

12.4 EXPECTATIONS

Economic theorists began to see that the key to understanding the changing set of tradeoffs between inflation and unemployment was in how people formed their expectations of future inflation. If they thought that fiscal policies would lead to higher prices, then they would anticipate and behave accordingly, for example by demanding wage increases that would keep up with the expected increase in prices. A central question that emerged from this line of reasoning was about the actual process people used to form expectations. There

[1] Milton Friedman (1968) presciently explained why there is not a stable, long run, tradeoff between inflation and unemployment.

are many ways to model expectations formation and here was an opportunity for economic assumptions of rationality to begin to influence thinking on the macroeconomy. What better way to form expectations than to assume that everyone used all available information to form their ideas. That is what a rational person would do, and even if no one is precisely accurate in their guesses about future inflation, there is a kind of wisdom in crowds such that one person's underestimate will be offset by another person's overestimate. We all miss, but our errors cancel out because our misses are random and not systematic. This assumption was labeled "rational expectations" and was grafted onto economic theory in the late 1970s and early 1980s, during the Great Inflation.[2]

If the breakdown in the stable tradeoff between inflation and unemployment undermined the usefulness of Keynesian fiscal policy as a short run stabilizer, the assumption of rational expectations could be used to kill it altogether. The necessary next step was to ask what a rational consumer would do in the face of increased budget deficits caused by government spending designed to end a recession. The answer was obvious: They would cut back on their consumption spending in order to prepare for the higher future taxes they will be charged as a result of the deficit. Hence, government spending crowds out private spending, completely, and we are back to the pre-Keynesian era thinking about government expenditures. And, it was argued that recessions would disappear on their own because rational utility-maximizing consumers and rational profit-maximizing businesses know what is happening, they adjust their expectations of prices and wages accordingly, and the economy is reset at its long run natural rate of unemployment. If a recession comes, the lack of spending will cause prices and wages to decline, and then employment will increase back to its pre-recession level as lower wages induce firms to hire more workers. If government tries to boost the economy, prices and wages will

2 The foremost thinker in the "rational expectations revolution" was John Muth (1961). His work was ignored for many years, however, until economists began to look for better ways to model expectations.

increase as everyone recognizes the coming inflation. Doing nothing lets the economy seek its own equilibrium where employment is at the "Goldilocks" rate, not too high, not too low, and inflation is stable. The conclusion of this line of inquiry and theorizing was that government spending has little or no effect on the real economy. It affects prices and wages, but not real output. Hence, the multiplier is zero.

By the mid1980s, criticisms of Keynesian analysis had taken their toll. Keynesian fiscal policy was too cumbersome to implement. It was inflationary. It caused budget deficits. It led to unwanted government programs and inefficient economic interventions. And, theoretically, it was not capable of curing a recession. Each of these points has some validity, just not all the time or in every case. Keynesian stimulus can be implemented relatively quickly when the minds of legislators and the chief executive are focused on a rapidly collapsing economy;[3] stimulus spending can be inflationary, but when consumers and businesses are sitting on the sidelines and there is slack in the economy, there is a lot of room for increasing demand before prices begin to take off; stimulus spending usually increases the deficit in the short run, but if it aids in economic recovery, deficits in the long run will be less than they would have been; stimulus is a government intervention, but it can be done in ways that minimize distortions, such as repairing crumbling infrastructure; and there are theoretical holes in Keynesian models, but that mainly testifies to the limits of our understanding of economic forces and our limited abilities to model the economy. There is no doubt that the macroeconomics of a crisis is complicated and our ability to implement policies is not the same as following a recipe with clear directions and known outcomes. Still, it can be and has been done.

12.5 KEYNESIANS AND ANTI-KEYNESIANS

The difficulties and confusions of modeling and then implementing policy contributed to the dismissal of Keynesian modes of analysis, but at bottom, the dialogue between Keynesians and anti-Keynesians

[3] The Obama Administration's stimulus, called the American Recovery and Reinvestment Act of 2009, was implemented less than a month after they took office.

is not about those problems. It is more about a style of modeling and economic philosophy. Anti-Keynesians, mostly in the camp of the New Classical economists, prefer economic models of the macroeconomy to be built up from the microdecisions of individuals, households, and firms. In their view, the macrolevel outcomes we observe must be understood as the result of the millions of decisions at the microlevel. Furthermore, individuals, households, and firms are rational, meaning that they act in ways that further their own interests. The goal of New Classical economists is to build a model of the macroeconomy on the foundation of millions of decisions made by rational profit-maximizing and utility-maximizing businesses and households. Philosophically, economists in this school tend to prefer small government and to think of it as more likely to be an obstacle to prosperity rather than a support. On the other hand, while their views on smaller versus bigger government vary, the current generation of Keynesians, often referred to as New Keynesians, have models that are not all-encompassing. They have acknowledged holes in their models because they are not trying to model the entire economy but usually just pieces of it, and because they recognize that there are important economic phenomena that are not well understood. For example, it is not entirely clear why wages and prices do not fall as easily as they rise – why is there no symmetry? New Classical economists assume there is symmetry and build that into their models, while New Keynesians recognize that the world is different from a theoretical model, that wages and prices are in fact asymmetric in their movement up and down, and that economies sometimes do not easily move past recessions.

The track records of the two schools of thought could not have been more different than they were during the Great Recession. New Classical economists consistently predicted rising inflation, a falling dollar, and no positive benefits from either monetary or fiscal stimulus. New Keynesian models showed that when the economy is at or near a zero interest rate during a period of recession caused by a lack of demand, economic stimulus will not have a major impact on price inflation, the dollar will not experience any major decline, and there will be significant positive effects on output from the stimulus. After the economic stimulus package was passed in 2009 and implemented in stages over the succeeding few years, inflation remained low and the recovery in the United States was stronger than in most other countries hit by the recession. It is rare that events provide a direct test of economic theories, but the Great Recession allowed both camps to mark their predictions to actual economic outcomes and the results were not close.

Between the early 1980s and the Great Recession, the White House, Congress and the Federal Reserve, did not need to solve the riddle of who was right and who was wrong about fiscal policy and multipliers. Most forecasters continued to use some form of Keynesian multiplier analysis, but management of the macroeconomy was done through monetary policy instead. As long as the Federal Reserve kept the economy on an adequate growth track and inflation remained bottled up, presidents and Congress did not have to argue about economic stimulus or the size of the multiplier. Academic economists were divided on this issue, but their world was mostly contained in journals and conferences, and the advice they dispensed was largely in line with what politicians preferred to hear.

Fair-minded economists took seriously the work of both camps when it was produced to a high quality. Although data was lacking to support New Classical positions, the theoretical elegance, internal consistency, and mathematical sophistication of their models were greater. Their ideas implied that the multiplier was zero, possibly even negative at times, but it did not matter to anyone's real economy as long as it was an academic exercise. It began to matter deeply, however, when the financial crisis hit, and Western Europe and the United States fell into severe recessions.

One of the strongest characteristics of financial crises is that they produce large budget deficits, primarily due to the collapse of economic activity which leads to a decline in government revenue, and secondarily due to the increase in automatic expenditures that support income and other social programs (Reinhart and Rogoff, 2009a). The financial crisis of 2007–2009 was no exception and shortly after the worst of the crisis passed, governments began to worry about their deficits. Deficits and debt can be serious problems because they can intensify a crisis and make it more difficult to escape the downturn, while at the same time they nearly always increase a country's vulnerability to sudden shifts in capital flows.

12.6 TESTING IDEAS WITH A CRISIS

If the Keynesian multiplier for government expenditures is zero, or near zero, then it also implies that cuts in expenditures have no impact on GDP. Theoretically, the effects must be symmetrical and if increased expenditures have little or no impact, then decreased expenditures do not either. This was the perspective of the IMF and European policymakers, derived from the sophisticated, cutting-edge theories of the New Classical economists. The New Classical economists went one step further than the claim that expenditure cuts by governments would have no impact and began to assert that the effects would actually be positive. In other words, it is not that Keynesian analysis is irrelevant, but in their view it was exactly backward: Expenditure cuts were expansionary. Not surprising this was quickly labeled expansionary austerity and became a favorite policy recommendation of conservatives and libertarians interested in reducing the size of government and expanding the role of markets.

By 2010, as the worst of the crisis passed, governments in the United States and Western Europe pivoted away from economic stimulus and toward deficit reduction. The idea of expansionary austerity provided the most vocal proponents of small government with an argument for the idea that reduced expenditures would increase economic output and growth. The proposition that federal budget deficits were holding back the recovery ran counter to basic economic theory, but in a move that was reminiscent of the pre-Keynesian analysis of the 1930s, proponents of expansionary austerity argued that businesses wanted governments to balance budgets more than anything else, that they lacked confidence in government and in the future so long as deficit spending was happening, and once the deficits were eliminated, there would be a greater incentive for business investment. To support their views, the more academically inclined cited a widely disseminated paper by two economists that studied a number of cases in which government budgets were cut and economies grew (Alesina and Ardagna, 2010).

The working paper was widely cited by policy makers who were interested in cutting government spending and were opposed to using fiscal stimulus to help end the slow economic growth that followed the worst of the recession. In their paper, Alesina and Ardagna argued that their sample of countries, where spending cuts or tax increases were enacted to counter government budget deficits, did not show a pattern of decline in economic growth and, in some cases, showed an increase. They attributed the positive growth effect to a positive impact of austerity on business confidence. This was music to the ears of austerians and became a strong part of an argument for cutting spending and raising taxes even if the recession was not over or was barely ended.

The problems with the idea of expansionary austerity are numerous. First, it stood economic theory on its head. While economists were not sure of the magnitude of the effect on real GDP of changes in government spending, mainstream economic theory held that cuts in spending were contractionary, not expansionary, and increases in spending were expansionary. So, expansionary austerity proposed a new theory without a new model or a new theoretical framework. Second, the empirical data used to support the idea of expansionary austerity was deeply flawed (IMF, 2010; Ball, Leigh, and Loungani, 2011; Blanchard and Leigh, 2013; Krugman, 2013). It confused different types of cases and did not distinguish between budget cuts made during a strong economic expansion and cuts made during a contraction. The state of the economy matters. For example, the Clinton Administration imposed budget cuts during a strong economic expansion in the 1990s; given that the economy was growing, the reduction of government spending freed up resources for the private economy and overall growth was unaffected by the spending cuts. Cuts during a recession, or when recovery is still in its early phase, are another matter. When unemployment is high and business investment is weak, there is little or no competition between government and the private sector, and cuts in government spending simply reduce demand for output and lead to further declines in production. In contrast, increases in government spending may stimulate the demand for goods and services enough to increase private investment. Increases in government spending will crowd out private investment when the economy is near full employment, but it can crowd in private spending when there many idle resources and a lack of demand.

The United States, the United Kingdom, and the European Union adopted the policies of expansionary austerity in 2010. Not surprisingly, the United Kingdom and the European Union fell back into recession. The United States did better, mostly because of the unconventional monetary policies pursued by the Fed and the fact that some of the stimulus passed in 2009 was spread over subsequent years. Still, political forces in the United States, as in Europe, opposed further stimulus and prevented any new spending programs. Federal Reserve Chairman Bernanke described fiscal policy in the United States after 2010 as an adverse headwind that prevented the economy from escaping the recession sooner, and as a force that undermined some of the stimulus effects of his monetary policies (Bernanke, 2015: 504).

The Eurozone was another matter. Debt levels had become unsustainable in Greece, and were rising rapidly in other parts of the Eurozone periphery. The IMF and the European Commission were deeply worried by the deficits and accumulating debt, and budget cuts became inevitable. Cuts were proposed as a way to restore the confidence of the private sector and, hopefully, encourage investment. Again, the impact on real GDP was assumed to be small.

Very few economists thought spending had no effect, but many assumed that the fiscal multipliers from government spending were very small, so cuts would not have strong effects on GDP. That assumption proved to be a costly mistake. The reduction in government expenditures in the Eurozone caused declines in real GDP and prolonged the recession in several countries. In 2014, the IMF's Evaluations Office looked at the advice it gave in 2010, and acknowledged that the turn toward austerity was premature and that further economic stimulus would have reduced the length and severity of the crisis (Independent Evaluations Office, 2014). IMF researchers have shown that the larger the reduction in budget deficits, the larger the negative impact on real GDP, and have acknowledged that the IMF and others seriously underestimated the size of the multiplier (Blanchard and Leigh, 2013).

At first glance, it should be relatively easy to measure the size of government spending multipliers. The question is straightforward: How much does real GDP change if government spending changes? The answer is complicated by several factors, however, as noted in the Chapter 11. First, there is a time element in measuring GDP, including the speed of any changes and whether they are temporary or permanent. Second, the multiplier for an economy near full employment, when little additional output can be produced, cannot be the same as the multiplier during a recession, when workers, factories, farms and other resources are unemployed or underutilized. Several studies note that a number of variables cause multipliers to be different in different places and in the same place at different points in time (Auerbach and Gorodnichenko, 2012; Blanchard and Leigh, 2013). Even if it is unreasonable to put a single value on the multiplier, we can safely say that they are much larger in a recession and that it was a mistake to think that cuts in government spending and tax increases would somehow pull us out of a recession. In fact, they did just the opposite, as some countries were thrown back into recession and all countries suffered slower growth and a much longer recovery period than necessary.

13 Monetary Integration Requires Fiscal Integration

13.1 THE GRAND EXPERIMENT

With the exception of the common currency, the euro, all members of the European Union are required to follow the rules and regulations of the economic union. To date, nineteen of the current twenty-eight members of the European Union have given up their national currencies. The incentive to adopt the euro is the belief that a common currency will increase prosperity and promote deeper integration and closer political ties. A common currency reduces costs by eliminating the need for travelers to change their money when they cross borders, and for businesses to keep multiple accounts or currencies for receipts and payments. A further benefit for business is that a common currency eliminates exchange rate risk. The most important trading partners for EU countries are other EU countries so the elimination of exchange rate fluctuations provides an added degree of stability in payments and receipts. In the 1990s, as the euro project was negotiated and developed, proponents also hypothesized that it would cause there to be more trade and investment between member countries and that the ties binding together EU countries would strengthen.

When countries share a currency they also share a one-size-fits-all monetary policy since it is impossible to have multiple policies tailored to regional differences in economic conditions. This is the central issue in the viability of a single currency such as the euro. Large countries with multiple regions and a single currency, for example the United States or China, have a variety of mechanisms, both fiscal and institutional, to manage regional economic variations and their attendant political pressures. They have a substantial degree of fiscal integration with regional transfers, and key sectors such as banking and finance have significant institutional integration. The lack of fiscal and institutional integration across the various countries sharing the euro make the common currency in Europe a grand experiment in monetary integration. Prior to its introduction, there are no examples of democratic societies spread across multiple geographic and economic regions that attempted to introduce a single currency without the support of fiscal and institutional integration. Without those supports, the inevitable rise of regional differences in economic conditions has the potential to become politically contentious in ways that threaten not just membership in the single currency, but the overall economic union itself. Essentially, this is the problem that has plagued the Eurozone since 2010, when fiscal rules pushed more austerity and monetary policy was ineffective, at best, and counterproductive at worst. To see why a fiscal union matters, consider the imperfect example of the United States.[1]

13.2 THE UNITED STATES IS A MONETARY AND FISCAL UNION

During the financial crisis, home prices collapsed in several states, especially the sand states of Florida, Arizona, Nevada, and California. One of the hardest hit cities, Las Vegas, experienced a 62 percent decline in home prices from their peak in 2008 to the bottom in 2012. Prices in other cities also fell dramatically, although not as much: 50 percent in Miami; 43 percent in Los Angeles; 56 percent in Phoenix. Some US cities such as Dallas and Denver fared much better

1 Peter Kenen (1969), an American economist, noted these risks in 1969 when he analyzed the idea of a single currency. Reading his work today makes one realize how strange it must have seemed to have a single currency without fiscal integration. Kenen was primarily concerned with the question of whether different regions in a fiscal system should share a common currency or have their own, with their own exchange rates. The problems that might arise if the opposite existed, a currency without fiscal integration, was never directly addressed.

or were barely touched by the crisis, while most cities were intermediate between Dallas and Las Vegas (S&P Dow Jones Indices, 2015).

The economic fallout from the housing bubble was severe, particularly in states where house prices collapsed the most. Falling prices froze credit markets and real estate activity and pushed the United States into a recession. The decline in tax revenues caused large deficits in state and city budgets, and states and cities responded with spending cuts and tax increases aimed at restoring mandated balanced budgets. Budget cuts and tax increases worsened macroeconomic conditions, as teachers, health care providers, and government workers were laid off. Adding to the complications of a slowing economy, problems in the financial sector caused a spike in the number of banks that either failed or needed financial assistance to remain in operation. In 2007, three institutions failed or needed assistance but by 2010, the annual number of failures in institutions covered by deposit insurance had grown to 157 (FDIC, 2017).

As bad as conditions were, they would have been much worse in Florida and the other hard-hit states, if they had not been part of a fiscal union. When the financial crisis began and banks collapsed, federal deposit insurance protected all depositors in FDIC-regulated banks, regardless of location, and no state government needed to assume the debts of its failing banks. Retired and disabled people on federal programs such as Social Security and Medicare received pensions and health care benefits despite state budget problems, and Congress passed extra unemployment benefits to supplement and extend state unemployment insurance programs. In a fiscal union, a crisis in one place is not the sole responsibility of its residents but is the responsibility of all the residents of the union. In this way, a fiscal union creates a form of risk sharing, or insurance, so that disasters, whether natural or man-made, are a joint responsibility of everyone. In effect, people who live in places that are less affected by economic decline help out the people in places that are hit harder.

In the United States, the fiscal union moves resources in ways that the average citizen does not notice. Less well-off states routinely receive more in federal grants, contracts, direct payments, and insurance coverage than they pay while better-off states pay more than they receive. The coverage is not perfect, but it is an advantage in both good times and bad. These transfers occur automatically, year-in and year-out, based partly on differences in short-run economic conditions and partly on longer run structural conditions. For example, when a US state experiences a loss of income due to a localized slowdown in its economy, tax payments to the federal government decline while receipts go up, partially offsetting some of the cyclically caused income decline. Estimates of the amount of the decline in state income offset by federal transfers vary between 28 percent and 40 percent (Sala-i-Martin and Sachs, 1991; Bayoumi and Masson, 1995). In addition and over the long-run, some states receive permanently higher levels of support from the federal government because the state economy is less prosperous.

Suppose this were not so. As a thought experiment, suppose that states shared a common currency but did not make or receive payments to and from the federal government. It is certain that the negative effects of the housing crisis on many state budgets would have been much more severe. Large state deficits would have forced cuts in pensions and health care benefits and deeper cuts in education and public safety. Unemployment insurance would have run out in the worst-hit states, and other support programs would have been impossible. Further, lacking federal insurance on bank deposits, banks caught in the crisis and forced out of business would possibly have taken some or all of their depositor's money, depending on the depth of the crisis and the strength of possible state deposit insurance schemes. State support for failing banks would add to the already precarious deficits in state budgets and might have caused some states to leave credit markets, no longer able to borrow given their large and unsustainable deficits. The loss of pension incomes, health care, unemployment insurance, and cash in bank accounts, would have begun a vicious downward economic spiral. High and rising unemployment would have worsened the situation as more people found themselves without income and spending ability. While this thought experiment is only imaginary, it is the unfortunate reality for some countries that share the euro.

13.3 THE EURO AND OPTIMAL CURRENCY AREAS

The theory of a shared currency did not begin with the Eurozone project but dates back several decades before the euro's debut in 1999. Beginning in the 1960s, researchers began to look at the economic theory of common currencies. The first modern work in this area, by Robert Mundell, focused on the requirements that had to be met for a common currency to work better than separate currencies (Mundell, 1961). Economists refer to the geographic region that meets the requirements for using a single currency as an optimal currency area. An example is the area that comprises New York and New Jersey, since (by assumption) they are both better off with a common currency. It is an open question whether the entire United States is an optimal currency area, since it is conceivable that some states might be better off with their own currency. For example, would California, Texas, or Alaska be better off if they had its own money? This is the type of question Mundell sought to answer.

Mundell's work is straightforward and has a relatively clear answer to the question about regions that should share a common currency. There are two main criteria for adopting a single currency: synchronized business cycles, so that recessions and expansions begin and end at more or less the same time; and mobile labor and capital so that workers and savings can migrate to places where jobs and investment opportunities are more plentiful. If business cycles are synchronized, then mobile labor and capital are less necessary, but if cycles are not synchronized, mobility is a way to smooth out the differences between regions, as mobile labor and capital move from places they are not needed to more dynamic areas with better opportunities. Business cycles in Europe are not synchronized and while there are plentiful cross border capital flows, migration is dampened somewhat by language, cultural, and historical differences. This is particularly the case for unskilled workers who have a more difficult time migrating under any circumstances. Compared to the costs and effort to move from Idaho to Texas, which is not without costs, the move from Portugal to Germany is more difficult and expensive for most people.[2] As discussions of the euro began, the absence of synchronized business cycles and easy labor mobility in Europe was a red flag for economists and caused many of them to oppose the adoption of the euro. Political voices were stronger, however, and the idealist vision of a more integrated Europe prevailed.

13.4 PROMOTING THE EURO

The idea of a single currency in Europe was on the minds of the founders of European project after World War II. In 1970, the Council and Commission of the European Communities produced the Werner Report on the degree of fiscal and institutional integration necessary for successful monetary integration. Mundell did not theorize about fiscal integration, in part because his analysis was primarily concerned with areas that were already fiscally integrated and he wanted to ask if it was optimal for them to share a common currency. The authors of the Werner Report assumed fiscal integration would follow the introduction of a common currency because they believed the latter was not possible without the former. Delivery of the Werner Report in 1970 was followed by additional reports in 1975 and 1977 that also assumed fiscal integration was a necessary component of a common currency area and even estimated the necessary size of

2 Historically, labor in general is less mobile in the European Union than in the United States, although there are big differences between skilled and unskilled workers (Eichengreen, 1991). This might be changing as US households have become significantly less mobile in recent decades.

a European federal budget.[3] Subsequent events have shown that a common currency can work in the absence of fiscal integration only as long as business cycles remain synchronized and there are no significant divergences in economic conditions among member countries. In a crisis, or even a recession that affects some regions and not others, the lack of fiscal integration is corrosive for political collaboration and rather than pushing countries toward needed fiscal integration, regional divergences harm solidarity, particularly if there are prolonged recessions in some but not all of the single currency countries.

While fiscal integration helps overcome problems that arise when regional economic divergences appear, the degree of integration necessary is not precisely defined in terms of specific taxes or expenditures. The key idea, however, is that fiscal integration links a shared responsibility for economic conditions with a collective ability to act in a crisis. For example, individual states and cities in the United States maintain a variety of their own taxes and expenditures on infrastructure, schools, health care, and other items, but the degree of federal taxation and expenditure provides a degree of risk sharing and collective responsibility during hard times. In the Eurozone, as the Subprime Crisis deepened into a debt crisis, each country was responsible for its own anti-recession measures and for handling the doom loop described in Chapter 7.

3 The Werner Report (Council and Commission of the European Communities, 1970) assumes that a single currency would eventually cause member states to develop a common fiscal policy. The findings of the Werner Report were supported and extended in the Marjolin Report (Marjolin, 1975) and the MacDougall Report (European Commission, 1977). All assumed fiscal integration with an expanded European authority to control a much larger budget, and that member states would cede some sovereignty to a European entity in order to make it possible. Individual economists warned of the dangers of the common currency shortly after the Werner Report was issued. Among others, Nicholas Kaldor's article (1971) in the *New Statesman* expressed the problems of monetary union clearly: ".... the objective of a full monetary and economic union is unattainable without a political union; and the latter pre-supposes fiscal *integration*, and not just fiscal *harmonization*." Ashoka Mody (2018: Chapter 1) provides a detailed history of the discussions that led up to the adoption of the single currency.

Leaders in leading EU countries, especially in Germany and France, wanted the euro as a means to encourage further integration. They continued the push toward a single currency even as it became increasingly clear that deeper political integration with some degree of fiscal coordination and risk sharing was beyond the range of possible outcomes. As they moved forward, little consideration was given to problems that might arise if some parts of the currency area fell into a recession while others did not, or what would happen if there was a severe financial crisis. The hope and the belief among politicians was that Europe would muddle through any crisis that arose and, in the end, would be more integrated with a stronger union. Jean Monnet, one of the founders and inspirations for the European Union, wrote in his memoirs that "Europe will be forged in crisis, and will be the sum of the solutions adopted for those crises" (Barroso, 2011). Politicians who created the monetary union sincerely believed that any potential crisis would cause governments to strengthen their ties and to exercise greater solidarity in order to solve common problems. In their beliefs, the forces of nationalism and separatism would be submerged for the greater good.[4]

Negotiations to adopt the euro began in 1992. In anticipation of its implementation, interest rates throughout the Eurozone began to converge to the rates in countries with the lowest rates. The Greek government, for example, paid over 23 percent on its ten year government bonds in 1993 while the German government paid 6.5 percent. The differential fell during the fifteen years before the Subprime Crisis, and by 2007 Greek rates were at 4.5 percent and German rates were 4.2 percent. Interest rates in most countries trended down during this period, but the large currency and country risk premiums

4 Following the Werner Report (Council and Commission of the European Communities, 1970) EU leaders held to the idea that the single currency, while problematic, would cause the European Union to "fall forward" into deeper integration (Mody, 2018: chapter 1). When asked in an interview to name which of the many cognitive biases he would eliminate if it were in his power, Daniel Kahneman, psychologist and Nobel Laureate in Economics, replied that he thought human society would benefit the most from eliminating overconfidence (Shariatmadari, 2015).

between Greece and Germany (and other leading economies) was completely eliminated by the late 1990s.[5]

From the outset, the leadership of fiscally conservative countries worried that governments in less conservative countries would use the euro to borrow large sums at low interest rates and cause rates to be higher than they would have been for the stronger countries alone. In effect, the decline in borrowing costs for some countries would come at the price of higher costs for others, and was unacceptable to low interest countries. Nor was it acceptable that anyone would expect EU support, including bailouts, if the heavy borrowers were in fiscal trouble. Hence, the negotiations led to the "No bailouts" clause which prohibited the new European Central Bank from lending to governments that are at risk of default.

In addition to the no bailout clause, the fear that weaker countries might impose costs on stronger ones led to a set of rules and criteria for joining the Eurozone, called the convergence criteria. These are rules to limit budget deficits to no more than 3 percent of GDP, limit debt to a maximum of 60 percent of GDP, and establish maximum allowable inflation rates and currency fluctuations in the years before joining the euro. The goals were intended to ensure that governments were capable of prudent financial management and to prevent weaker economies from imposing costs on stronger ones by running large deficits that generate inflation and push up interest rates throughout the single currency region. Proponents of the convergence criteria believed that if individual countries could meet the criteria and align their most important fiscal indicators with the rest of the Eurozone, then they were prepared for euro adoption.

From a macroeconomic perspective, whenever business cycles across the Eurozone begin to diverge, the convergence criteria are guaranteed to worsen economic conditions and intensify the divergence. The normal pattern in countries entering a recession is that budget deficits appear, or increase if already present. Tax revenues

5 This is the average daily secondary market yield on ten-year fixed-rate government bonds as reported by the International Monetary Fund, 2017a.

decline and social expenditures such as unemployment insurance automatically increase as workers are laid off and business slows. The convergence criteria framework, however, requires cuts in government expenditures and/or tax increases to reduce the widening deficit, even if it is caused by a recession. Those policies further depress the economy and exacerbate the differences between countries. Without a fiscal union of one sort or another, there is no way around this problem: Countries either follow the rules, as German policymakers demand, or they switch to a politically determined and context-sensitive set of policies in times of stress, as French policymakers prefer.

13.5 MISSING INSTITUTIONS

Mundell's work on currency areas primarily focused on the choice between fixed or flexible exchange rates and the implications for economic stability. He did not discuss institutions for fiscal redistribution or banking unions, although he mentions fiscal unions. His analysis is concerned with regions and geography, where a region is defined as an area with a relatively uniform economic profile and therefore a synchronized business cycle. Mundell considered geography because he viewed it as an important determinant of the boundaries between economic regions and business cycles. In effect, he was asking if states of the United States benefit from sharing a common currency. Critics of the euro project questioned whether it was truly an optimal currency area given that it did not meet the criteria laid out by Mundell and others. The Werner Report and the other studies conducted by the European Commission were used to raise questions about missing institutions for fiscal redistribution.

In 1970, at the time of the Werner Report, the issue of missing institutions seemed abstract and theoretical, with no sense of urgency given that the single currency was only an idea. In the lead-up to adoption of the euro, both proponents and opponents argued that deeper political integration was necessary for a single currency to work properly. That was too far a reach for the member countries, however, and the proponents clung to their belief in the path laid out by Monnet and the other architects of the European Union who had argued that a currency union would have the political will to resolve problems when they arose, and would develop new institutions and deeper levels of integration if needed.[6] Critics of the single currency were divided between agnostics who believed a deeper political integration was possible but not certain, and nonbelievers who thought it was beyond the reach of European politics.[7] In general terms, the division between euro-proponents and euro-skeptics cut across political ideologies and was related more to geographical location. American economists tended to be more skeptical of the euro project and were criticized by some European proponents for holding blindly to Mundell's theory of optimal currency areas and for not understanding the evolving nature of politics and political commitments in the European Union (Junong and Drea, 2010).

In addition to the need for fiscal integration, the financial crisis has clarified the need for a set of rules to integrate the banking sector. Banking integration, or a banking union, has three components: a common deposit insurance program, a common bank regulator, and a common resolution process. In 2015, the European Union proposed the creation a banking union. Soon after, it implemented rules primarily covering the largest or most systemically important institutions, while leaving most rules for smaller national banks in the hands individual national authorities (European Commission, no date). Until the next crisis, it is impossible to say if this is adequate to prevent a banking crisis from spilling across national boundaries, or

6 Junong and Drea (2010) favored the creation of new institutions and the euro; Eichengreen and Freiden (1994) opposed adoption of the euro but agreed that it might further political integration.

7 Critics who thought deeper integration could not be forced by adoption of the euro included Dornbusch (1996) and Feldstein (1997); Feldstein was also among those who noted a potential problem given the absence of any mechanisms for fiscal redistribution, along with Salvatore (1997) and Tobin (2001).

to prevent the doom loop between government finances and bank solvency of the last crisis.[8]

Regardless of how one thought about the euro in the 1990s and early 2000s, as the financial crisis enveloped the Eurozone, missing institutions proved to be deeply harmful to the well-being of several countries and by the 2010s, questions were being asked about the costs of staying in the euro versus the costs of leaving. Greece is the main example, but behind it were a number of other potential euro-leavers, particularly if Greece left and subsequently did better. As of mid-2018, the answer to the question of the cost of leaving versus staying still has not been settled as, so far at least, no country has left. In reality, no one knows if Greece would have recovered more quickly if it left the euro in 2012 or 2013, but the point is moot because it chose to stay.

The biggest question for the Eurozone is how to move forward and develop the institutions it needs to make the euro workable for all its members. While leaving the Eurozone is not off the table and future crises are all but guaranteed as long as the region lacks a credible fiscal and banking union, the challenges of making the currency work require further institutional development. The primary obstacle is that the Eurozone members, like all nation-states, are highly resistant to ceding sovereignty over their internal fiscal systems to a supranational authority. In the United States, Californians and New Yorkers do not resist paying taxes to benefit Mississippians or Alabamians, probably because they mostly do not realize they are doing so and because it is a system they inherited from the past. If US citizens in richer states were asked to vote on paying new taxes for schools or pensions in poorer states, or to help those states

8 In contrast, the United States has a common deposit insurance program (FDIC) that shares the costs of protecting the deposits of a failed bank. The other elements of a banking union are less than perfect, to say the least. There are four bank regulators, including the FDIC, the Board of Governors of the Federal Reserve, the Office of the Comptroller of the Currency, and the National Credit Union Administration. Whether this constitutes a "unified regulatory framework" is open to question. The Dodd–Frank reforms establish a clearer set of rules for the resolution of failed banks but, as in the Eurozone, it will require another crisis to know whether they are adequate.

overcome their budget shortfalls, many, if not most, would probably vote against the measure. Similarly, German and Dutch citizens are not amenable to higher taxes to help Greece or other struggling countries.

In 2017, the budget of the European Union was less than 1 percent of the GDP of its member countries, while national budgets averaged over 45 percent of GDP.[9] The European Commission's 1977 MacDougall Report on the requirements for deeper fiscal integration to support a single currency concluded that prior to launching the currency, the European fiscal authority would need resources equal to 2–2.5 percent of the region's gross product, and that fiscal integration after the currency was launched would require a minimum of 7–7.5 percent of regional gross product. Full integration on the order of the United States would take 20–25 percent of regional gross product (European Commission, 1977). Even the 2–2.5 percent level seems beyond reach as it would require more than doubling of the EU budget. This is particularly the case given the collapse of solidarity in the wake of the financial crisis and the long standing and widespread view that large transfers within the EU would lead to significant inefficiencies.[10]

With genuine fiscal integration off the table, efforts at resolving the problem of missing institutions have focused on new rules rather than mechanisms for fiscal transfers. The Subprime Crisis exposed the weakness of this approach, however, when market forces overwhelmed the capacity of budget rules to contain divergences among the member economies and made deficits worse by hurting economic growth. Prior to the crisis, higher growth rates in the peripheral booming countries such as Greece, Spain, and Portugal, inevitably led to capital inflows from Northern Europe, higher wages and prices, and, consequently, declining competitiveness. Once the crisis began, countries that had experienced relatively greater price and wage

9 The budget of the EU in 2017 was 157.9 billion euros, or less than 1 percent of the total GDP of the EU countries which is estimated to be 13,677 billion euros. Data for the budget are from European Union, 2017; GDP data from IMF, 2017b.

10 For example, Giovannini (1990: 267) expressed this view as early as 1990, as the discussions around the idea of a common currency were just beginning.

increases before the crisis, were less competitive and more deeply indebted. As countries across the Eurozone implemented austerity programs, in large part to comply with the deficit limits set by the European Union, the needed increase in demand from the countries that first recovered from the crisis never materialized. Nor were there common fiscal institutions to provide assistance to the countries that suffered deep job losses and prolonged negative growth. If the Eurozone has no real lender of last resort, no mechanisms for supporting credit systems, and no way to make large income transfers, how can it respond? Individual countries cannot devalue their currency and have no monetary policy tools. In the slow and negative growth countries, rules about deficits are likely to make conditions worse since they will mandate expenditure cuts precisely when the economy is in need of more spending. At this point, events have shown that it is impossible to manage the single currency successfully with strict rules and without significant transfers during the inevitable recessions and crises that occur in all market economies.

14 Open Capital Markets Can Be Dangerous

14.1 ASSUME THERE ARE BENEFITS

It is easy to tell a story about the benefits of capital flows and open capital markets. The free movement of financial capital lets the receiving countries obtain more resources for investment while businesses and individuals in the sending countries earn higher returns. History is full of examples. In the nineteenth century, the United Kingdom invested its savings in infrastructure projects around the world, but especially in its colonies and former colonies where British savings were used to build the railroads, seaports, mines, urban sanitation systems, and other major projects. British investors were not alone in investing in the Americas, Asia, and Africa, but were joined by German, French, Dutch, and others lenders and investors.[1]

The images of nineteenth century English townspeople providing funds for the construction of Buenos Aires' new sewer system, or for a rail connection from Mexico City to the port of Veracruz, are ones where the benefits of global financial flows are obvious. Capital-scarce regions with obvious needs receive funding while people in capital-rich countries earn a better return on their savings and enjoy more comfortable lives. Global financial markets are beneficial because they move savings from regions with relatively abundant capital resources to relatively scarce regions, exactly as markets are expected to do. It is important to keep this scenario in mind even while it may be idealized and lacking in details. It is important because it illustrates

[1] Obstfeld and Taylor (2004, chapter 2) estimate that UK capital flows to the world averaged 4.5 percent of GDP from 1870 to 1914 and reached 8–10 percent in some years. Bordo and Meissner (2010) estimate that up to 20 percent of late nineteenth century investment in developing countries was from the United Kingdom, and accounted for half the foreign investment in Australia, Canada, Argentina, and Brazil.

the essential function of beneficial financial globalization and conveys the reasoning behind the widely held preference for keeping financial markets open to international capital flows. Few would argue that there should be no limits on international financial flows, and few would take the other side that that flows should not be allowed. Differences in opinions have usually been over the degree of openness and the types of controls that should be put into place.

14.2 CAPITAL MARKET LIBERALIZATION DEFINED

Most countries are members of the IMF. Established at the Bretton Woods Conference in 1944, the goal of the creators of the IMF was to avoid a return to the international financial instability of the 1930s. The primary functions of the organization are to provide technical and financial assistance to countries needing help managing their exchange rate or their international payments. As a secondary goal, the IMF encourages trade and discourages trade restrictions, even though it does not have a direct say in trade policy. In part, it does this by requiring countries to open their financial markets to transactions on the current account of the balance of payments.[2] Since the current account is primarily a measure of trade flows, the rule is designed to prevent IMF members from stopping financial flows associated with imports or exports. Other types of nontrade related international financial transactions such as foreign investment, speculation, buying and selling foreign securities, making or receiving foreign bank loans, are not counted in the current account and are not included in this rule. Given the distinction between payments and receipts for imports and exports, and financial flows for investment or

2 A country's balance of payments is an accounting record of its transactions with the rest of the world. There are two main components of the balance of payments. The first is the current account which records exports and imports, net income from existing foreign investments, and foreign aid. The second component is the financial account which is a record of all asset purchases and liabilities incurred. There is a (usually) small third account consisting of transfers of non-financial assets. Throughout this chapter, financial globalization implies transactions on the financial account, which is to say, purely financial transactions not associated with trade.

speculation, a country joining the IMF is not required to open to all international financial transactions.

During the Bretton Woods era (1950–1973), most countries maintained some controls on the movement of capital and few, if any, had completely open capital markets. In part, this was necessitated by the Bretton Woods fixed exchange rate system, in conjunction with a desire to maintain independent monetary policies as a stabilization tool. A fundamental constraint in international financial relations is the inability of countries to have open capital markets if they also want to have both independent monetary policies and fixed exchange rates. This is known as the trilemma of international finance and is an inherent limitation, not a legal rule.[3] If capital is completely free to move, then inflows and outflows will affect the value of the domestic currency through changes in its supply and demand. With a fixed exchange rate, the country's monetary authority is not free to ignore those changes but must make adjustments to the money supply in order to maintain a stable exchange rate and to prevent deviations away from the fixed value. Monetary policy, then, is in service of the exchange rate and is not free to stabilize the macroeconomy if doing so would conflict with the fixed exchange value. On the other hand, they can have an independent monetary policy with a fixed exchange rate, but only if they limit capital inflows and outflows. This frees monetary policy from the conflict between maintaining a fixed exchange rate (external equilibrium) and supporting adequate economic growth (internal equilibrium). This may sound familiar since it is a reflection of the same dilemma that confronted the Federal Reserve during the Great Depression, described in Chapter 3. During the Great Depression, when capital markets were open, the Federal Reserve remained focused on supporting the dollar's fixed value and was not free to use its monetary policy tools to fight the Great Depression.

3 This point was made by Robert Mundell (1963) and J. Marcus Fleming (1962), two of the key economists in post-War international macroeconomics. Obstfeld and Taylor (2004) test the empirical relevance of the trilemma in global finance.

After the breakdown of the Bretton Woods exchange system in the early 1970s, industrial economies gradually moved to floating exchange rate systems, so the possibilities for open capital markets became a possibility. Even so, many countries in Western Europe retained controls on the flow of capital as late as 1992.[4] The United States and the United Kingdom, both at the center of global finance, were open by choice and by necessity since without capital market openness, their financial services sectors would not thrive and the dollar and the pound would not have been as widely used in international transactions. Gradually, the presumed benefits of open capital markets became embedded in the advice given to countries by the IMF and the US Treasury Department, and on the eve of the Asian Crisis in 1997, the IMF was formally promoting open capital markets as a best practice. A few years later, in the aftermath of the Asian Crisis, the IMF began to reconsider the advice and encouragement it was giving to countries, and after several more years of research, it openly acknowledged that some controls on capital flows can be beneficial at times.

In retrospect, it seems odd that capital market openness ever became a mantra of the economics profession. To be sure, there were always dissenters and it was never a subject in which there was a consensus among academic economists. For the most part, open capital markets seem to have been promoted by the financial services industry and government officials, some of whom were undoubtedly subject to regulatory capture by the former. Academic economists are also subject to a form of regulatory capture although it is probably more accurate to call it research capture since the problem is not so much that academicians leave their posts for Wall Street jobs (although it happens) as much as it is a case of wanting to keep the flow of large research grants coming. But as was noted, there was never

4 In 1992, the Single European Act (SEA) was implemented in the European Union. The goal was to create a single market and a single European identity that transcended national limits through the implementation of the "four freedoms": free movement of goods, services, people, and capital.

a consensus among economists about this issue, mainly because money is not the same as goods and services and the theory of international trade favoring generally open markets does not apply to the theory of international capital flows, or trade in financial assets. The tools used to analyze imports and exports do not carry over to the analysis of buying and selling financial products across international borders. Goods and services are in the present moment, while financial assets are representations of expected future values and are subject to many more market distortions and other problems. A promise to pay an amount in the future cannot be evaluated in the same way as an imported car you can drive today. Given that financial assets are a promise, there is always the possibility that the promise may not be kept and the scope for information asymmetry and other market failures is much greater.

Capital is also far more liquid than goods and services. This gives it the ability to move quickly, either into or out of a country. The sudden flight of capital into a country can lead to a credit boom and excessive lending, while the flight of capital out can disrupt financial markets through the severing of credit links and pressures on the value of the domestic currency. With capital flight, domestic banks and other lenders sometimes find their sources of financing suddenly gone, along with the ability to make payments to their creditors.

14.3 FROM OPEN CAPITAL MARKETS TO A FINANCIAL CRISIS

There is a widespread consensus that open capital markets increase the probability of a financial crisis. This is a viewpoint supported by quantitative historical analysis, economic theory, and policy studies. The main mechanism is from a capital inflow to a credit boom to over leveraging and maturity mismatches that eventually result in a crisis. The link between capital inflows and credit booms is the increase in liquidity caused by the inflow. The rise in liquidity often gives rise to increased bank lending, depending on the receiving country's policies, including the degree and types of financial sector supervision and regulation. Not every inflow leads to an increase in bank lending, however. Foreign direct investment, for example, increases expenditures in the receiving country, but does not directly expand bank loans or other forms of debt unless the investment increases the size of the financial sector, for example the establishment of a new bank. Similarly, a capital inflow used to purchase equities can expand the receiving companies' expenditures but will not usually result in a direct expansion of bank loans or leverage.

The riskiest type of inflow is related to an increase in debt. Debt can take many different forms, from bank deposits or bank loans to much more exotic forms involving the purchase of securitized derivatives. The form of debt that led to the Latin American Debt Crisis was direct loans by banks in New York and other money centers to governments, parastatals, and private firms throughout Latin America, often with an explicit government guarantee of repayment. In the lead up to the Asian Crisis, Thai banks received large quantities of short term loans from abroad and became increasingly dependent on them to maintain growth in their real estate projects and other long term investments. In the years before the Subprime Crisis, the United States, Spain, the United Kingdom and other countries received large inflows from abroad that were used among other purposes, to purchase equities and securitized assets, including mortgage backed securities, or that were used to make simple bank loans for financing real estate and other projects. The capital inflows were savings from one part of the world that were lent in another part. The countries that received the savings from abroad increased their dependence on debt to the point that its cessation triggered a crisis.

Other problems often follow from large capital inflows. Latin America and the Asian economies caught in the debt and banking crises of 1982 to 1989 and 1997 to 1998 also experienced currency crises as the inflows reversed and caused investors, both foreign and domestic, to sell assets, convert them into a reserve currency, and take them out of the country. Capital flight exhausted the reserves of dollars in the borrowing countries, and forced the monetary authorities to devalue. Devaluations were exceptionally harmful given that countries in Latin America and Asia had borrowed in dollars or another international currency and were required to repay in the foreign currency.

The United States and Europe were over-leveraged and suffered banking crises during the Subprime Crisis and its aftermath, but they did not have currency problems. In the case of the United States, there are two reasons why the dollar did not fall. One, the debt obligations of borrowers were in dollars. As is the case with US government debt, private sector debts in the United States are almost exclusively in dollars. Therefore, there is not a wedge between the value of the domestic currency and the value of the debt. And two, the United States has a privileged position in international financial markets due to the fact that the dollar is the world's main reserve currency. During times of crisis and uncertainty, when households, businesses, and governments look for a safe place to store financial assets, the United States is the main recipient of funds, even when the crisis arises first in the United States. There is absolutely no guarantee that this will continue, but since World War II, it has been a major characteristic of international financial relations.

In the case of Europe, the crisis countries had debts that were also mainly in their own currency, the euro. Most of the debts owed by Greece and Spain and Ireland and others were intra-European Union, so there was no question of a wedge between the size of their debt and the value of their currency. Confidence in the euro did flag, however, between 2008 and 2010, and doubts about its ability to survive the crisis were openly expressed. Nevertheless, it never suffered a loss in value comparable to the currency declines in Latin America and East Asia during their periods of crises.[5]

5 Between a June, 2001, and July, 2008, the euro gained value against the dollar. At that point, it was probably overvalued. In 2008 and 2009, during the middle of the crisis, it lost about 20 percent of its value. From that point, it bounced around without a trend, until 2014, when it lost another 15 percent. Other factors besides the crisis were most likely the main causes.

Researchers looking at a variety of time periods and with different sets of countries have come to similar conclusions about the link from capital inflows to financial crises. For example, Bordo and Meissner (2010) associate large capital inflows with an increased probability of a crisis during the height of Britain's investment abroad prior to World War I. Bordo and Eichengreen (2002) show that for a sample of twenty-one countries from 1880 to 1997, and seventy-seven countries from 1973 to 1997, a boom in international lending is highly correlated with the onset of a crisis. Demirgüç-Kunt and Detragiache (1999) measure the effects of financial liberalization across many countries and find that it leads to a significant increase in banking crises, particularly if the financial liberalization occurs prematurely before the establishment of adequate supervisory and regulatory institutions. Eichengreen (1999) compares the Baring Crisis of 1890 in Argentina to the Peso Crisis of 1994 to 1995 in Mexico and sees a significant role for large capital inflows in the two cases separated by more than a century. Claessens and Kose (2014) review the literature on the link between credit booms and international capital flows, and Schularick and Taylor (2012) find that credit growth is a strong predictor of crises. There are many other studies that find similar results.[6]

Triggers of capital inflows are varied, but include financial liberalization, capital market opening, and strong economic growth. These are not necessary nor sufficient causes of a crisis, but occur with enough frequency to be viewed as a typical first step toward a crisis when one occurs. For example, Carmen Reinhart and Kenneth Rogoff (2009a) summarize the prototypical sequence of a financial crisis as beginning with financial liberalization that results in a banking crisis and leads into a currency crisis. Their database covers every known crisis since 1800 (as of the publication of their work in 2009). A database put together by the IMF covers 170

6 See, for example, Rancière, Tornell, and Westermann (2008) and Goodhart and Delargy (1998). Gorton's (2012) detailed economic history of financial crises asserts that many are preceded by a credit boom. This is the fundamental idea of Minsky (1977) and Kindleberger (1978).

countries and identifies 175 credit booms. The booms were all started by some combination of the three triggers: financial liberalization, capital market opening, and economic growth. In their sample, 57 of 175 credit booms (one-third) resulted in a financial crisis and 121 had either a crisis or several years economic growth well below average after the credit boom ended. (Laeven and Valencia, 2013; Dell'Ariccia, et al., 2014: 333).

Not all credit booms are fueled by capital from abroad, and local or national credit conditions are perfectly capable of triggering a boom in lending. Nevertheless, a great many lending booms, including the Subprime Crisis, the Latin American Debt Crisis, and the East Asian Crisis, were significantly encouraged by inflows of foreign capital. How the inflows develop into a credit boom, and whether the boom leads to a crisis depends on numerous other factors, most especially the financial sector's structure and incentives. Financial innovation and the regulatory environment are important, as are more fundamental elements of the financial sector's architecture. If financial firms compete aggressively, for example, the availability of new sources of funding from abroad leads to a more dramatic expansion of credit.[7] The degree to which aggressive competition among lenders leads them to become over-leveraged and vulnerable in a cyclical downturn depends in part on the types of regulation and its enforcement. As discussed in Chapter 8, the notion that banks and other intermediaries can self-regulate becomes all the more tenuous when faced with large increases in the availability of funds and a need to earn higher returns than their competitors.

14.4 OPEN CAPITAL MARKETS AND ECONOMIC GROWTH

An increase in the probability of a crisis when capital markets are open does not lead to the conclusion that countries should avoid opening them. There are several reasons for this, the most basic of which was described at the beginning of this chapter and is simply

[7] Firms with significant charter values and protected markets are less likely to compete aggressively in the expansion of credit. See Chapter 10.

the recognition that capital inflows provide financial resources that can be used to promote economic growth if deployed correctly. If crises are infrequent and the damages are minimal, they are conceivably a price worth paying for the added economic growth. Furthermore, if it is possible to completely avoid crises caused by capital inflows, then there is no need to weigh the gains against losses and inflows are strictly beneficial. After all, not all inflows result in a crisis.

Theoretically, it is possible that crisis avoidance policies will develop in the future so that inflows are managed prudently and no crisis takes place. It should be clear by now, however, that we are a long ways away from that possibility. It is perhaps tempting to believe that advanced economies with sophisticated financial markets and the resources to deploy well informed, skilled regulators and supervisors within an overall regulatory framework that minimizes the likelihood of crises, are not subject to the mistakes or problems of less developed economies or emerging markets. The Subprime Crisis should disabuse everyone of that view. High income countries and sophisticated financial systems do not outgrow the risk of financial crises, nor do they automatically develop the regulatory and risk management systems that enable them to avoid crises. Lobbying by financial services industries in high income countries, for example, persuaded academics, government agencies, politicians, and international organizations such as the IMF, that open capital markets were inherently superior to the use of controls on capital flows. After several crises, there has been a lot of reconsideration.

The right question to ask is fundamentally an empirical question about the relationship between open capital markets and economic growth: Do countries with open capital markets grow faster, and if so, does it make up for any setback they might experience from financial crises? It turns out that this is a complicated question to answer since it requires agreement about the definition of open capital markets, the causes of crises, and the start and stop dates of crises. Hence, no one study by itself should be considered definitive and the answer depends on the weight of multiple analyses and the patterns they demonstrate.

There are two separate questions that must be answered in order to have a clear picture of the relationship of open capital markets and economic growth. First, do countries with open capital markets grow faster? And second, if they do, then is the added growth sufficient to compensate for the higher probability of a financial crisis? The first question has generated a variety of answers but the weight of the responses seems to favor the "no extra growth" view. For example, a comprehensive meta-analysis of the growth effects of open capital markets finds that they provide little in the way of extra economic growth (Jeanne, Subramanian, and Williamson, 2012).[8] This may seem counter-intuitive, but there is no theory explaining how an increase in financial resources contributes to growth (Stiglitz, et al., 2006). One can imagine specific country cases where there are potential benefits to having additional financial resources, but also other cases where the capital inflows are not used productively or are acquired in a way that increases risk and inefficiencies and causes lower economic growth than average. This latter possibility was shown by researchers at the IMF to occur in about two-thirds of the cases with credit booms (Dell'Ariccia, et al., 2014).

One of the results of looking at the relationship between financial globalization and economic growth is the recognition that there are thresholds in institutional quality and the development of the financial system. Systems with lower quality institutions, where the rule of law is weaker and monitoring of financial intermediaries is constrained by politics or other factors, where macroeconomic decisions are ideological or politically determined rather than based on sound analysis, where trade integration is limited, usually do not generate benefits from financial globalization (Kose, et.al, 2009;

8 Schularick and Steger (2010) find an empirical link from open capital markets to growth in the first wave of globalization, but not currently. They hypothesize that the difference between the two periods was related to the link between capital flows and investment.

Kose, Prasad, Taylor, 2011). The effects of different types of financial flows appear to depend on different threshold levels for institutional development, with lower institutional development requirements for foreign direct investment (FDI) to be beneficial than for portfolio investments or bank loans. That is not surprising, perhaps, given that FDI entails the direct acquisition of firms or new plants and equipment, whereas portfolio investments and loans must take additional steps before they are turned into physical assets.[9]

14.5 SHOULD COUNTRIES CLOSE THEIR CAPITAL MARKETS?

Regardless of the answer to the question posed in this section, it is highly unlikely that advanced economies such as the United States, the European Union, or Japan, would ever consider it necessary to close their economies to foreign capital flows. They are too highly integrated into the world economy and have the additional buffer of their currencies serving as reserve currencies, One would have to imagine a world very different from the present to see their disengagement from international financial integration as a possibility. On the other hand, countries less well integrated into the global economy, or newcomers such as China, often have a variety of barriers blocking the free flow of capital across their national borders. In essence, the question posed in this section is about the potential utility or disutility of controls on capital flows, particularly for developing countries and emerging markets. Should the IMF and other agencies encourage countries to open their capital markets, or should they advise that selected controls on capital flows are desirable at times?

This is an area of active research but several points seem to be agreed. First, analysts have broken the idea of controls into two major possibilities: controls on the inflow of capital and controls on the outflow. There is a consensus that controls on outflows are a crisis

9 Note that Jeanne, Subramanian and Williamson (2012) are not in complete agreement. They see very little connection between financial liberalization and economic growth except, possibly, in equity markets.

management strategy, while controls on inflows are crisis avoidance. Second, there is some evidence that controls on capital outflows hurt economic growth if they are used during normal (non-crisis) times, which is why the IMF and others have until recently opposed their use.[10] And third, there is substantial evidence that capital controls on inflows can be a prudential measure to help countries reduce the amount of risk-taking by financial intermediaries. The bottom line is that the best policy depends on the depth of the financial system, the quality of institutions, and whether there is a crisis or not. There is no such thing as a one-size-fits-all policy, nor is there any such thing as a best policy for all time.

10 See Eichengreen and Leblang (2003). Bordo, et al. (2001) show that capital controls reduce the number of banking crises but are associated with an increase in currency crises. They reason that this may be the result of countries adopting riskier exchange rate regimes when they have controls in place.

15 Not All Debt Is Created Equal

15.1 FEAR OF A US DEBT CRISIS

During the Subprime Crisis and its aftermath, the US federal debt ratcheted up dramatically. By 2012 it was equal to almost 100 percent of GDP and in the next year it crossed that symbolic level.[1] While the ratio of debt to GDP was climbing before the crisis, the increase in both deficits and debt during the crisis created a political backlash. Conservatives and deficit hawks opposed any further increases in spending and tried to cut both discretionary spending and mandatory entitlements.

Relative to the size of the economy, the largest debt in recent US history was just over 118 percent of GDP in 1946. Most observers probably justified wartime expenditures as warranted given the existential threat of Nazism, but the debt accumulated during the Subprime Crisis did not have a similar rationale, particularly when it was assumed that it was largely due to bailouts of financial institutions, auto companies, and other private enterprises. When the Republican party gained control of Congress in 2010, their opposition to nonmilitary spending led to compromise legislation and a freeze on all new discretionary spending. On an annualized basis, the deficit began to fall in 2010, and continued decreasing until 2016. Since then, it has increased each year and is projected to continue increasing for at least five years.[2]

1 US federal debt began a more rapid increase after the second quarter of 2008, as the country entered the worst of the crisis and recession (FRB St. Louis and OMB, 2017; US Department of Treasury, 2018a). Note that this is total federal debt, including the part held by federal agencies. Federal debt held by the public is a smaller share of GDP but is expected to cross the 100 percent threshold shortly after 2028 (CBO, 2018).

2 The deficit is much larger than the average during an economic expansion. This poses potential problems when the expansion ends because there will be less "fiscal space" for stimulus spending (CBO, 2018; US Department of Treasury, 2018a).

The Subprime Crisis was a typical financial crisis in terms of its effects on government budget deficits. To the casual observer it probably appeared that the reason for the ballooning deficit was mainly the increased spending on bailouts and financial supports given to banks and other businesses. Bailout costs, however, were relatively small compared to the loss of tax revenue and in this respect at least, the Subprime Crisis was a relatively typical financial crisis.[3] The amount disbursed by the US federal government through the various bailout programs came to $626.9 billion, by no means a small number, but in most cases the spent dollars gave the federal government claims against the future earnings of the firms it saved. As of April, 2018, these claims have returned $713.4 billion to the US Treasury, for a net profit of $86.6 billion.[4] By comparison, if US federal tax receipts had remained at their 2007 level, they would have brought in over a trillion additional dollars during the subsequent four years.

Congress' heated rhetoric about government deficits and debt was a political argument disguised as an economic one. The Congressional majority used large budget deficits as a means to oppose the policies of the White House and as a way to promote smaller government and reduced social spending.[5] It was a political argument but it also reflected the fact that debates over the size of deficits and other politically contentious issues tend to become overheated and polarized in the aftermath of financial crises (Mian, Sufi, and Trebbi, 2014).

Deficit hawks may overstate the potential risks of rising debt during a crisis, but government deficits and debt do have consequences and risks. Risk assessment, however, first requires

3 Reinhart and Rogoff (2009a, 224) estimate that government debt has increased an average of 86 percent in post-World War II banking crises.

4 Payouts include the Troubled Assets Relief Program and the rescue of the government sponsored enterprises, Fannie Mae and Freddie Mac. Earnings are refunds of money lent, dividends, interest payments and other proceeds (ProPublica, 2018).

5 Republican support for the 2017 tax cuts illustrates this point. Although the tax cuts are guaranteed to increase the deficit, they passed with only one dissenting vote from the Republican party. In justification, politicians favoring the tax cuts dragged out the tired and empirically unsupported idea that they would pay for themselves.

recognition of the variations across countries. Variations in risk are so large that it is impossible to make generalizations or hard rules about debt levels or to define threshold levels where debt becomes too great. For example, Japan's central government debt is currently above 200 percent of its GDP. By historical standards and in comparison to other nations, this level of debt is nearly unique and would probably be ruinous for most countries, yet Japan continues to borrow at low costs. Perhaps that will change someday, but the debt has continued to grow without significant problems for several decades. Another interesting case is the debt history of the United Kingdom. Its total public sector debt was above 200 percent of GDP in 1822, after which it had an industrial revolution and established *Pax Britannica*. The United Kingdom paid down its debt over the nineteenth century and grew its economy so that by 1913, the debt-to-GDP ratio was 28 percent. Then, the combined effects of World War I, the Great Depression, and World War II pushed its debt up again, this time above 250 percent of GDP in 1946. By the 1990s, it was once again back to moderately low levels at 25 percent of GDP. As in the United States and many other countries affected by the Subprime Crisis, UK debt levels rose again during the financial crisis and are approximately 90 percent of GDP today (Bank of England, 2018).

High debt does not necessarily result in a default, although it may create other problems which are discussed below. Nearly the opposite is true as well: Low debt levels do not guard against defaults. Over 50 percent of all sovereign defaults since 1970 have occurred in countries with debt levels less than 60 percent of GDP and 19 percent have been in countries with debt less than 40 percent of GDP (Reinhart and Rogoff, 2009a: 24). If some countries can carry debt-to-GDP levels of 100 or 200 percent, seemingly without trouble, but others default with debt less than 40 percent of GDP, then it must be the case that the potential dangers of debt vary greatly by country. The United States and Japan are not the same as Guatemala or Cambodia in their ability to handle debt, just as Warren Buffet and

Bill Gates do not have the same vulnerabilities to debt as, say, the average college professor.

15.2 HOUSEHOLDS, BUSINESSES, AND GOVERNMENTS

Debt is a useful tool for managing financial affairs through time. Households, businesses, and governments acquire debt so they can have or do things today that their current income does not allow. The simplest and easiest examples of useful debts are cases where countries, businesses, or individuals incur debt in order to pay for things that make the borrower more productive in the future – education, infrastructure, capital equipment, new technologies, and other expenditures that are not possible with current income or savings. These expenditures require debt today but the benefit and tradeoff is that they also contribute to future productivity. This is the correct use of debt, as opposed to borrowing for consumption that does not leave the borrower better off and more able to repay debt in the future. The distinction between borrowing for investment or borrowing for consumption seems simple, but many cases are intermediate, such as borrowing for housing, or borrowing for investment that does not lead to the expected increases in productivity.

When the discussion is about government borrowing, the greatest fear is of a sovereign debt crisis, defined as the situation where an independent national government cannot make a scheduled payment on the interest or principal it owes. The discussion in Chapter 4 of Latin America's Lost Decade describes the most dramatic cases in recent history. Countries borrowed in order to maintain spending, much of which did not contribute to growth through increases in skills or infrastructure. Furthermore, most of the debt was external. External debt often intensifies and prolongs a crisis due to the fact that the borrowed money is denominated in a foreign currency, and the terms and conditions are set in New York, London, and other markets outside the borrowing countries. If debt is incurred in domestic currencies rather than foreign, it is more manageable as the borrowing countries have more options.

Too much government debt, however, is not the only kind of debt that causes problems. There are numerous cases, including the Subprime Crisis, where collapsing real estate or other asset prices made debt repayment impossible and triggered a financial crisis. The Subprime Crisis began with household defaults, which were also a characteristic of the Great Depression, along with farm defaults.[6] Defaults by homeowners or farmers are problems in the private market economy. Similarly, banking crises are usually classified separately from debt crises but they are a type of crisis caused by debt, in this case owed to depositors or other lenders. Failure in the shadow banking sector also stemmed from the inability of private firms to pay the debt they owed. Shiller (2012: 155–57) hypothesizes that debt may be at the source of many more crises than generally recognized.

Debt levels in the private sector can trigger a crisis but they can also affect the recovery. When households and businesses begin a crisis period with already high debt levels, they are in a weakened position and will experience delayed and slower recoveries. Debt overhang is the term used to describe debt that is so burdensome that it discourages new spending on investment and consumer goods by businesses and households. When emerging from a crisis with high debt levels, households and businesses alike tend to use a large share of their earnings to reduce debt and are cautious about making new investments or purchases. The lack of new expenditure in the recovery phase adds contractionary forces to the macroeconomy and helps explain why a number of recoveries were slower than expected. Debt overhang probably played a role in the Great Depression and was almost certainly an obstacle for Japan during its decade-long stagnation in the 1990s. It also helps explain the slow

6 Persons (1930), Fisher (1933) and Olney (1999) describe the role of private debt in the Great Depression and Glick and Lansing (2010) and IMF (2012a) show that countries with the largest increases in household debt were hardest hit by the Subprime Crisis. Mian and Sufi (2014) explore in depth the relationship between household debt and macroeconomic fragility.

recovery of several newly independent states after the break up of the Soviet Union.[7]

15.3 SOVEREIGN DEBT CRISES

Sovereign debt crises occur when an independent government misses an interest or principal payment on its debt. In most cases, an agreement is negotiated with creditors and the debt may be partially forgiven, rescheduled, or some combination of the two. The frequency of sovereign debt crises is perhaps higher that commonly believed. According to Reinhart and Rogoff (2009a) and Laeven and Valencia (2014), there were sixty-three defaults and reschedulings during a thirty-four year span from 1975 to 2008, which is nearly two a year. The timing of defaults is not evenly distributed over that period, however, with more in the 1980s during the Latin American Debt Crisis.

Beyond the number and frequency of sovereign debt crises, there are a few additional questions that researchers would like to have answered, if possible. Why do some government's default with relatively low debt levels and others seem able to carry extraordinarily high levels without an apparent problem? What factors other than the amount of debt are associated with an increase in the probability of a debt default? What policies have countries used to reduce their debt and to alleviate the problems caused by a default?

To begin to address some of these issues, it is useful to say a few words about debt measurement. Debt can be reported in absolute value or relative value, and as gross or net debt. The absolute value of debt is its monetary value, usually measured in domestic currency or US dollars. The relative value of debt is usually the debt to GDP measurement used here, and is considered more meaningful than absolute debt since it puts the level of debt in the context of the size

[7] Koo (2008) analyzes the role of debt overhang in the suppression of Japanese investment and growth. He also makes the argument that debt overhang in the 1930s explains the lack of growth in the first recession, 1929 to 1933. Jordà, Schularick, and Taylor (2011) study a large number of recessions in fourteen advanced countries between 1870 and 2008 and show that debt build up before a crisis significantly increases the depth of a crisis-associated recession.

of the economy. Debt to GDP is also useful when the goal is to compare country debt levels, as when, for example, Japan's debt level of more than 200 percent of GDP is compared to Germany's 60 percent of GDP. Gross sovereign debt is the total debt owed by a government, while net debt equals gross debt minus financial assets owned by (owed to) the government. For example, the IMF's estimate of Japan's gross debt in 2017 was 240 percent of GDP, and net debt was half that level, at 121 percent.[8]

By nearly any measure, Japan's level of debt is extraordinarily high yet there are no signs of looming default. Similarly, US debt is high by historical standards, at 108 percent gross and 82 percent net in 2017. This level is below that reached in the aftermath of World War II, in spite of major tax cuts in 2001, 2003, and 2018, and the Subprime Crisis' impact on tax revenues. Between 1946 and 1981, gross debt as a percentage of GDP fell from 119 percent to 31 percent of GDP before beginning a long climb back above 100 percent. The United States's post-World War II experience roughly parallels that of the United Kingdom, mentioned earlier (FRB St. Louis and OMB, 2017; Bank of England, 2018).

The common thread in the Japanese, United Kingdom and United States cases is that debt is entirely, or nearly entirely, in their domestic currency. In that sense, the owner of the debt is relatively less important, no matter whether it is a Chinese bank, a US hedge fund, a foreign government, or a US pension fund. The nationality of the owner of debt turns out to be much less important than the currency denomination of the debt and the repayment rules, including dispute resolution requirements. Japan owes yen, the United States owes dollars, and the United Kingdom owes pounds, while disputes between those governments and their lenders will be settled in the

8 The IMF's *World Economic Outlook Database* defines net debt as "gross debt minus financial assets corresponding to debt instruments. These financial assets are: monetary gold and SDRs, currency and deposits, debt securities, loans, insurance, pension, and standardized guarantee schemes, and other accounts receivable" (International Monetary Fund, 2017b). The IMF debt figures are "general government debt" and include all levels of government. Normally, when discussing debt, the more relevant concept is central government debt. Countries vary in the level of responsibility national governments have for local and provincial government debt.

courts of the issuing countries. During the Latin American Debt Crisis discussed in Chapter 4, the defaulting countries owed mostly dollars and the rules were set in New York, London, and other financial centers outside Latin America.

Internal or domestic debt is almost always debt that is owed in the domestic currency and is adjudicated in the courts of the borrowing country if disputes arise. External debt for most countries without reserve currencies, is usually borrowed from foreigners, nearly always in a foreign currency (often dollars), and is adjudicated in the courts of the lending country.[9] These differences between internal and external debt make their riskiness very dissimilar since internal debt can be paid back with domestic currency and is governed by national rules applied in national courts. Not only does the borrowing government have the capacity to print the money it owes, but its monetary policies can influence the inflation rate and directly change the real value of the debt. Given these considerations, it is not surprising that external debt is much riskier than internal debt and that defaults can occur at levels of debt that seem to be relatively low. As noted earlier, over half of all defaults by middle income countries between 1970 and 2008 were cases where the level of external debt was below 60 percent of national income, and in nearly 20 percent of cases, was below 40 percent. It is possible that there is an interaction between internal and external debt which explains why some defaults on external debt occur at relatively low levels. Countries with high levels of internal debt may be less able to manage the added burden of servicing their external debt and are more likely to default. Reinhart and Rogoff (2009a) refer to this as "debt intolerance."

With external debt, the debt-to-GDP ratio is informative, but sometimes less meaningful than alternative measures such as debt-to-exports, or debt-servicing-to-exports. Not infrequently, the size of the

[9] There is another category: foreign currency denominated domestic debt. This is debt created when a country agrees to repay in a foreign currency, but the rules and legal arrangements governing the debt are domestic. For the purposes of this chapter, it is of lesser importance and is ignored. It did play a significant role in Mexico's debt and currency crisis of 1994–1995.

debt relative to the size of the economy does not clearly signal the ability of a country to pay. As noted in Chapter 4, South Korea's debt-to-GDP ratio in 1980 was nearly the same as Argentina's, while Brazil and Mexico both had debt ratios that were significantly lower. Nevertheless, South Korea escaped the debt crisis, while Argentina, Brazil, and Mexico did not. One major difference was that South Korea's ability to earn dollars by selling exports to the rest of the world gave it a much greater capacity to pay interest and principal on its external debt. In 1980, two years before the Latin American Debt Crisis began, South Korea's ratio of debt-to-exports was 131 percent, while in Argentina, Brazil, and Mexico it was 242 percent, 301 percent, and 233 percent respectively (World Bank, 1987).

One of the most contentious issues related to government debt is the idea of debt thresholds beyond which economic growth slows significantly. Economists have spent a fair amount of energy trying to understand if debt thresholds exist and if so, then at what level. Higher debt levels are likely to raise borrowing costs through an increase in interest rates, and to reduce spending, particularly on investment goods, while increasing uncertainty. All of these factors might affect the rate of economic growth. Conversely, causation from debt to growth may be in the other direction since it is likely that slow growth causes debt levels to rise. Consequently, an observation of high debt and slow growth could have causation running in either direction. The problem of causation has been difficult to disentangle and there is no clear consensus as to whether debt causes slower growth or vice versa.[10] Researchers at the IMF (2012b: 106–09), for example, cite

10 For example, Carmen Reinhart and Kenneth Rogoff (2010), the two economists who are perhaps most responsible for making known the wide variation in debt levels at the time of default, believe their data shows a threshold at a debt-to-GDP level of 90 percent. Above that, they argue, average annual growth slows by about 1 percent per year in both advanced and emerging economies. Herndon, et. al. (2013) criticized Reinhart and Rogoff for having coding errors, selective omissions of available country data, and some statistical problems with the way they weighted their data. Rogoff (2013) responded with a detailed, point by point critique of the critique. Does debt above some level cause economic growth to slow? All we can say for certain is that we don't know.

empirical works demonstrating a negative growth-debt correlation and other works showing no correlation. In their analysis, the effects of debt on growth are mediated by a number of important variables, such as the stance of monetary and fiscal policies, inflation rates, trade balances, and exchange rates.

Analysis is complicated by the fact that rich and poor countries respond to debt differently. Reinhart and Rogoff, for example, argue that advanced economies "graduate" from the possibility of a sovereign debt crisis, although not completely and not in all cases.[11] Individual country characteristics matter and those with long histories of multiple defaults and high inflation find it harder to graduate. Clearly, however, countries that are able to borrow in their own currencies are less likely to default since they can print money. (Borrowing in your own currency is different, however, when your country is part of a monetary union, as Greece and other Eurozone countries demonstrate.) This is one of the primary reasons why emerging markets have tried to reduce their dollar denominated borrowing in favor of borrowing in their domestic currency.

15.4 A SECOND LOOK AT THE UNITED STATES

The United States has the exorbitant privilege of being the only supplier of the world's largest reserve currency and, along with its relatively strong institutions such as the rule of law, contract enforcement, and open and liquid financial markets, has a unique position in today's global economy, even as there is no guarantee that these conditions will last, nor that a rival won't emerge with better opportunities and lower transaction costs for investment, security, and growth. The point is not that the United States can ignore the constraints that affect other countries, but rather that its current position in the world economy is unique. While its privileges

11 While they argue that high income or advanced economies tend to "graduate" from debt crises (Reinhart and Rogoff, 2009a: 151), there is no evidence that they ever graduate from banking crises. Note however that they analyze a large number of defaults by the world's leading economies, including the United States, in the wake of World War I and II (Reinhart and Rogoff, 2014).

are shared by a few other countries, the others are not quite as free from many of the constraints as is the United States. Consequently, recognition of the United States's unique position in the world economy is important to an understanding of its debt and deficits.

If pushed, the United States can pay nearly any size debt because it can create the dollars needed. That would not be an optimal monetary policy and it raises issues of equity and fairness but it at least rules out a sovereign debt crisis. Furthermore, long before such a radical response becomes necessary, markets would signal with higher interest rates that the world economy no longer wants to buy US government bills. To date, the US government has not experienced any difficulties in borrowing despite the fact that the US debt is the highest it has been since the end of World War II. Interest rates continue to be below historical averages, so much so that the Federal Reserve is worried that it will not have space to lower them when the next recession starts.

If the problem of a sovereign debt crisis is off the table, at least in the short and medium terms, and low market interest rates continue to signal that the US Treasury can sell its debt cheaply, then how about the burden-on-future-generations-argument against debt? Do not large debts today place a burden on future generations that will have to repay the debt? The answer to this question is not completely obvious. First, the United States does not have to repay all its debt but can continue to carry it forward by borrowing more to pay off principal when it is due. In this sense, it may seem that governments are not like households, but in fact the same applies to a majority of households. Most people probably spend most of their life with at least some debt in the form of mortgages, car loans, credit cards, and student loans. Few of us ever pay off our debt completely, nor do we need to. We only have to service the debt. Second, future generations will inherit the bonds that are sold today, so while they are paying off old debt, they will also be the recipients of most of the payments. There are distributional issues between taxpayers and bondholders, some of whom are the same and some of whom are not, but most future payments will be made to residents of the United States. Third, if debt today is used to increase the productivity of the economy, then repayment in the future will be easier. If, however, debt today is incurred for nonproductive uses, then the future inherits debt without an enhanced ability to service it. The distributional issue of debt uncovers the political nature of the discussion. Decisions about taxation and public spending priorities are at the core of most people's interest in deficits and debt, and the later are often a rhetorical device to oppose or support the former. In spite of the fact that arguments about deficits and debts are often vigorous and passionate, they are usually of secondary importance to the policy change under consideration. Most people seem perfectly willing to shift their stance on deficits and debt if a preferred policy requires them to do so.

Even though a lot of the discussion of debt is politically motivated by other concerns, it does not mean that debt is a nonproblem in the United States and other advanced economies. The most important issue about debt is long term and demographic in nature. Population in most high income countries is aging and over the next few decades, depending on the country, there will be fewer working age people per retired person. Pension and health care systems will be under pressure to adjust to increased needs at the same time there are fewer working people paying into the systems. If countries have high levels of debt as they move down this demographic path, then they will have fewer options for adjustment. This is a serious problem since tax burdens could end up quite high or the generational compact between retirees and workers could be broken. Nevertheless, as with the other issues, the solution is in the realm of politics and involves societal choices about taxes, benefits, and intergenerational transfers.

A relevant question for the United States and all countries is whether debt levels are sustainable.[12] This is the question of debt thresholds again, and in general, there is not a well established rule

12 The World Bank defines external public debt as sustainable "... when it can be serviced without resort to exceptional financing (such as debt relief) or a major future correction in the balance of income and expenditures" (World Bank, 2006).

for determining the amount of debt a country can incur without running the risk of default. The World Bank, for example, has a set of rules for determining debt sustainability for individual countries, but ultimately "staff judgments" play an important role.[13] Consequently, about all we can say for certain is that, all else being equal, less debt is safer than more debt. Another way to come at this problem, however, is to ask what level of debt can be sustained over some period of time. In many respects this is the same as asking if there is a crisis threshold, but it is more subtle since the concept of debt sustainability recognizes that countries may have a level of debt that cannot be sustained but that does not imply a pending crisis. A common indicator of debt sustainability is related to the rate of increase of a country's debt level: How fast is it growing? The relevant benchmark for sustainability is that it is growing less rapidly than the country's GDP. As long as that is the case, the debt-to-GDP ratio shrinks and debt becomes more manageable under most conditions.

A deficit hawk who reads this may surmise that the arguments presented are intended to dismiss the problem of debt. That is not the intention. Debt can cause severe problems, as illustrated by government debts during the Latin American Debt Crisis and private debts during the Subprime Crisis. The key issue is stressed in every elementary economics text: debt is beneficial when it is used to increase productivity and is potentially harmful when it is used to increase

13 The World Bank program to assess debt sustainability in low income countries (Low Income Country Debt Sustainability Framework, or LIC DSF) uses an index of policy and institutional strength assessments (Country Policy and Institutional Assessment, or CPIA) along with macroeconomic projections and staff judgments to estimate sustainability thresholds for low income country debt. There is a great deal of guesswork in this methodology, however, from construction of the CPIA index to forecasts of macroeconomic conditions and overall judgment of conditions. As noted by the World Bank, "Baseline macroeconomic projections and stress test scenarios are evaluated relative to these thresholds, and used in conjunction with staff judgment to assign risk ratings of external debt distress. The value of these risk ratings is, of course, dependent on the realism of medium- to long-term macroeconomic projections .... " One might add that they are dependent on the staff judgments as well (World Bank, 2017b).

consumption or to buy assets such as houses that cannot be traded internationally.

15.5 GETTING OUT OF DEBT

Another contentious issue, but one with more definite historical lessons is the type of policies countries should follow in order to get out of a public debt crisis or to remove a potentially serious debt problem. Since this is a question of policy and affects many countries, there are strongly held beliefs about the right and wrong kind of actions countries should follow. Fears of moral hazards and the desire to avoid rewards for irresponsible financial management guide one set of observers, while others worry about punitive policies that in the end are ineffective at crisis resolution and may even cause an increase in debt levels. Both the European Union and the United States cut stimulus spending too soon and, as a result, experienced abnormally slow recoveries. Frequently, debt incurred through spending to end a recession causes tax revenues to rebound more quickly and avoids the losses of skills, labor, and technology that occur during a prolonged recession. In this case, the fear of deficit spending slows the recovery and in the long run, increases debt by more than additional spending would have.

Most policy advice for managing a debt crisis or reducing a country's level of debt tries to lower the ratio of debt to GDP. Since it is a ratio, there are two main approaches and both are visible in the historical record. One approach is to shrink the debt directly. In this strategy, governments are encouraged to run primary surpluses with some combination of tax increases and/or cuts in public spending.[14] An alternative is to generate more GDP growth and to grow out of the debt. While these two approaches are often used in combination, both are problematic. Cuts in spending and tax increases can be counterproductive if applied too vigorously because they shrink GDP. Countries may successfully reduce their debt level, but

14 The primary budget balance is the surplus or deficit when interest on the debt is omitted.

if GDP falls, then the burden of debt measured by the debt-to-GDP ratio may actually increase. As discussed in Chapters 7 and 13, this happened in the Eurozone, and it may have been a factor in the rise in US debt levels. Austerity as a solution to a debt crisis has a very poor record and can even cause long run damage. If austerity causes a recession, depending on its depth and length, long term effects that permanently shrink the capacity of the economy are possible. When people lose jobs, their skills atrophy, and some workers chose to permanently leave the labor force while others migrate. Similarly, machinery depreciates in idle factories, and in the end, the capacity of the economy to produce may be less than before austerity was imposed. Ultimately, the ability of the economy to manage a given level of debt is impaired rather than enhanced.

This argues for an approach to debt relief which tries to support GDP and GDP growth. Clearly, if growth can be restored then governments will have more resources for addressing their debt and the relative weight of debt declines. The main problem is that economic growth in a crisis and its immediate aftermath is difficult to achieve. Recessions that accompany financial crises, regardless of the type, are more severe and last longer, and the toolbox of policymakers is usually empty given that fiscal expansion is limited by the ability to borrow and monetary expansion is often ineffective or creates other problems. Furthermore, policy differences tend to become more contentious and politics more polarized during financial crises.

The options for debt reduction and GDP growth are limited and constrained by the usual asymmetry between borrowers who are vulnerable and lenders who are frequently better off and better organized. This is particularly true in the case of international debts when lenders are located in the world's money centers and can work with the governments of advanced economies to shape international economic policies. For example, during the Latin American Debt Crisis, lenders formed a cartel which had the explicit support of the United States and other advanced economy governments while borrowers had no similar organizing capability. For reasons that are not entirely clear, except perhaps because of this asymmetry, borrowers are usually viewed as responsible for a debt crisis even though lenders are equally to blame. The result is that there is a bias toward policies that reduce spending in the indebted country through some form of austerity. The Greek case in the Eurozone Crisis highlights both the asymmetry in policies toward lenders and borrowers and the preference for policies of austerity. The negative and ineffective results of austerity were more easily dismissed due to the fact that Greece mismanaged and fraudulently reported its fiscal accounts prior to the crisis and some kind of punishment seemed justified by those living in the countries where lenders were at risk of losing money on the risky bets they had made.

In practice, a common escape route from unsustainable domestic debt is a steady dose of inflation, often accompanied by financial repression.[15] Inflation increases nominal GDP which shrinks the debt-to-GDP level. Obviously it is not a solution for external debt owed in a foreign currency, but it has been widely used throughout history for domestic currency debt, from the sweating and clipping of metallic coins by European sovereigns, to the European and Japanese inflations after World Wars I and II. Financial repression that accompanies inflation serves as a mechanism to remove pressure on debt repayment by forcing domestic interests to buy government debt. For example, banks, pension funds, and insurance companies can be forced to hold some or all of their reserves in the form of government bills.[16]

While inflation may reduce debt denominated in domestic currency, it does not reduce external debt denominated in a foreign currency, and will actually increase the debt burden if it leads to

15 Reinhart and Rogoff (2014: 147) suggest that there are five ways to reduce debt: growth, austerity, default or restructuring, inflation, and financial restrictions on banking and finance accompanied by inflation. They note that growth is a relatively rare solution to debt.

16 Financial repression also includes measures to limit international capital flows, limit bank interest rates, and others that more closely tie together the banking system and government.

a currency devaluation. In the end, however, debt that cannot be paid will not be paid. Consequently the solution to an external debt crisis usually requires some degree of debt reduction through a combination of rescheduling to lengthen the repayment period and lower the individual payments, lowering of interest rates, and outright debt forgiveness.[17] Debt forgiveness or restructuring as methods of managing a crisis raise moral hazard issues and are unpopular with lenders, yet they are very commonly used to end or reduce the severity of a debt crisis, primarily because there are no other options.

17 In discussing debt restructuring, Das, Papaioannou, and Trebesch (2014: 595) note that there have been "more than 600 individual cases in 95 countries since 1950."

Conclusion

> Every change in financial institutions is an experiment, and only after many years of experience with any institution do we know how well it will work.
>
> Robert J. Shiller (2012: 177)

It is too soon to know if the financial controls implemented in the wake of the recent Subprime Crisis are as robust as the reforms put into place after the Great Depression. It seems unlikely, however, that the next seventy-five years will be free from a systemwide crisis like the seventy-five years from the Great Depression to the Subprime Crisis. The complexity of finance, together with its international linkages, rapid development of new technologies such as blockchain and risk models, and institutional innovations such as the various forms of shadow banking, seem to argue against another long period of relative quiet.

There are plenty of possibilities for another crisis. China has accumulated massive amounts of internal debt in its shadow banks and state owned enterprises. The Eurozone will continue to create divergences between weak and strong economies, along with pressures to implement austerity in countries already suffering from slow or negative growth. The reactions against international trade and finance by populists and authoritarians in Europe and the United States pose an uncertain future for value chains, trade relations, and the liberal democratic order. As ever, financial interests continue to push for more deregulation in financial markets. Cyberwar and cyberattacks against financial systems could create massive disruptions. A financial meltdown in a leading emerging market such as Turkey could spill across borders and disrupt trade and finance in unexpected places. And these are just some of the obvious cases in 2019. Most likely, the next systemic crisis will be the result of forces few are thinking about today.

The lessons of the past are nearly impossible to learn due to our tendency to think we are different from our predecessors. In the age of electronic communications and increased international integration, this tendency causes us to see ourselves as unique in history and it obscures the ways in which we live the same patterns as people before us. The Eurozone could have learned from Latin America and other historical episodes that austerity is rarely if ever a solution to debt, and Thailand could have learned from the Mexican experience in the early 1990s that large capital inflows and real appreciation are very dangerous to economic health. The United States should have known that a nationwide decline in housing prices is not impossible and the IMF, the European Union, and the United States should all have remembered the lessons of the 1930s, that the escape from the Great Depression ultimately happened through public spending that made up for missing private spending.

To be sure, some lessons have been learned. In the United States, the Subprime Crisis resulted in the Great Recession, not another Great Depression. Criticisms of Federal Reserve policy aside, the US credit system did not collapse as it did in the 1930s because there were targeted efforts to keep it operating. In spite of the constant push toward deregulation in financial markets, there are new approaches, including macroprudential regulation and plans for the orderly liquidation of failing systemically important institutions. Until there is a crisis we cannot know how well these systems will work, but at a minimum, there is recognition of some of the problems and with any luck, the new systems will protect us from the worst.

Part 3 discussed eight specific lessons from the perspective of economic and financial analysis. It did not try to analyze whether these lessons have been learned and incorporated into new regulatory systems or new rules for managing financial services. The lessons are known by economists but are not necessarily reflected in our institutions and several have serious political obstacles to acceptance. Nevertheless, some of the lessons have been incorporated into policy. For example, the first three lessons are prominent in the 2010 Dodd–Frank financial reform legislation passed by the United States. The long run tendency toward less financial regulation has been reversed and belief in a self-regulating financial system now seems exotic and a bit odd. Progress is not linear, but even with current conditions in US politics and its backsliding toward less regulation, there is a new wariness toward unregulated financial markets. Debates over the efficacy of particular regulations will no doubt continue, and corrections to the Dodd–Frank legislation must continue to be debated and implemented where necessary, but the powers granted the FDIC and the FSOC to designate systemically important businesses and to impose tougher standards share widespread support. Similarly, the European Union created the European Systemic Risk Board to guard against bubble-like problems and other systemwide risks. These new authorities also incorporate the second lesson that shadow banks operate in ways that are essentially similar to legally designated banks and must be subject to some oversight. The FSOC, along with rules governing capital levels, required liquidity, and transparency in derivative markets are efforts to pull shadow banks out of the shadows and to create oversight and supervision similar to that in the regular banking sector. While Dodd–Frank in the United States and the Basel III agreement for Europe raised capital standards for banks and other important financial enterprises, there continues to be a great deal of uncertainty around the optimal levels of capital and debt. European standards are lower than in the United States, and both are below what some academics regard as optimal.

Lessons four through six are mostly not incorporated into new rules or policies. Lessons four and five, on monetary and fiscal policies are not directly related to crisis prevention but concern crisis mitigation or crisis management. Considering monetary policy first, central banks have learned (relearned is probably more accurate) that financial stability must be one of their goals. The Federal Reserve of the United

States was established in large part to support greater financial stability. The Panic of 1907 caused bank failures, a steep decline of the money supply in New York where the financial stress was greatest, a collapse in asset prices, and a recession. The establishment of the Federal Reserve Bank in 1914 was a response. Over the subsequent decades, however, the financial stability role of the Federal Reserve diminished as it became more focused on its role as a lender of last resort and as a supporter of economic growth with stable prices. Adding financial stability back into the list of Federal Reserve responsibilities is absolutely necessary, but is not an easy task given that their tools are limited to monetary policy and some regulatory powers. When monetary policy becomes relatively ineffective as interest rates approach zero, its options become more and more limited and results are less certain. The Federal Reserve, the Bank of England, and the ECB, all used unconventional monetary policy to buy private assets, often long term ones rather than short term, and in order to provide liquidity, support credit markets, and influence long run interest rates. Most analysis shows some positive effects, although the evidence is not overwhelming. Central banks would prefer to be able to use conventional monetary policy, but given our current state of knowledge, no amount of legislation or rule changing will turn ineffective monetary policies into suddenly effective ones or make financial stability an easy target for monetary policy. In this respect, the Federal Reserve's participation in the FSOC, and the creation of the European Systemic Risk Board are positive steps toward financial stability, but neither will make monetary policy better or provide an alternative to the times when it is ineffective.

Lesson five on fiscal multipliers is far from being absorbed. The Eurozone and the United Kingdom continue to promote austerity as a path to prosperity in spite of the empirical evidence. Furthermore, there seems to be an effort to ignore the fact that every European government that could, implemented expansionary policies in 2008 and 2009. That is, when the crisis was most intense, they knew what the right policies were, but they were unable to resist premature tightening as the worst passed even though their economies were still fragile and weak. The shift to austerity in late 2009 and 2010 was most damaging to economies where capital inflows had been strongest prior to the crisis and where the crisis was most severe: Cyprus, Greece, Ireland, Italy, Portugal, and Spain. Ireland has been hailed as the star of this group since it recovered its precrisis level of GDP before the others and has grown relatively rapidly since then. However, even the star performer took seven years to recover its precrisis level of real GDP. And in the other countries, it took nine years (Spain) or ten years (Cyprus and Portugal), while in two countries (Greece and Italy) real GDP is still below the 2007 level (as of 2018).[1] All countries recover from negative shocks sooner or later but this recovery is much slower than normal, and is so slow that it is worse than the United States's recovery from the Great Depression, which took seven years to climb back to the 1929 precrisis peak.

The need for fiscal integration as a complement to monetary integration is also a long way from being resolved and continues to sporadically flare-up into potential crises and serious worries about euro viability. The latest flare-up (2018) is related to Italy's populist movements and the difficulties of forming a government. Most of these storms will pass, but that will not be the case indefinitely. The lack of fiscal integration is a weakness at the core of the common currency and, to date at least, there appears to be no prospect to change that fact and therefore no way to avoid the problems that emerge when economic conditions diverge. Countries have no tools to combat a recession and the Stability and Growth Pact demands that they balance their budgets when deficits grow, as they inevitably do during a recession. Researchers may be exploring ways to reconcile the diverse political opinions regarding austerity and risk sharing, but political leaders are not yet ready to move away from austerity as

1 Data are constant price gross domestic product in national currency from the IMF's World Economic Outlook Database (April 2018). Portugal and Cyprus are estimated by the IMF to recover their 2008 precrisis levels in the current year (2018). The IMF forecasts extend to 2023; Greece is not expected to recover by then while Italy is estimated to regain its precrisis GDP in that year.

a one-size-fits-all solution to economic divergences (Bénassy-Quéré, et al., 2018).

The last two lessons, on international capital flows and debt, have seen definite progress, albeit less so in the case of debt. Prior to the Subprime Crisis, and partly in response to the East Asian Crisis, the IMF and the US Treasury began to adjust their positions on open capital markets. Policymakers and advisers are much more cautious about pushing countries to completely open their financial markets to international capital flows, while researchers are keen to define the policies that capture the benefits but avoid the dangers. In addition, the potential to use capital controls or restrictions during a crisis in order to mitigate some of the damage continues to be an important topic of investigation.

The issue of debt is probably one of the oldest issues in economics, but that does not mean that there is a great deal of agreement. We know, for example, that countries that borrow in their own currencies cannot experience a Greek-style default since they can always print money to pay off their bond holders. And we know that countries in a similar position to the United States, with strong institutions and the ability to borrow in their own currency, do not face the same pressures or vulnerabilities as other countries. That can change, however, as foreign holders of debt may not be content to hold the same assets indefinitely into the future, particularly if there are reevaluations of the role of leading economies. British exit from the European Union, a decline in US reliability and leadership, or other factors could cause a shift in opinions over time, and a shift in the willingness of foreigners to finance the debts of those countries.

The introduction to this book argued that financial crises are a natural part of market economies. It argued that crises are embedded in market relations, and whether they are caused by too much debt, overvalued currencies, financial liberalization, or some other vulnerability, it is certain there will be more crises. It is impossible to predict where the next one will start, or what will trigger it. Legislative and regulatory remedies to avoid the next crisis are worthy efforts, but usually we do not see a crisis coming until it is upon us. The Dodd–Frank legislation was designed to prevent another Subprime Crisis, not to anticipate where the next one starts or how it will be transmitted. By the time we grasp the full significance of new financial innovations, or understand their limits, the excesses can grow beyond the ability of public authorities and private interests to protect against the fallout. New direct bank loans to Latin America, or emerging market investment vehicles, or shadow banks in the United States, quietly offered new ways to move capital from one place to another, feeding economic growth and conveying a sense of innovation with widespread, tangible, benefits: more investment in Latin America, greater financial depth in East Asia, and more mortgages and home ownership in the United States.

All economies need finance. They need to be able to store wealth for future use and to move wealth from one place to another so it can be put to more productive uses. Financial globalization is part of an ongoing process of international economic integration that has resulted in larger movements of people, goods, and services. New technologies have facilitated these movements and have created a number of challenges for governments, businesses, and households. While we may sometimes wish to stop the relentless pace of change, that is not a realistic option, even as the changes brought by new technologies and increased integration are disruptive and make many people uncertain about their futures. In order to deal with the changes, we must find ways to reduce the insecurity generated by new technologies and new movements of capital, goods, services, and people. A good place to begin is with recognition of the constant risks inherent in market economies, and in the development of policies that protect people against the fallout when there is a crisis. We should not accept the view that nothing can be done to prevent or ameliorate crises nor should we accept the idea that risk reduction is inherently harmful to markets. Globalization in general, and financial globalization in particular, have contributed to the reduction in global poverty and improvements in living standards and we should try to protect those benefits, while looking for ways to reduce the human and financial costs of crises.

Abbreviations and Acronyms

ABCP	Asset backed commercial paper
ABMI	Asian Bond Market Initiative
ADB	Asian Development Bank
AIG	American International Group
AIIB	Asian Infrastructure Investment Bank
AMF	Asian Monetary Fund
ASEAN	Association of Southeast Asian Nations
BNL	Banca Nazionale del Lavoro
BNP	Banque Nationale de Paris
CDO	Collateralized debt obligation
CEPR	Centre for Economic Policy Research
CFPB	Consumer Financial Protection Bureau
ECB	European Central Bank
ECLA	Economic Commission on Latin America
EMS	European Monetary System
EMU	Economic and Monetary Union
FCIC	Financial Crisis Inquiry Commission
FDI	Foreign direct investment
FDR	Franklin D Roosevelt
FDIC	Federal Deposit Insurance Corporation
FHFA	Federal Housing Finance Agency
FRB	Federal Reserve Bank
FRBSF	Federal Reserve Bank of San Francisco
FSOC	Financial Stability Oversight Council
GATT	General Agreement on Tariffs and Trade
GDP	Gross domestic product
GIIPS	Greece, Ireland, Italy, Portugal, and Spain
GSE	Government sponsored enterprises
HPAE	High Performance Asian Economies

IGM	Initiative on Global Markets
IMF	International Monetary Fund
ISI	Import substitution industrialization
MBS	Mortgage backed securities
OMT	Outright Monetary Transactions
QE	Quantitative easing
SIB	Systemically Important Bank
SIFI	Systemically Important Financial Institutions
SMP	Securities Markets Program
SPG	Stability and Growth Pact
S&P	Standard and Poors
VW	Volkswagen
WTO	World Trade Organization

Bibliography

Admati, A. (2014). "Seeing through 'the banker's new clothes": Anat Admati at TEDxStanford". www.youtube.com/watch?v=s_I4vx7gHPQ

Admati, A., and Hellwig, M. (2013). *The Bankers' New Clothes: What's Wrong with Banking and What to Do about It*, Princeton, NJ: Princeton University Press.

Akerlof, G. and Romer, P. (1993). Looting: The economic underworld of bankruptcy for profit. *Brookings Papers on Economic Activity*, 2, 1–73.

Akerlof, G. and Shiller, R. (2015). *Phishing for Phools: The Economics of Manipulation and Deception*, Princeton, NJ: Princeton University Press.

Alesina, A.F. and Ardagna, S. (2010). Large Changes in Fiscal Policy: Taxes versus Spending. In J. R. Brown, ed., *Tax Policy and the Economy, Vol. 24*. Cambridge, MA: National Bureau of Economic Research, 35–68.

Anginer, D., Demirgüç-Kunt, A. and Zhu, M. (2014). How does deposit insurance affect bank risk? Evidence from the recent crisis. *Journal of Banking and Finance*, 48, 312–321.

Asian Development Bank (2017). Free trade agreements. Asia Regional Integration Center. https://aric.adb.org/fta

Auerbach, A., and Gorodnichenko, Y. (2012). Measuring the output responses to fiscal policy. *American Economic Journal – Economic Policy*, 4, 1–27.

Bagehot, W. (1873). *Lombard Street: A Description of the Money Market*. London: Henry S. King & Co.

Baldwin, R. and Giavazzi, F., editors (2015). Introduction. In R. Baldwin and F. Giavazzi, eds., *The Eurozone Crisis: A Consensus View of the Causes and a Few Possible Remedies*. London: CEPR Press. A VoxEU.org eBook: http://voxeu.org/content/eurozone-crisis-consensus-view-causes-and-few-possible-solutions

Ball, L. (2016). The Fed and Lehman Brothers: A new narrative. Vox CEPR Portal. August. https://voxeu.org/article/fed-and-lehman-brothers

(2018). *The Fed and Lehman Brothers: Setting the Record Straight on a Financial Disaster*. Cambridge, UK: Cambridge University Press

Ball, L., Leigh, D. and Loungani, P. (2011, September). Painful medicine. *Finance & Development*, 48:3. www.imf.org/external/pubs/ft/fandd/2011/09/ball.htm

Bank of England (2018). Public sector debt outstanding in the United Kingdom [PSDOTUKA]. Retrieved from FRED, Federal Reserve Bank of St. Louis; https://fred.stlouisfed.org/series/PSDOTUKA, Last accessed May 17, 2018.

Bank for International Settlements (2016). *Triennial Central Bank Survey*. www.bis.org/publ/rpfx16.htm

Barnichon, R., Matthes, C., and Ziegenbein, A. (2018). The financial crisis at 10: Will we ever recover? *Economic Letter*. 2018–19. Federal Reserve Bank of San Francisco.

Barr, M. D. (2000). Lee Kuan Yew and the "Asian values" debate. *Asian Studies Review*, 24:3, 309–334.

Barroso, J. M. (2011). "A Europe for all weathers." Speech delivered to EU Heads of Delegation. November 30. Available: europa.eu/rapid/press-release_SPEECH-11-838_en.doc

Bartholomew, P.E., Mote, L.R., and Whalen, G. (1995). The definition of systemic risk. Washington, DC: U.S. Office of the Comptroller of the Currency, Department of Economic and Policy Analysis, Bank Research Division.

Bayoumi, T. and Masson, P. (1995). Fiscal flows in the US and Canada: Lessons for monetary union in Europe. *European Economic Review*, 39: 253–274.

BBC News. (2010, 2 May). Eurozone approves massive Greece bail-out. http://news.bbc.co.uk/2/hi/europe/8656649.stm

(2018, 22 June). Greece hails "historic" debt relief deal. www.bbc.com/news/business-44573548

Bénassy-Quéré, A., Brunnermeier, M.K., Enderlein, H., et al. (2018). Reconciling risk sharing with market discipline: A constructive approach to euro area reform. *CEPR Policy Insight No. 91*. https://cepr.org/sites/default/files/policy_insights/PolicyInsight91.pdf

Bernanke, B. (1983). Nonmonetary effects of the financial crisis in the propagation of the Great Depression. *American Economic Review*, 73:3, 257–276.

(1995). "The Macroeconomics of the Great Depression: A Comparative Approach." *Journal of Money, Credit and Banking*. 27:1. 1–28.

(2000a). Japanese monetary policy: A case of self-induced paralysis? In A. Posen and R. Mikitani, eds., *Japan's Financial Crisis and Its Parallels to US Experience*. Washington, DC: Peterson Institute for International Economics. 149–166.

(2000b). Nonmonetary effects of the financial crisis in the propagation of the Great Depression. In Bernanke, ed., *Essays on the Great Depression (Chapter 2)*. Princeton, NJ: Princeton University Press. 41–69.

(2005). The global saving glut and the US current account deficit. Sandridge Lecture. Virginia Association of Economists, Richmond, Virginia. www.federalreserve.gov/boarddocs/speeches/2005/200503102/

(2012). The aftermath of the financial crisis. *Bernanke College Lecture Series.* Board of Governors of the Federal Reserve System. www.federalreserve.gov/aboutthefed/educational-tools/lecture-series-the-aftermath-of-the-crisis.htm.

(2015). *The Courage to Act: A Memoir of a Crisis and its Aftermath.* New York: W.W. Norton & Company.

Bernanke, B. and James, H. (1991). The gold standard, deflation, and financial crisis in the Great Depression: An international comparison. In R.G. Hubbard, ed., *Financial Markets and Financial Crises.* Chicago, IL: University of Chicago Press 33–68.

Bértola, L. and Ocampo, J.A. (2012). *The Economic Development of Latin America since Independence.* Oxford, UK: Oxford University Press.

Bilefsky, D., and Thomas Jr., L. (2010, May 2). Greece takes its bailout, but doubts for the region persist. *New York Times.* https://nyti.ms/2r1ik0N

Blanchard, O. and Leigh, D. (2013). Growth forecast errors and fiscal multipliers. *International Monetary Fund Working Paper* WP/13/1. www.imf.org/external/pubs/ft/wp/2013/wp1301.pdf

Blinder, A. (2013). *After the Music Stopped: The Financial Crisis, the Response, and the Work Ahead.* New York: Penguin Books.

Blustein, P. (2001). *The Chastening: Inside the Crisis That Rocked the Global Financial System and Humbled the IMF.* New York, N.Y.: Public Affairs.

Board of Governors of the Federal Reserve. (2015). Total assets of the Federal Reserve, credit and liquidity programs and the balance sheet. www.federalreserve.gov/monetarypolicy/bst_recenttrends.htm

(2017a). Foreign exchange rates—H.10. www.federalreserve.gov/releases/h10/hist/default.htm

(2017b). Malaysia / U.S. Foreign Exchange Rate [EXMAUS], retrieved from FRED, Federal Reserve Bank of St. Louis; https://fred.stlouisfed.org/series/EXMAUS.

(2017c). South Korea / U.S. Foreign Exchange Rate [EXKOUS], retrieved from FRED, Federal Reserve Bank of St. Louis; https://fred.stlouisfed.org/series/EXKOUS.

Bolt, J. and van Zanden, J. L. (2014). The Maddison Project: collaborative research on historical national accounts. *Economic History Review.* 67:3. 627–651. https://onlinelibrary.wiley.com/doi/abs/10.1111/1468-0289.12032

Bordo, M. (2008). Growing up to financial stability. *Economics.* 2:2008–12.1—17. www.economics-ejournal.org/economics/journalarticles/2008-12

Bordo, M. and Eichengreen, B. (1999). "Is our current international economic environment unusually crisis prone?" In D. Gruen and L. Gower, eds., *Capital Flows and the International Financial System.* Reserve Bank of Australia. www.rba.gov.au/publications/confs/1999/bordo-eichengreen.html

(2002). "Crises now and then: What lessons from the last era of financial globalization?" National Bureau of Economic Research Working Paper No. 8716.

Bordo, M., Eichengreen, B., and Irwin, D. (1999). "Is globalization today really different from globalization a hundred years ago?" *Brookings Trade Forum, 1999*. Washington, D.C.: The Brookings Institution. 1–50.

Bordo, M., Eichengreen, B., Klingebiel, D., and Martinez-Peria, M.S. (2001). "Is the crisis problem growing more severe?" *Economic Policy*. 16: 32. 53–82.

Bordo, M. and Meissner, C. (2010). Foreign capital and economic growth in the first era of globalization. National Bureau of Economic Research Working Paper 13577.

Borio, C., Erdem, M., Filardo, A., and Hofmann, B. (2015). "The costs of deflations: A historical perspective." *BIS Quarterly Review*. March18. 31–54. Available: www.bis.org/publ/qtrpdf/r_qt1503e.pdf

Boughton, J. (2001). *Silent Revolution: The International Monetary Fund 1979–1989*. Washington, DC: The International Monetary Fund.

Brown, E.C. (1956). Fiscal policy in the 'thirties: A reappraisal. *The American Economic Review*, 46:5. 857–879. Retrieved from www.jstor.org/stable/1811908

BLS (Bureau of Labor Statistics). (2016). Consumer price index for all urban consumers: All items [CPIAUCSL], retrieved from FRED, Federal Reserve Bank of St. Louis; https://fred.stlouisfed.org/series/CPIAUCSL.

(2017). Seasonally adjusted unemployment level and seasonally adjusted unemployment rate. Labor Force Statistics from the Current Population Survey. Series Id: LNS13000000 and LNS14000000.

Calvo, G. A. (1998). Capital flows and capital-market crises: The simple economics of sudden stops. *Journal of Applied Economics*. 1:1. 35–54.

Capie, F. H. (1992). "British economic fluctuations in the nineteenth century: Is there a role for money?" In S.N. Broadberry and N.F.R. Crafts, eds. *Britain in the International Economy*. New York: Cambridge University Press. 80–97.

Caprio, G. (1998). *Banking on crises: expensive lessons from recent financial crises*. World Bank, Development Research Group, Finance.

Caprio, G. and Klingebiel, D. (1997). "Bank insolvency: Bad luck, bad policy, or bad banking?" *Annual World Bank Conference on Development Economics 1996*. World Bank: Washington DC.

(2002). Episodes of systemic and borderline banking crises. In D. Klingebiel and L. Laeven, eds., *Managing the Real and Fiscal Effects of Banking Crises*. Discussion Paper 428. Washington, DC: World Bank. 31–49.

Carney, M. (16 June, 2014). Taking shadow banking out of the shadows to create sustainable market-based finance. *Financial Times*.

Case-Shiller (S&P Dow Jones Indices LLC, S&P/Case-Shiller U.S. National Home Price Index). (2017). [CSUSHPINSA], retrieved from FRED, Federal Reserve Bank of St. Louis; https://fred.stlouisfed.org/series/CSUSHPINSA

CFPB (Consumer Finance Protection Bureau). (2018). www.consumerfinance.gov. [Accessed date July 18, 2018]

Chanda, N. (2007). *Bound Together: How Traders, Preachers, Adventurers, and Warriors Shaped Globalization.* New Haven: Yale University Press.

Chandler, A.D. (1977). *The Visible Hand: The Managerial Revolution in American Business.* Cambridge, MA: Belknap Press.

(1990). *Scale and Scope: The Dynamics of Industrial Capitalism. Cambridge,* MA: Belknap Press.

Claessens, S., Kose, M.A. and Terrones, M.E. (2009). What happens during recessions, crunches, and busts? *Economic Policy.* 24:60. 653–670.

Claessens, S. and Kose, M.A. (2014). Financial crises: Explanations, types, and implications. In S. Claessens, M.A. Kose, L. Laeven, and F. Valencia, eds., *Financial Crises: Causes, Consequences and Policy Responses.* Washington, DC: International Monetary Fund. 3–59. (Also published in 2013 as an IMF Staff Working Paper, WP/13/28.)

Cline, W. (1984). *International Debt: Systemic Risk and Policy Response.* Institute for International Economics: Washington DC.

(1995). *International Debt Reexamined.* Washington DC: Institute for International Economics.

(2017). *The Right Balance for Banks: Theory and Evidence on Optimal Capital Requirements.* Washington DC: Peterson Institute for International Economics

Cline, W. and Gagnon, J.E. (2013). Lehman died, Bagehot lives: Why did the Fed and Treasury let a major Wall Street bank fail? Policy Brief PB13-21. Peterson Institute for International Economics.

CBO (Congressional Budget Office). (2018). Chapter 4: The outlook for deficits and debt. *The Budget and Economic Outlook: 2018 to 2028.* www.cbo.gov/system/files/115th-congress-2017–2018/reports/53651-outlook.pdf

Council and Commission of the European Communities. (1970). *Report to the Council and the Commission on the realisation by stages of economic and monetary union in the Community* (Werner Report). October 8, 1970. http://aei.pitt.edu/1002/1/monetary_werner_final.pdf

Council on Foreign Relations. (2017). Greece's Debt. www.cfr.org/timeline/greeces-debt-crisis-timeline

Das, U., Papaioannou, M.G., and Trebesch, C. (2014). Restructuring sovereign debt: Lessons from recent history. In S. Claessens, M.A. Kose, L. Laeven, and F. Valencia, eds. *Financial Crises: Causes, Consequences and Policy Responses*. Washington, DC: International Monetary Fund. 593–620.

Dell'Ariccia, G., Igan, D., Laeven, L., and Tong, H. (2014). Policies for macro-financial stability: Dealing with credit booms and busts. In S. Claessens, M.A. Kose, L. Laeven, and F. Valencia, eds. *Financial Crises: Causes, Consequences and Policy Responses*. Washington, DC: International Monetary Fund. 325–364.

DeLong, J.B. (2013, 17 September). Let Me Sharply, Sharply Dissent from William Cline and Joe Gagnon on Paulson, Bernanke, and Geithner's Actions vis-a-vis Lehman in 2008. Blog: Grasping Reality with at Least Three Hands. http://delong.typepad.com/sdj/2013/09/let-me-sharply-sharply-dissent-from-william-cline-and-joe-bagnon-on-paulson-bernanke-and-geithners-actions-vis-a-vis-lehm.html.

DeLong, J.B., and Tyson, L.D. (2013, 5 April). Discretionary fiscal policy as a stabilization policy tool: What do we think now that we did not think in 2007? U.C. Berkeley. Draft 1.21. www.imf.org/external/np/seminars/eng/2013/fiscal/pdf/tyson.pdf.

Demirgüç-Kunt, A. and Detragiache, E. (1997). The determinants of banking crisis: Evidence from industrial and developing countries. World Bank Policy Research Working Paper 1828. Washington, DC: World Bank.

(1999). Financial liberalization and financial fragility. Policy Research Working Paper 1917. World Bank.

Diaz-Alejandro, C. (1985). Good-bye financial repression, hello financial crash. *Journal of Development Economics*. 19: 1/2.1–24.

Dornbusch, R. (1996). Euro fantasies. *Foreign Affairs* 75:5. 110–124.

Dornbusch, R., and Edwards, S. (1990). The macroeconomics of populism. In R. Dornbusch and S. Edwards, eds., *The Macroeconomics of Populism in Latin America*. Chicago: University of Chicago Press. 7–13.

Dornbusch, R. and Werner, A. (1994). Mexico: Stabilization, reform and no growth. *Brookings Papers on Economic Activity, 1:1994*. 253–315.

Dottle, R., King, R., and Koeze, E. (2017). Hurricane Harvey's impact – and how it compares to other storms. FiveThirtyEight Blog. https://fivethirtyeight.com/features/hurricane-harveys-impact-and-how-it-compares-to-other-storms/. [Accessed date March 29, 2018].

Dowd, K., Cotter, J., Humphrey, C., and Woods, M. (2008). How unlucky is a 25-Sigma? *arXiv, e-print*. Cornell University Library. arxiv.org/pdf/1103.5672.pdf

Draghi, M. (26 July, 2012). Speech by Mario Draghi, President of the European Central Bank at the Global Investment Conference in London. www.ecb.europa.eu/press/key/date/2012/html/sp120726.en.html

Easterly, W. (2013). *The Tyranny of Experts: Economists, Dictators, and the Forgotten Rights of the Poor*. New York: Basic Books.

Edwards, S. (1989). "Structural adjustment policies in highly indebted countries. In J. Sachs, ed., *Developing Country Debt and Economic Performance, Volume 1: The International Financial System*. Chicago, IL: University of Chicago Press. 159–207.

(1995). *Crisis and Reform in Latin America: From Despair to Hope*. World Bank: Washington DC.

(2010). *Left Behind: Latin America and the False Promise of Populism*. Chicago: University of Chicago Press.

Eichengreen, B. (1991). Is Europe an optimum currency area? National Bureau of Economic Research Working Paper No. 3579. Cambridge, MA: NBER

(1992). *Golden Fetters: The Gold Standard and the Great Depression, 1919–1939*. New York: Oxford University Press.

(1999). The Baring Crisis in a Mexican Mirror. *International Political Science Review*. 20:3. 249–270.

(2008). *Globalizing Capital: A History of the International Monetary System*. Princeton, NJ: Princeton University Press.

(2015). *Hall of Mirrors: The Great Depression, the Great Recession, and the Uses —and Misuses—of History*. New York: Oxford University Press.

Eichengreen, B. and Sachs, J. (1985). Exchange rates and economic recovery in the 1930s. *Journal of Economic History*. 45:4. 925–946.

Eichengreen, B. and Portes, R. (1989). Settling defaults in the era of bond finance. *The World Bank Economic Review*. 3:2. 211–239.

Eichengreen, B. and Frieden, J. (1994). The political economy of European monetary integration. In B. Eichengreen and J. Frieden, eds., *The Political Economy of European Monetary Unification*. Boulder, CO: Westview Press. 1–21.

Eichengreen, B. and Leblang, D. (2003). Capital account liberalization and growth: Was Mr. Mahathir right? National Bureau of Economic Research Working Paper No. 9427. Cambridge, MA: NBER

Eichengreen, B., Rose, A., and Wyplosz, C. (1995). Exchange market mayhem: The antecedents and aftermath of speculative attacks. *Economic Policy*. 10:21. 249–296.

European Commission. (No date). Banking Union. https://ec.europa.eu/info/business-economy-euro/banking-and-finance/banking-union_en.

(1977). *Report of the study group on the role of public finance in European integration, Volume 1: General Report*. (Called the MacDougall Report). Economic and Financial Series, 1977. http://aei.pitt.edu/36433/1/Report.study.group.A13.pdf

(2017). How is the EU budget spent? https://europa.eu/european-union/about-eu/money/expenditure_en

(2018). The history of the European Union, https://europa.eu/european-union/about-eu/history_en.

Fama, E. (2010, January 13). Interview with Eugene Fama by John Cassidy. *The New Yorker Blog*. www.newyorker.com/news/john-cassidy/interview-with-eugene-fama

FDIC (Federal Deposit Insurance Corporation). (2017). Failures and assistance transactions of all institutions for the United States and other areas. [BNKTTLA641 N], retrieved from FRED, Federal Reserve Bank of St. Louis; https://fred.stlouisfed.org/series/BNKTTLA641N

Feinstein, C.H., Temin, P., and Toniolo, G. (2008). *The World Economy between the World Wars*. New York: Oxford University Press.

Feldstein, M. (1997). The political economy of the European economic and monetary union: Political sources of an economic liability. National Bureau of Economic Research Working Paper No. 6150. Cambridge, MA: NBER.

Ffrench-Davis, R. (1998). The Latin American economies, 1950–1990. In Leslie Bethell, ed., *Latin America: Economy and Society Since 1930*. Cambridge, UK: Cambridge University Press. 159–250.

Ffrench-Davis, R. and Griffith-Jones, S. (2011). Taming capital account shocks: Managing booms and busts. In J.A. Ocampo and J. Ros, eds., *The Oxford Handbook of Latin American Economics*. New York: Oxford University Press. 161–186.

FHFA (US Federal Housing Finance Agency). (2017). All-transactions house price index for California [CASTHPI], retrieved from FRED, Federal Reserve Bank of St. Louis; https://fred.stlouisfed.org/series/CASTHPI.

Financial Crisis Inquiry Commission (FCIC). (2011). *Financial Crisis Inquiry Report: Final Report of the National Commission on the Causes of the Financial and Economic Crisis of the United States*. US Government Printing Office: Washington DC.

Fisher, I. (1933). The debt-deflation theory of great depressions. *Econometrica*. 1:4. 337–357.

Fleming, J.M. (1962). Domestic financial policies under fixed and under floating exchange rates. International Monetary Fund Staff Papers, 9. 369–79.

FRB Minneapolis. (2018). The Minneapolis Plan to end too big to fail. www.minneapolisfed.org/news-and-events/news-releases/minneapolis-fed-releases-final-plan-to-end-too-big-to-fail.

FRB New York. (No date). Actions related to AIG. www.newyorkfed.org/aboutthefed/aig

FRB St. Louis. (No date, a). Timeline: Federal Reserve Bank of St. Louis' financial crisis timeline. https://fraser.stlouisfed.org/timeline/financial-crisis

(No date, b). Financial crisis of 2007–2009. https://fraser.stlouisfed.org/theme/103

(2017a). Excess reserves of depository institutions [EXCSRESNS], retrieved from FRED, Federal Reserve Bank of St. Louis; https://fred.stlouisfed.org/series/EXCSRESNS.

(2017b). Federal Reserve Bank of St. Louis, St. Louis Fed Financial Stress Index© [STLFSI], retrieved from FRED, Federal Reserve Bank of St. Louis; https://fred.stlouisfed.org/series/STLFSI.

FRB St. Louis and U.S. Office of Management and Budget. (2017). Gross federal debt as percent of gross domestic product [GFDGDPA188S], retrieved from FRED, Federal Reserve Bank of St. Louis; https://fred.stlouisfed.org/series/GFDGDPA188S.

Freixas, X. and Laux, C. (2012). Disclosure, transparency and market discipline. In M. Dewatripont and X. Freixas, eds., *The Crisis Aftermath: New Regulatory Paradigms*. London: Centre for Economic Policy Research (CEPR).

French, K.R., et al. (2010). *The Squam Lake Report: Fixing the Financial System*. Princeton, NJ: Princeton University Press.

Frieden, J. (2018). A plan to save the euro. *Vox: CEPR Policy Portal.* https://voxeu.org/article/plan-save-euro

Friedman, M. *(1953)*. The case for flexible exchange rates. *Essays in Positive Economics*. Chicago, IL: University of Chicago Press. 157–203.

(1968). The role of monetary policy. *The American Economic Review*. 58:1. 1–17.

Friedman, M. and Schwartz, A. (1963). *A Monetary History of the United States: 1867–1960*. Chicago: University of Chicago Press.

Friedman, W. (2013). *Fortune Tellers: The Story of America's First Economic Forecasters*. Princeton, NJ: Princeton University Press.

Furman, J., and Stiglitz, J.E. (1998). Economic crises: Evidence and insights from East Asia. *Brookings Papers on Economic Activity, 1998, 2*. 1–135

Gadea, L., Gomez-Loscos, A., and Pérez-Quirós, G. (2015, 26 October). On the greatness of the great moderation. VOX. www.voxeu.org/article/greatness-great-moderation.

Galbraith, J. K. (1955). *The Great Crash, 1929*. Boston: Houghton Mifflin.

Geithner, T. (2014). *Stress Test: Reflections on Financial Crises*. New York: Crown Publishing.

Gerber, J. (2007). Import substitution industrialization. In W. Kerr and J. Gaisford, eds. *Handbook on International Trade Policy*. London: Edward Elgar. 441–449.

Gerber, J. and Passananti, T. (2015). The economic consequences of financial regimes: A new look at the banking policies of Mexico and Brazil, 1890–1910. *America Latina en la Historia Económica*. 22:1. 35–58.

Giovannini, A. (1990). European monetary reform: Progress and prospects. *Brookings Papers on Economic Activity* 2. 217–291

Glick, R. and Lansing, K.J. (2010). Global household leverage, house prices, and consumption. *FRBSF Economic Letter*. San Francisco: Federal Reserve Bank of San Francisco. www.frbsf.org/economic-research/publications/economic-letter/2010/january/global-household-leverage-house-prices-consumption/

Goetzmann, W.N. (2015). Bubble investing: Learning from history. National Bureau of Economic Research Working Paper No. w21693. Cambridge, MA: NBER.

Goodhart, C. and Delargy, P.J.R. (1998). Financial crises: Plus ça change, plus c'est la meme chose. *International Finance* 1. 261–287.

Google (2018). Emerging markets. Google Ngram Viewer. https://books.google.com/ngrams

Gordon, R.J. (2016). *The Rise and Fall of American Growth*. Princeton, NJ: Princeton University Press.

Gorton, G. (2009, 11–13 May). Slapped in the face by the invisible hand: Banking and the Panic of 2007. Conference on Financial Innovation and Crisis. Federal Reserve Bank of Atlanta.

(2010). *Slapped in the Face by the Invisible Hand: The Panic of 2007*. New York: Oxford University Press.

(2012). *Misunderstanding Financial Crises: Why We Don't See Them Coming*. Oxford University Press: New York.

Greenspan, A. (1997, 12 April). Speech to the Annual Conference of the Association of Private Enterprise Education. www.federalreserve.gov/boarddocs/speeches/1997/19970412.htm.

Guttentag, J. (1994, September). Debt, financial fragility, and systemic risk: A review. *Journal of Economic Literature*. 32:3. 1238–40.

Hellman, T., Murdock, K., and Stiglitz, J. (1997). Financial restraint: Toward a new paradigm. In M. Aoki, H.K Kim, and M. Okuno-Fujiwara, eds. *The Role of Government in East Asian Economic Development: Comparative Institutional Analysis*. Oxford: Clarendon Press.

Herndon, T., Ash, M., and Pollin, R. (2013). Does high public debt consistently stifle economic growth? A critique of Reinhart and Rogoff. Political Economy Research Institute, Working Paper Series, 322. Amherst, MA: University of Massachusetts, Amherst. www.peri.umass.edu/fileadmin/pdf/working_papers/working_papers_301-350/WP322.pdf

Hoshi, T. (2011). Financial regulation: Lessons from the recent financial crisis. *Journal of Economic Literature*. 49:1. 120–128.

IGM Forum. (2012, 15 February). Economic stimulus. IGM Economic Experts Panel. University of Chicago, Booth School of Business. www.igmchicago.org/surveys/economic-stimulus.

(2014a, 29 July). Economic stimulus (revisited). IGM Economic Experts Panel. University of Chicago, Booth School of Business. www.igmchicago.org/surveys/economic-stimulus-revisited

(2014b, 28 January). Chairman Bernanke. IGM Economic Experts Panel. University of Chicago, Booth School of Business. www.igmchicago.org/igm-economic-experts-panel/poll-results?SurveyID=SV_1GF6NyHSVWhEtN3. November 4, 2015.

(2017, 17 October). Factors contributing to the 2008 global financial crisis. IGM Economic Experts Panel. University of Chicago, Booth School of Business. www.igmchicago.org/surveys-special/factors-contributing-to-the-2008-global-financial-crisis-2

Independent Evaluation Office of the International Monetary Fund. (2014). *IMF Response to the Financial and Economic Crisis*. Washington, DC: IMF.

IMF (International Monetary Fund). (2010). Chapter 3: Will it hurt? Macroeconomic effects of fiscal consolidation. *World Economic Outlook*. Washington, DC: International Monetary Fund.

(2012a). Chapter 3: Dealing with household debt. *World Economic Outlook*. Washington, DC: International Monetary Fund.

(2012b). Chapter 3: The good, the bad, and the ugly: 100 years of dealing with public debt overhangs. *World Economic Outlook*. Washington, DC: International Monetary Fund.

(2014a) *Annual Report on Exchange Arrangements and Exchange Restrictions, 2014*. Washington, DC: International Monetary Fund. www.imf.org/external/pubs/nft/2014/areaers/ar2014.pdf.

(2014b). *Global Financial Stability Report: Moving from Liquidity- to Growth-Driven Markets*. Washington DC. https://www.imf.org/en/Publications/GFSR/Issues/2016/12/31/Moving-from-Liquidity-to-Growth-Driven-Markets

(2016, October). *World Economic Outlook Database*. October, 2016. www.imf.org/external/pubs/ft/weo/2016/02/weodata/index.aspx.

(2017a). *International Financial Statistics*. http://data.imf.org/?sk=4C514D48-B6BA-49ED-8AB9-52B0C1A0179B

(2017b). *World Economic Outlook Database*. April, 2017 release. www.imf.org/external/pubs/ft/weo/2017/01/weodata/index.aspx.

(2018). *World Economic Outlook Database.* April, 2018 release. www.imf.org/external/pubs/ft/weo/2018/01/weodata/index.aspx

Jeanne, O., Subramanian, A., and Williamson, J. (2012). *Who Needs to Open the Capital Account?* Washington, DC: Peterson Institute for International Economics.

Jonung, L. and Drea, E. (2010). It can't happen, it's a bad idea, it won't last: U.S. economists on the EMU and the euro, 1989–2002. *Econ Journal Watch.* 7:1. 4–52

Jordà, Ò., Richter, B., Schularick, M., and Taylor, A.M. (2017). Bank capital redux: Solvency, liquidity, and crisis. National Bureau of Economic Research Working Paper, No. 23287. Cambridge, MA: NBER.

Jordà, Ò., Schularick, M., and Taylor, A.M. (2011). When credit bites back: Leverage, business cycles and crisis. National Bureau of Economic Research Working Paper, No. 17621. Cambridge, MA: NBER.

(2013). Sovereigns versus banks: Credit, crises, and consequences. National Bureau of Economic Research Working Paper, No. 19506. Cambridge, MA: NBER.

(2016.) Bubbles, credit, and their consequences. *Economic Letter.* 2016–2027. Federal Reserve Bank of San Francisco.

Joyce, J.P. (2013). *The IMF and Global Financial Crises: Phoenix Rising?* New York: Cambridge University Press.

Kaag, J. (2016). *American Philosophy: A love story.* New York: Farrar, Strauss, and Giroux

Kahneman, D. (2011). *Thinking, Fast and Slow.* London: Penguin Books.

Kaldor, N. (1971). The dynamic effects of the Common Market. *New Statesman.* March 12. 329–340. Reprinted in *Further Essays on Applied Economics.* New York: Holmes and Meier Publishers, Inc. 187–220.

Kaminsky, G. and Reinhart, C. (1999). The twin crises: The causes of banking and balance-of-payments problems. *American Economic Review.* 89:3. 473–500.

Kaufmann, D., Kraay, A., and Mastruzzi, M. (2010). The Worldwide Governance Indicators: Methodology and analytical issues. World Bank Policy Research Working Paper No. 5430. Washington, DC: World Bank.

Kawai, M. and Wignaraja, G. (2010). Asian FTAs: Trends, prospects, and challenges. ADB Economic Working Paper Series, No. 226. Manila: Asian Development Bank.

Kay, J. (2015). *Other People's Money: The Real Business of Finance.* New York: Public Affairs.

Kenen, P. (1969). The theory of optimum currency areas: An eclectic view. In R. Mundell and A. Swoboda, eds., *Monetary Problems of the International Economy.* Chicago: University of Chicago Press. 41–60.

Keynes, J.M. (1936). *The General Theory of Employment, Interest, and Money*. New York: Harcourt Brace.

Kindleberger, C.P. (1973 [2013]). *The World in Depression, 1929–1939*. 40th Anniversary Edition. Berkeley, CA: University of California Press.

(1978). *Manias, Panics, and Crashes: A History of Financial Crises*. New York: Basic Books.

(1984). *A Financial History of Western Europe*. London: Routledge.

Konczal, M. (2015, 11 June). Two opposing methods tell us the too big to fail subsidy has collapsed. Next New Deal: The Blog of the Roosevelt Institute. http://bit.ly/1PjYmDm

Koo, R. (2008). *The Holy Grail of Macroeconomics: Lessons from Japan's Great Recession*. Hoboken, NJ: Wiley and Sons.

Kose, M.A., Prasad, E., Rogoff, K., and Wei, S.-J. (2009). Financial globalization: a reappraisal. *IMF Staff Papers*. 56:1. 8–62.

Kose, M.A., Prasad, E., and Taylor, A.D. (2011). Thresholds in the process of international financial integration. *Journal of International Money and Finance*. 30:1. 147–179.

Krugman, P. (1994). The myth of Asia's miracle. *Foreign Affairs*. 73:6. 62–78.

(1996). Are currency crises self-fulfilling? In B. Bernanke and J. Rotemberg, eds., *NBER Macroeconomics Annual*. Cambridge MA: MIT Press.

(1998). Its baaack: Japan's slump and the return of the liquidity trap. *Brookings Papers on Economic Activity: 2*. 137–205.

(2013, 6 June). How the case for austerity has crumbled. *New York Review of Books*. www.nybooks.com/articles/archives/2013/jun/06/how-case-austerity-has-crumbled/?pagination=false&printpage=true

Laeven, L. and Valencia, F. (2013). Systemic banking crises database. *IMF Economic Review*. 61:2. 225–270.

(2014). Systemic banking crises. In S. Classens, M.A. Kose, L. Laeven, and F. Valencia, eds., *Financial Crises: Causes, Consequences and Policy Responses*. Washington, DC: International Monetary Fund. 61–137.

Lewis, M. (1989). *Liar's Poker*. WW Norton Company: New York.

(2010). *The Big Short*. New York: W.W. Norton & Company.

Lindert, P. and Morton, P. (1989). How sovereign debt has worked. In J. Sachs, ed., *Developing Country Debt and Economic Performance, Volume 1: The International Financial System*. Chicago, IL: University of Chicago Press. 39–106.

Lo, A. (2012). Reading about the financial crisis: A twenty-one-book review. *Journal of Economic Literature*. 50:1. 151–178.

Lowenstein, R. 2000. *When Genius Failed: The Rise and Fall of Long-Term Capital Management*. New York: Random House.

Lucas, R. (2003). Macroeconomic priorities. *American Economic Review*. 93:1.1–14. [Presidential Address, January 4, 2003]

(2012). Robert Lucas on modern macroeconomics. *Society for Economic Dynamics*. 14: 1.Online: www.economicdynamics.org/interviews/

Lustig, N. (1998). *Mexico: The Remaking of an Economy (2e)*. Washington DC: Brookings Institution Press.

(1990). Economic crisis, adjustment and living standards in Mexico, 1982–85. *World Development*. 18:10. 1325–1342.

Maddison, A. (1982). *Phases of Capitalist Development*. New York: Oxford University Press.

(1991). *Dynamic Forces in Capitalist Development: A Long-Run Comparative View*. New York: Oxford University Press.

(2006). *The World Economy*. Paris: OECD.

Maddison Project Database. (2013). Groningen, NL: University of Groningen, Groningen Growth and Development Center. www.rug.nl/ggdc/historicaldevelopment/maddison/releases/maddison-project-database-2013.

Malmendier, U. and Tate, G. (2008). Who makes acquisitions? CEO overconfidence and the market's reaction. *Journal of Financial Economics*. 89:1. 20–43.

Marjolin, R. (1975). *Report of the Study Group "Economic and Monetary Union 1980" and Annex I. 8 March 1975*. (Called the Marjolin Report). Accessed February 6, 2019: http://aei.pitt.edu/1009/

Mbaye, S., Moreno Badia, M., and Chae, K. (2018). Global debt database: Methodology and sources. IMF Working Paper WP 18/111. International Monetary Fund: Washington DC.

Medley, B. (2013). Volcker's announcement of anti-inflation measures. Federal Reserve History. Available: www.federalreservehistory.org/Events/DetailView/41.

Meltzer, A. (2005). Origins of the Great Inflation. *Federal Reserve Bank of St. Louis Review*, 87:2(Part 2). 145–175.

Mian, A., and Sufi, A. (2014) *House of Debt: How They (and You) Caused the Great Recession and How We Can Prevent It from Happening Again*. Chicago, IL: University of Chicago Press.

Mian, A., Sufi, A., and Trebbi, F. (2014). Resolving debt overhang: Political constraints in the aftermath of financial crises. *American Economic Journal: Macroeconomics*. 6:2. 1–28.

Minsky, H.P. (1975). *John Maynard Keynes*. New York: Columbia University Press.

(1977). The Financial Instability Hypothesis: An interpretation of Keynes and an alternative to 'standard' theory. *Challenge*. 20:1. 20–27.

Minsky, H. (1986). *Stabilizing An Unstable Economy*. A Twentieth Century Fund Report. New Haven, CT: Yale University Press.

Mishkin, F. and Eakins, S. (2015). *Financial Markets and Institutions. 8e*. Boston, MA: Pearson.

Modigliani, F. and Miller, M. (1958). The cost of capital, corporation finance and the theory of investment. *American Economic Review*. 48:3. 261–297.

Modigliani, F., Fitoussi, J.-P., Moro, B., Snower, D., Solow, R., Steinherr, A., and Labini, P.S. (1998). An economists' manifesto on unemployment in the European Union. *BNL Quarterly Review*. 51:206. 327–361.

Mody, A. (2018). *EuroTragedy, A Drama in Nine Acts*. New York: Oxford University Press.

Montevideo-Oxford Latin America History Database. (2016). Nominal exchange rates, local currency units per US dollar. Available: http://moxlad-staging.herokuapp.com/home/en.

Mundell, R. (1961). A theory of optimum currency areas. *The American Economic Review* 51:4. 657–665.

(1963). Capital mobility and stabilization policy under fixed and flexible exchange rates. *Canadian Journal of Economics and Political Science*. 29:4. 475–85.

Muth, J. (1961). Rational expectations and the theory of price movements. *Econometrica*. 29:3. 315–335.

NBER (National Bureau of Economic Research). (2010). US business cycles expansions and contractions. Cambridge, MA: NBER. www.nber.org/cycles.html.

(2016a). Index of farm prices of crops for United States [M04059USM323NNBR], retrieved from FRED, Federal Reserve Bank of St. Louis; https://fred.stlouisfed.org/series/M04059USM323NNBR.

(2016b). Index of wholesale prices of commodities other than farm products and foods for United States [M04193USM350NNBR], retrieved from FRED, Federal Reserve Bank of St. Louis; https://fred.stlouisfed.org/series/M04193USM350NNBR.

(2016c). Index of wholesale prices, all commodities (20 foods, 25 raw materials) for France [M04057FRM360NNBR], retrieved from FRED, Federal Reserve Bank of St. Louis; https://fred.stlouisfed.org/series/M04057FRM360NNBR.

(2016d). Bonds outstanding, straight, par value, all industries for United States [Q10084USQ311NNBR], retrieved from FRED, Federal Reserve Bank of St. Louis; https://fred.stlouisfed.org/series/Q10084USQ311NNBR.

(2016e). Gross national product in constant dollars for United States [Q0896AUSQ240SNBR], retrieved from FRED, Federal Reserve Bank of St. Louis; https://fred.stlouisfed.org/series/Q0896AUSQ240SNBR.

(2016f). Unemployment rate for United States [M0892AUSM156SNBR], retrieved from FRED, Federal Reserve Bank of St. Louis; https://fred.stlouisfed.org/series/M0892AUSM156SNBR.

(2016g). Number of suspended banks, all banks for United States [M09036USM155NNBR], retrieved from FRED, Federal Reserve Bank of St. Louis; https://fred.stlouisfed.org/series/M09036USM155NNBR.

(2016h). Index of the general price level for United States [M04051USM324NNBR], retrieved from FRED, Federal Reserve Bank of St. Louis; https://fred.stlouisfed.org/series/M04051USM324NNBR.

Neumann, M. (1992). Seigniorage in the United States: How much does the U.S. government make from money production? *Federal Reserve Bank of St. Louis Review*. 74:2. 29–40.

Noyes, A. (1909). A year after the Panic of 1907. *Quarterly Journal of Economics*. 23:2. 185–212.

Obstfeld, M. (1996). Models of currency crises with self-fulfilling features. *European Economic Review*. 40:3–5.1037–1047.

Obstfeld, M. and Taylor, A.M. (2004). *Global Capital Markets: Integration, Crises, and Growth*. Cambridge, UK: Cambridge University Press.

OECD (Organization for Economic Cooperation and Development). (2017). National Currency to US Dollar Spot Exchange Rate for Indonesia [CCUSSP02IDQ650 N], retrieved from FRED, Federal Reserve Bank of St. Louis; https://fred.stlouisfed.org/series/CCUSSP02IDQ650N.

(2018). Quarterly GDP (indicator). doi:10.1787/b86d1fc8-en.

Olney, M. (1991). *Buy Now, Pay Later: Advertising, Credit, and Consumer Durables in the 1920s*. Chapel Hill, NC: University of North Carolina Press.

(1999). Avoiding default: The role of credit in the consumption collapse of 1930. *Quarterly Journal of Economics*. 114:1. 319–35.

Olivera, J. (1967). Money, prices and fiscal lags: A note on the dynamics of inflation. Banca *Nazionale del Lavoro Quarterly Review*. 20:82. 258–267.

Oppenheimer, L., Kessler, J., and Liner, E. (2014, 18 November). Demystifying Dodd-Frank: Fourteen ways it reforms the financial system. *Third Way*. www.thirdway.org/report/demystifying-dodd-frank-14-ways-it-reforms-the-financial-system

Quiggin, J. (2010). *Zombie Economics: How Dead Ideas Still Walk Among Us*. Princeton, NJ: Princeton University Press.

Paulson, H. (2010). *On the Brink: Inside the Race to Stop the Collapse of the Global Financial System*. (Fifth Anniversary Edition). New York: Business Plus.

Persons, C.E. (1930). Credit expansion, 1920 to 1929, and its lessons. *The Quarterly Journal of Economics*, 45:1. 94–130.

Phillips, A.W. (1958). "The relation between unemployment and the rate of change of money wage rates in the United Kingdom, 1861–1957. *Economica* (New Series). 25: 100.283–299.

ProPublica. (2018). Bailout tracker. http://projects.propublica.org/bailout/

Rajan, R. (2011). *Fault Lines: How Hidden Fractures Still Threaten the World Economy*. Princeton, NJ: Princeton University Press.

Rancière, R., Tornell, A., and Westermann, F. (2008). Systemic crises and growth. *The Quarterly Journal of Economics*. 123:1. 359–406.

Rauchway, E. (2015). *The Money Makers: How Roosevelt and Keynes Ended the Depression, Defeated Fascism, and Secured a Prosperous Peace*. New York: Basic Books.

Reinhart, C. and Rogoff, K. (2009a). *This Time Is Different: Eight Centuries of Financial Follies*. Princeton, NJ: Princeton University Press.

(2009b). The aftermath of financial crises. *American Economic Review*. 99:2. 466–472.

(2010). Growth in a time of debt. *American Economic Review: Papers & Proceedings*. 100:2. 573–578.

(2014). Financial and sovereign debt crises: Some lessons learned and those forgotten. In S. Claessens, M.A. Kose, L. Laeven, and F. Valencia, eds., *Financial Crises: Causes, Consequences and Policy Responses*. Washington, DC: International Monetary Fund. 141–155.

Rodgers, M.T., and Payne, J.E. (2015). Was the Panic of 1907 a global crisis? Testing the Noyes Hypothesis. Workshop on Monetary and Financial History, Federal Reserve Bank of Atlanta. https://www.frbatlanta.org/-/media/documents/news/conferences/2015/0511-workshop-on-monetary-and-financial-history/papers/rodgers-payne-noyes-hypothesis.pdf

Rogoff, K. (2013). FAQ on Herndon, Ash and Pollin's critique. Updated with 2015 Addendum. http://scholar.harvard.edu/rogoff/publications/faq-herndon-ash-and-pollins-critique

Romer, C.D. (1993). The nation in depression. *The Journal of Economic Perspectives*. 7:2. 19–39.

(1990). "The Great Crash and the onset of the Great Depression. *Quarterly Journal of Economics*. 105:3. 597–624.

(2005). Commentary. *Federal Reserve Bank of St. Louis Review*. 87:2(Part 2). 177–185. https://research.stlouisfed.org/publications/review/05/03/part2/Romer.pdf

Ruggie, J.G. (1982). International regimes, transactions, and change: Embedded liberalism in the postwar economic order. *International Organization*. 36:2. 379–415.

S&P Dow Jones Indices. (2015). S&P/Case-Shiller 20-City Composite Home Price Index. McGraw Hill Financial. http://us.spindices.com/indices/real-estate/sp-case-shiller-20-city-composite-home-price-index

Sachs, J. (1988). Recent studies of the Latin American Debt Crisis. *Latin American Research Review*. 23:3. 170–179.

(1989). Introduction. In J. Sachs, ed., *Developing Country Debt and Economic Performance, Volume 1: The International Financial System*. Chicago, IL: University of Chicago Press. 1–35.

Sala-i-Martin, X. and Sachs, J. (1991). Fiscal federalism and optimum currency areas: Evidence from Europe and from the United States. National Bureau of Economic Research Working Paper No. 3855. Cambridge, MA: NBER.

Salvatore, D. (1997). The common unresolved problem with the EMS and EMU. *American Economic Review*. 87:2. 224–226.

Schularick, M. and Taylor, A.M. (2012). Credit booms gone bust: Monetary policy, leverage cycles, and financial crises, 1870–2008. *American Economic Review*. 102:2. 1029–61.

Schularick, M. and Steger, T.M. (2010). Financial integration, investment, and economic growth: Evidence from two eras of financial globalization. *The Review of Economics and Statistics*. 92: 4.756–768.

Securities and Exchange Commission. (2015). *Annual Report on Nationally Recognized Statistical Ratings Agencies*. www.sec.gov/ocr/reportspubs/annual-reports/2015-annual-report-on-nrsros.pdf

Sen, A. (1997). Human rights and Asian values. Sixteenth Annual Morgenthau Memorial Lecture on Ethics and Foreign Policy. Carnegie Council for Ethics in Human Affairs, May 25. www.carnegiecouncil.org/publications/archive/morgenthau/254

Shariatmadari, D. (2015, 18 July). Daniel Kahneman: 'What would I eliminate if I had a magic wand? Overconfidence. *The Guardian*. www.theguardian.com/books/2015/jul/18/daniel-kahneman-books-interview

Shiller, R. (2005). *Irrational Exuberance*, 2e. Princeton, NJ: Princeton University Press.

(2012). *Finance and the Good Society*. Princeton, NJ: Princeton University Press.

(2013). Online data for *Irrational Exuberance*. Princeton, NJ: Princeton University Press. www.irrationalexuberance.com.

(2013b). Reflections on finance and the good society. *The American Economic Review*. 103:3. 402–405.

Skidelsky, R. (2009). *Keynes: The Return of the Master*. New York: Public Affairs.

Smith, A. (1776 [1937]). *An Inquiry into the Nature and Causes of the Wealth of Nations*. New York: The Modern Library.

Stallings, B. and Peres, W. (2000). *Growth, Employment, and Equity: The Impact of the Economic Reforms in Latin America and the Caribbean*. Washington, DC and Santiago, Chile: Brookings Institution Press and Economic Commission for Latin America and the Caribbean.

Stiglitz, J., Ocampo, J.A., Spiegel, S., Ffrench-Davis, R., and Nayyar, D. (2006). *Stability with Growth: Macroeconomics, Liberalization and Development*. Oxford: Oxford University Press.

(2010). *Freefall: America, Free Markets, and the Sinking of the World Economy*. New York: W.W. Norton & Company.

(2016). *The Euro: How a Common Currency Threatens the Future of Europe*. New York: W.W. Norton & Company.

Tallman, E.W. and Wicker, E.R. (2010). Banking and financial crises in United States history: What guidance can history offer policymakers? Federal Reserve Bank of Cleveland, Working Paper 10–09.

Tarullo, D.K. (2012, 12 June). Shadow banking after the financial crisis. Conference on Challenges in Global Finance: The Role of Asia, San Francisco, California. Federal Reserve Bank of San Francisco. www.federalreserve.gov/newsevents/speech/tarullo20120612a.htm

(2013, 13 November). Shadow banking and systemic risk regulation. Americans for Financial Reform and Economic Policy Institute Conference. Washington, D.C. www.federalreserve.gov/newsevents/speech/tarullo20131122a.htm#fn1

Temin, P. (1976). *Did Monetary Forces Cause the Great Depression?* New York: W.W. Norton & Company.

(1989). *Lessons from the Great Depression*. Cambridge, MA: MIT Press.

Temin, P. and Vines, D. (2013). *The Leaderless Economy: Why the World Economic System Fell Apart and How to Fix It*. Princeton, NJ: Princeton University Press.

Thorp, R. (1998). *Progress, Poverty and Exclusion: An Economic History of Latin America in the 20th Century*. Inter-American Development Bank: Washington, DC.

Tobin, J. (1978). A proposal for international monetary reform. *Eastern Economic Journal*. 4:3–4.153–159.

(2001, 1 May). Currency unions: Europe versus the United States. *Policy Options*. http://policyoptions.irpp.org/magazines/one-world-one-money/currency-unions-europe-vs-the-united-states/

UNCTAD (United Nations Conference on Trade and Development). (2018). Foreign direct investment. http://unctadstat.unctad.org/wds/ReportFolders/reportFolders.aspx

Urban Institute. (2017). Housing finance at a glance: A monthly chartbook. Housing Finance Policy Center. www.urban.org/sites/default/files/publication/91506/june_chartbook_2017.pdf

US Department of the Treasury. (2018a). Fiscal service, federal debt: Total public debt [GFDEBTN], retrieved from FRED, Federal Reserve Bank of St. Louis; https://fred.stlouisfed.org/series/GFDEBTN.

(2018b). Major foreign holders of treasury securities. Treasury International Capital System. http://ticdata.treasury.gov/Publish/mfh.txt

(No date). Financial Stability Oversight Council. https://home.treasury.gov/policy-issues/financial-markets-financial-institutions-and-fiscal-service/fsoc

US Government Accountability Office. (2009). *Financial Markets Regulation: Financial Crisis Highlights Need to Improve Oversight of Leverage at Financial Institutions and across System*. GAO-09–739. www.gao.gov/new.items/d09739.pdf

Wallach, P. (2015). *To the Edge: Legality, Legitimacy, and the Response to the 2008 Financial Crisis*. Brookings Institution Press: Washington, DC.

Wallison, P. (2015). *Hidden in Plain Sight: What Really Caused the World's Worst Financial Crisis and Why It Could Happen Again*. New York: Encounter Books.

Weitzman, H. (2012). *Latin Lessons: How South America Stopped Listening to the United States and Started Prospering*. John Wiley and Sons: Hoboken, NJ.

Westphal, L. (1990). Industrial policy in an export propelled economy: Lessons from South Korea's experience. *The Journal of Economic Perspectives*. 4:3. 41–59.

Williamson, J. (1994). In search of a manual for technopols. In J. Williamson, ed., *The Political Economy of Policy Reform*. Washington DC: Institute for International Economics. 9–28.

World Bank. (1987). *World Debt Tables*, 1986–87 Edition. Washington DC: The World Bank.

(1993). *The East Asian miracle: Economic growth and public policy*. (World Bank policy research report). New York, N.Y.: Oxford University Press.

(2006). How to do a debt sustainability analysis for low-income countries. http://siteresources.worldbank.org/INTDEBTDEPT/Resources/DSAGUIDE_EXT200610.pdf

(2014). *World Development Indicators*. Washington DC: The World Bank.

(2017a). *World Development Indicators*. Washington DC: The World Bank.

(2017b). *Review of the debt sustainability framework for low income countries: proposed reforms (English)*. Washington, D.C.: World Bank Group. http://documents.worldbank.org/curated/en/823731506617907804/Review-of-the-debt-sustainability-framework-for-low-income-countries-proposed-reforms

Wriston, W.B. (2007). Was I exacting? Sure. Was I occasionally sarcastic? Of course. Digital Collections and Archives, Tufts University. Available: http://hdl.handle.net/10427/36099 [Created from the article in Institutional Investor, 21:6. 1987.]

Yellen, J. (2013, 2 June). Regulatory landscapes: A US perspective. International Monetary Conference, Shanghai, China. www.federalreserve.gov/newsevents/speech/yellen20130602a.htm

Yergin, D. and Stanislaw, J. (1998). *The Commanding Heights: The Battle Between Government and the Marketplace That is Remaking the Modern World.* New York: Simon & Schuster.

Index

Admati, Anat, 223
adverse selection, 190
agricultural prices, 1920s, 75
Akerlof, George, 188
Albania, 39
Alesina and Ardagna, 249
American International Group (AIG), 154, 197
anti-Keynesian counter revolution, 228
Argentina, 38, 101, 102, 104, 105, 108
ASEAN+3, 138
Asian Bond Market Initiative (ABMI), 138
Asian Crisis, 13, 32, 62, 117
  austerity policy, 133
  capital market liberalization, 131, 132
  contagion, 128–129
  current account deficits, 129
  current accounts, 139–140
  Indonesia, 131
  international reserves, 127
  Korea, 131
  link to Subprime Crisis, 141–142
  Malaysia, 131
  post-crisis integration, 137–139
  post-crisis reserves, 141
  real appreciation, 129–130
  recovery, 134–135
  Thailand, 124
Asian Development Bank, 139
Asian Infrastructure Investment Bank (AIIB), 138
Asian Monetary Fund (AMF), 138
asset bubble, 23–28
  criticism of concept, 25
  Dotcom, 27
  equities versus housing, 26
  psychological factors, 25
  risks, 24
  US home prices, 144
asymmetric information, 7, 189, 190–192
  "bankruptcy for profit", 191
  "phishing for phools", 191–193
  adverse selection, 190
  moral hazard, 193
  mortgage originators, 191
  principal-agent problem, 192
  reputation mining, 192
austerians, 249
austerity, 299
  expansionary, 136, 179, 248
    critique, 249–250
    worsening problems in Eurozone, 251
  IMF's re-evaluation, 251
  impact on solidarity in Eurozone, 181

Bagehot, Walter, 83, 207
Bagehot's Rule, 83, 153–154
balance of payments crisis. *See* sudden stop crisis
bank failures, 1930s, 82
Bank for International Settlements, 63
Bank of England, 53, 153
banking crises
  high income countries, 187
banking crisis, **21**
  Bretton Woods Period, 56
  current period, 61
  frequency, 50
  high income countries, 65
  Interwar Period, 51
banking union, 262
banks
  capital levels, 161, 213
  capital requirements, 221
    risk reduction, 222
  implicit subsidies, 220–221
  optimal level of capital, 222
  retail versus investment, 209
  sources of funding, 212
Baring Crisis, 49, 273
Basel III, 214, 298
Bear Stearns, 19, 152, 153, 197

Bernanke, Ben, 69
  financial accelerator, 83, 208–209
  global savings glut, 141
  Japan's crisis, 233
BNP Paribas, 19, 152
Bolivia, 92, 101
Bordo, Michael, 273
Brady Plan, 114
Brazil, 101, 103, 105, 108
Bretton Woods, 10
  capital restrictions, 58, 60
  currency and banking crises, 59–60
  economic trends, 59
  end of, 59
  exchange rate system, 57–58
  goals, 56–57
  increase in international liquidity, 57
Bretton Woods Conference, 56
Buenos Aires Water Supply and Drainage Company, 49

capital controls, 277
capital flight, 32, 34
capital flows
  Eurozone, 169
  first and second globalization, 50
  return to Latin America, 1990s, 108
  short term, 63
capital market liberalization, 31–33
  benefits, 266–267
  Bretton Woods era, 268
  current period, 63
  effects on growth, 275–276
  IMF's assumptions, 269
  lack of consensus, 269–270
  links to crisis, 270–272, 273–274
  openness on current account, 267
  risks, 24
capital requirements
  optimal level, 222
  risk reduction, 222
CEPAL. *See* ECLA
CFPB, 162, 192
Chanda, Nayan, 46
Chandler, Alfred, 44
Chiang Mai Initiative, 138
Chicago Board of Trade, 47
Chile, 97, 105
China, 119, 125, 139, 141
  reserves accumulation, 149
Claessens, Stijn, 20, 273
Clinton Administration, 249
collateralized debt obligations (CDOs), 151
Colombia, 105
commercial paper, 199
  asset backed commercial paper (ABCP), 200
confirmation bias, 231
Consumer Financial Protection Bureau. *See* CFPB
cost of credit intermediation, 86
credit boom, 28–30
  Ireland and Spain, 2000s, 28–29
  Latin America, 1970s, 97
  loans to oil producers, 1970s, 97
  risks, 24
  United States, 2000s, 144–151
crisis risk factors, 23, *See* individual risk factors
  Latin America, 98
  Subprime Crisis, 151–152
crowding-in, 250
currency crisis, **21**
  Bretton Woods Period, 56
  current period, 61
  frequency, 50
  Interwar Period, 52

debt
  advantages of internal, 285
  Asian and Latin American compared, 287
  asymmetry, borrowers and lenders, 293
  country variation in risks, 282
  default with low levels, 281
  demographic challenges, 290
  external, 22
  external versus internal, 22
  external vs. internal, 39
  failure of austerity, 292–293
  frequency of sovereign defaults, 284
  graduation from debt crisis, 288
  gross, 285
  inflation, role, 294
  internal, 22
  Japan, 39
  measurment, public debt, 284–285
  net, 285
  political issues, 290
  private sector problems, 283–284
  private vs. public, 38

reducing, eliminating, 295
risk factor, 37–40
risks, 24
sustainability, 291
thresholds, 287
United Kingdom, 39
usefulness, 37, 282
debt crisis, **21**, 22
Bretton Woods Period, 56
current period, 61
Interwar Period, 52
sovereign, 282
frequency, 284
debt deflation, 27
debt intolerance, 286
debt overhang, 283
debt thresholds, 290
debt-to-exports ratio, 286
debt-to-GDP ratio, 38, 284
deceptive practices, 6
deflation
1920s, 51
impact on debt, 52
impact on production, 52
Demirgüç-Kunt, Asli, 273
Denmark, 33
deposit insurance, 206
derivative, 201
Detragaiche, Enrica, 273
Dodd-Frank, 159, 194, 298
capital requirements, 161, 222
Consumer Finance Protection Bureau (CFPB), 162–163
FSOC, 160
macroprudential regulation, 160
orderly liquidation, 161–162
Dodd-Frank Wall Street Reform and Consumer Protection Act. *See* Dodd-Frank
Draghi, Mario, 178

early warning indicators, 3, 40
ECB. *See* European Central Bank
ECLA, 96, 106
proposed economic reforms, 1960s, 96
Economic Commission on Latin America. *See* ECLA
economic growth
Bretton Woods Period, 59
emergence of modern era, 43
first era, 43
first wave of globalization, 43
five eras of modern growth, 43–44
Golden Age, 44
growth rates, different eras, 45–46
Interwar Period, 44
second wave of globalization, 44
economics
behavioral, 6–7
Keynesian, 227, 239–240
Keynesian models, 229
monetarism, 226
New Classical, 228
New Classical vs. New Keynesian, 229, 245–246
pre-Keynesian, 79
Ecuador, 39, 97
Eichengreen, Barry, 273
emerging markets, 115, 124
EU. *See* European Union
euro
assumptions of fiscal integration, 259
convergence criteria, 260
problems during a recession, 260–261
members, 166
negotiations, 259
worries of fiscal mismanagement, 260
European Central Bank, 168
emergency actions
Outright Monetary Transactions, 178
Securities Market Program, 178
lender of last resort, absence of, 168
monetary tightening, 173
no bailout clause, 260
single mandate, 173
European Systemic Risk Board, 298
European Union
expansionary austerity, 179–181
financial globalization, 171
focus on business confidence, 179
impossibility of transfers, 181
origins, 165
Stability Growth Pact, 172, 305
Eurozone, 11, 14
bailouts, 177–178
bank bailouts, debate, 171–172
borrowing patterns, pre-crisis, 172
budget, inadequate, 264

Eurozone (cont.)
capital flows, 2000s, 169
doom loop, 173, 174–175
expansionary austerity, 250
fear of contagion from bank failures, 172
interest rate convergence, 169, 259–260
loss of competitiveness in periphery, 170
missing institutions, 261–263
problem of sovereignty, 263–264
real appreciation, 2000s, 169–170
recovery from recession, 181
return of recession, 173–174
rise in debt levels
Ireland, 176
Spain, 176
rules versus institutions, 182, 264–265
excess reserves, 156
exchange rate
flexible, 61
post-Bretton Woods, 93
real appreciation, 33–34
exorbitant privilege, 288
expectations, modeling, 244
external debt, 22

Fama, Eugene, 25
Fannie Mae, 145–146
role in Subprime Crisis, 147–148
support for mortgage market, 146–147
takeover by US government, 154
FCIC, 196
FDIC, 90
creation, 87
Federal Deposit Insurance Corporation. *See* FDIC
Federal Home Loan Mortgage Corporation. *See* Freddie Mac
Federal Housing Finance Agency, 152
Federal National Mortgage Association. *See* Fannie Mae
Federal Reserve
failure during the Great Depression, 82
policy, 1920s, 74
Section 13, 154
Federal Reserve Bank of Minneapolis, 223
financial accelerator, 4, 83, 208–209
financial crisis, **4–5**
1970–2011, 2
categories, 20–22
contagion
common fundamentals, 128
international linkages, 128
costs, 1–2
end of the business cycle, 230
first wave of globalization, 49
measurement, 18–20
quantitative thresholds, 21
financial repression, 294
financial sector
economic models, 5, 8
Financial Stability Oversight Council. *See* FSOC
financial supervision, regulation
assumptions in high income countries, 30–31
fiscal integration, 300
fiscal union
risk sharing, 254, 258
role in US economy, 254–255
Fisher, Irving, 27, 207
fixed exchange rate. *See* exchange rate
flexible exchange rate. *See* exchange rate
foreign currency reserves, 34
France
deflation, 1920s, 52
support for euro, 259
Freddie Mac, 145–146
role in Subprime Crisis, 147–148
support for mortgage market, 146–147
takeover by US government, 154
Friedman and Schwartz hypothesis, 82–83, 85
gold standard, cost of credit intermediation, 86
Friedman, Milton
monetarism, 226
Monetary History of the United States, 81
role of Fed during the Great Depression, 82–83
FSOC, 160, 194
systemically important financial institutions, 160

GATT, 56, 60
Geithner, Timothy, 25
General Agreement on Tariffs and Trade. *See* GATT
Germany, 28, 51, 72
capital flows toward periphery, 169
deflation, 1920s, 52

economy during recession, 179
inflation, pre-crisis, 170
Stability and Growth Pact, 172
support for euro, 259
GIIPS, 166
global savings glut, 141, 149
impact on United States, 148–149
globalization
capital flows, 50–51
first wave, 31, 46–51
capital flows, 32, 47
frequency of crises, 49
gold standard, 48
large-scale projects, 47
products traded, 47
role of transportation and communication, 46
second wave, 61
causes of crises, 62–64
frequency of crises, 61–62
role of transportation and communication, 62
gold standard, 48
1920s, 73
internal versus external conditions, 48, 55
obstacle to economic recovery, 54, 87
Golden Age. *See* Bretton Woods
Goldman Sachs, 217
Gordon, Robert, 44
Gorton, Gary, 205
government sponsored enterprises (GSEs). *See* Fannie Mae; Freddie Mac
Great Depression, 11, 27, 41, 48 *See* Interwar Period; Roosevelt, Franklin
bank failures, 82
bank holiday, United States, 87
comprised of two recessions, 76–77
conflicting interpretations, 71
decline in demand, 78–79
economic growth, 76, 88
economic importance, 69–70
end of gold standard, United States, 87
financial accelerator, 84
fiscal policy, 89
Friedman and Schwartz hypothesis, 82–83
GDP decline, US, 78
international causes, 72–73
risk factors, 76
role of the Federal Reserve, 83, 85–86
second recession, 88
stock market crash, 77–78
Great Inflation, 240
causes, 240–241
Great Moderation, 230
Greece, 19, 250
austerity in return for bailout, 177
bailout, 177
borrowers vs. lenders, 294
fraudulent budget statistics, 180
inflation, pre-crisis, 170
interest rate convergence, 169, 259
loss of competitiveness, 170
rise in debt-to-GDP, 177
Greenspan, Alan, 185, 193
GSE. *See* Fannie Mae; Freddie Mac

Hellwig, Martin, 223
herd behavior, 6, 17, 25
Herzog, Jesús Silva, 92
High Performance Asian Economies. *See* HPAE
Hoover, Herbert, 81, 237
HPAE, 118
economic growth
debate, 121–123
institutions, 123–124
macroeconomic stability, 124
growth rates, 119
recovery from crisis, 134–135
Hungary, 29

IMF, 50, 60
assumptions about Latin American crisis, 94, 103
capital market liberalization, 135–136
creation, 56
re-evaluation of expansionary austerity, 251
response to Asian Crisis, 129, 133
criticism of response, 134, 136–137
response to criticisms, Asia, 137
Import substitution industrialization. *See* ISI
Indonesia, 118, 133
contagion, 131
inflation crisis, **21**
internal debt, 22

International Bank for Reconstruction and Development, 57
International Monetary Fund. *See* IMF
Interwar Period. *See* Great Depression
competitive devaluations, 1920s, 75
credit boom, 1920s, 75
deflation, 52, 74
Europe
decline in demand, 1920s, 79
frequency of crises, 52
international leadership, 74
overvalued British pound, 53–55
restoration of gold standard, 53, 73–74
Ireland
bailout, 177
credit boom, 28
inflation, pre-crisis, 170
support for banks, 176
irrational exuberance, 17
ISI, 106–107

Japan, 39, 114, 119
debt level, 281
debt overhang, 283
economic stagnation, 1990s, 232
problems, 1990s, 232–233
JP Morgan, 153

Kahneman, Daniel, 189
Keynes, J.M., 18, 79
absence of crowding out, 238
failure of self-correcting economy, 79–81, 238
General Theory of Employment, Interest, and Money, 79
government spending in a recession, 80
importance of aggregate demand, 86
uncertainty, 79
Keynesian multiplier, 241, 251
Keynesianism
New Classical critique, 244–245
problems of fiscal policy, 241–242
sticky wages and prices, 228
Kindleberger, Charles, 17, 18, 29
importance of international leadership, 73
Manias, Panics, and Crashes, 17
Kohl, Helmut, 172
Kose, M. Ayhan, 20, 273
Krugman, Paul, 232, 235

Latin America, 94
currency crises, 1980s, 102
economic populism, 95–96
impact of US disinflation, 99
import substitution industrialization (ISI), 107
Lost Decade, 99
real appreciation, 1980s, 101–102
seigniorage, 1980s, 100–102
soverign defaults, 1980s, 100
state-led development, 96
tecnopols, 109
urbanization after World War II, 93
use of currency as nominal anchor, 101–102
Latin American Debt Crisis, 12, 19
austerity, failure of, 109
borrowers versus lenders, 110–111
creditor cartel, 100
debt relief, 105, 107–108, 114
early diagnoses, 100
end of crisis, 108–109, 114
exposure of US banks, 103
first indicators, 92
growth of secondary debt market, 104
role of exports, 105–106, 114
stabilization and structural adjustment, 107–108
Lehman bailout, debate, 155, 197–198
Lehman Brothers, 19, 154
leverage, **214**, 217
disadvantages in a downturn, 215
effect on executive compensation, 216
liquidity trap, 231
London, 51
Lucas, Robert, 230

Macdougall Report, 264
macroprudential regulation, 194
Maddison Project Database 2013, 45
Maddison, Angus, 45
Malaysia, 118
capital controls, 136
Meissner, Christopher, 273
Mellon, Andrew, 81
Merrill Lynch, 154
Mexico, 94, 97, 100, 101, 103, 104, 105
capital inflows, 1990s, 115
economic reforms, 113, 114
emerging market, 115

oil boom, 92
onset of debt crisis, 92
peso crisis, 116–117, 273
real appreciation, 116
Minsky, Hyman, 18, 29, 30
financial instability hypothesis, 29
Modigliani-Miller Theorem, 219, 221
monetarism, **226**
monetary union
assumptions of EU leaders, 259
benefits assumed in EU, 252
Monnet, Jean, 259
Montague, Ashley, 74
moral hazard, 155, 162, **193**
bank executives, 214
deposit insurance, 206
mortgage backed securities (MBS), 27
multiplier, 242, 245, 248
Mundell, Robert, 256

narrative bias, 231
natural experiments, 41
natural rate of unemployment, 244
Netherlands, 28
New Classical synthesis, 228
Northern Rock, 153
Noyes, Alexander D., 49

Occam's razor, 218
October, 75
importance as cause of the Great Depression, 77
Olivera-Tanzi effect, 101
optimal currency area, 256
Mundell criteria, 256–257
need for fiscal integration, 258
requirements, 166–168
orderly liquidation, 161
overconfidence bias, 6, 13, 17, 217
overvalued currency, 33–35
risks, 24

Panic of 1907, 49, 299
pegged exchange rate. *See* exchange rate
Peru, 92, 97, 101, 108
Phillips Curve, 243
phishing for phools, 189, 191
Portillo, Lopez, 93
Portugal
bailout, 177
inflation, pre-crisis, 170
Postwar international organizations, 94 *See* IMF, GATT, World Bank
Prince, Charles, 6
principal-agent problem, 192
private debt
opacity, 38

quantitative easing, 156, 225, 233
inflation worries, 156

Rajan, Raghuram, 147
rating agencies
complexity of securities, 203–204
failures, 203
incentive problems, 203
justifications for ratings, 151
rational expectations, 244
real appreciation, 34
recessions
acts of nature, 237
Keynes' insight, 238
recycling of petrodollars, 97
Reinhart, Carmen, 20, 38, 273, 288
repo. *See* repurchase agreement
repurchase agreement, 200
reputation mining, 192
risk factors, 9, 22
risk models, 218–219
Rogoff, Kenneth, 20, 38, 273, 288
Roosevelt, Franklin, 87, 237
bank holiday, 87
budget orthodoxy, 89
monetary policy, 87

Schularick, Moritz, 273
Schwartz, Anna
Monetary History of the United States, 81
role of Fed during the Great Depression, 82–83
Securities and Exchange Commission, 90
securitization, 201
benefits and risks, 202
collateralized debt obligation (CDO), 201
collateralrized debt obligation (CDO), 203

securitization (cont.)
mortgage backed securities (MBS), 201
Sen, Amartya, 123
reasons for HPAE growth, 120
shadow banks, 199
bank panic, 205–207
compared to regular banks, 205
lenders, depositors, 204
need for short term assets, 210
regulation, 211
use of securities, 202
Shiller, Robert, 25, 188, 283
new era thinking, 1970s, 98
psychological factors in a crisis, 25
SIFI, 161, 194, *See* Dodd-Frank
Singapore, 119
six-sigma event, 217
Skidelsky, Robert, 239
Smith, Adam
regulation of banks, 187
South Korea, 105, 107, 114, 118
absence of capital controls, 136
sovereign defaults, 39
Spain
credit boom, 28
inflation, pre-crisis, 170
Squam Lake Report, 216
sticky wages and prices, 7, 228, 246
Strong, Benjamin, 74
Subprime Crisis, 11, 13, 14, 19, 26, 30, 65, 71
bailouts of financial institutions, 154–155
bank stress tests, 157
end of, 158
falling home prieces, US, 152
Federal Reserve balance sheet, 156
fiscal stimulus, United States, 157
liquidity trap, 234–235
new era thinking, 143
pre-crisis increase in home prices, 144
private debt, United States, 150–151
regulatory arbitrage, 151
spreading to Europe, 28
the Lehman debate, 155, 197–198
this time is different syndrome, 143
too big to fail, 207–208
unemployment, United States, 153
weak regulation, US, 150–151
sudden stop, **21**, 36
sudden stop crisis
current period, 61
systemically important financial institutions. *See* Dodd-Frank; SIFI

Taiwan, 119
Taylor, Alan M., 273
Thailand, 13, 62, 118
current account, 140
devaluation, 128
expectations of devaluation, 127–128
onset of Asian Crisis, 124
real appreciation, 125, 126–127
The Monetary History of the United States, 226
too big to fail, 160, 207–208
trade deficit, 35–37
need to finance, 35
policies to shrink, 36
risks, 24
Treaty of Rome, 166
Trichet, Jean-Claude, 172, 173
trilemma of international finance, 268
twin crises, 20

United Kingdom, 39
debt levels, 281
delfation, 1920s, 52
determination to restore gold standard, 73
gold standard, 48
official policy of deflation, 1920s, 53
return to the gold standard, 53
United States. *See* Subprime Crisis; Great Depression
1920s, 72
debt, 279
deflation, 1920s, 52
external debt, 22
fiscal and monetary union, 253
gold reserves, 1930s, 85
gold standard, 48
Great Moderation, 230
inflation, 1970s, 226
inflow of foreign savings, 148, 149
monetary policy cooperation with UK, 1920s, 74
recessions, 1980 and 1981–82, 95, 99
role in Bretton Woods exchange rate system, 57

tax loss due to recession, 280
trade deficit, 36
trade deficits under Bretton Woods, 58

Venezuela, 97, 104, 108
Viniar, David, 217
Volcker, Paul
disinflation policy, 99, 226

Washington Consensus, 12
weak institutions
risk factors, 30–31
risks, 24
Werner Report, 257, 261
World Bank, 50, 57, 60
The East Asian Miracle, 119
World Trade Organization. *See* WTO
World War I, 51
World War II, 55
Worldwide Governance Indicators, 123
Wriston, Walter, 110
WTO, 50, 56, 60